Pricing the Priceless

PRICING
THE
PRICELESS

Art, Artists, and Economics

WILLIAM D. GRAMPP

Basic Books, Inc., Publishers

NEW YORK

Library of Congress Cataloging-in-Publication Data

Grampp, William Dyer.
    Pricing the priceless: art, artists, and economics/William D.
Grampp.
    p. cm.
  Includes index.
  ISBN 0–465–06321–7
  1. Art as an investment. 2. Art—Marketing. I. Title.
N8680.G7 1989   89–42520
338.4'77—dc19   CIP

To my friends

in the

kingdom of the Annas

CONTENTS

PREFACE

THIS IS about art and artists, especially about painting and painters, and tries to say something that has not been said before or said in the same way. If it has succeeded, the reason is that it observes them from the point of view of neo-classical economics. That hardly ever has been done and probably never has been done in the way it is done here. Of course, neither is a sufficient reason for making the effort. I have made it in the belief that it will reveal things that are interesting, perhaps important, possibly useful. Whether that has been the result is for the readers to decide, and leaving the decision to them is an application of the neo-classical principle of consumer sovereignty.

My study would be much different, might not be at all, if in the course of making it I had not been assisted in many ways by many people, some of whom knew what I was doing and others of whom hadn't the slightest idea but were nevertheless helpful. Among the unknowing helpers have been librarians who located materials and reproductions; museum attendants who directed me to what I wanted to see and called my attention to things I might have missed, who turned on lights or turned them down, who explained arcane labels and identified work that had no label at all; writers in art periodicals who provided information that led me to conclusions they might abhor; art dealers who listened politely to the odd questions of a passer-by; and colleagues and students for their comments in seminars and at professional meetings where I have presented some of my findings.

Then there are those who did know what I was doing, and I thank them with the greatest of pleasure. They listened to my questions, heard my opinions, set me straight—or tried to—when they thought

I was going wrong, and, though none ever said it, must have wondered if I ever would finish what I had started out to do. They are the kind of people who are indispensable to one whose subject has rightly been called "the chilling skepticism." One thinks, if I can convince him or her of this, I will believe it myself. So they have provided me with moral assurance as well as with information. I must especially name Claire E. Friedland, Gilbert R. Ghez, Ronald P. Moses, and Roger W. Weiss. As I did not discuss everything with each of them or convince any of them of everything, none can be held responsible for all that I have said. But about what they did see and agree to they are not to go scot-free. If they let a blunder slip by or failed to notice any silly stuff, they share the responsibility with me. Another to whom I am indebted is Martin Kessler, the publisher of this book. He suggested (or was he prescribing?) ways in which the attention of the general reader could be engaged and by which information meant for thoughtful men and women could be made interesting as well as understandable. However, if they should not be continuously enraptured they are not to blame him (entirely) because he left most things to my judgment. Then there is the member of the publishing firm who suggested the title, possibly himself—he would not say. My only objection to it is that I did not think of it myself.

For particular thanks I must name my friends in Italy, Dottoressa Anna Bagiotti of the Rivista Internazionale di Scienze Economiche e Commerciali and Professoressa Anna Pellanda of the University of Padua. In addition to being grateful to them for their professional assistance, I am also grateful for their hospitality, which included providing me with a place to read, write, think, and observe, the one in Castione Andevenno, Valtellina, and the other in Venice on Dorsoduro. I could not have wished for more suitable and pleasant settings to do what I had in mind. For their hospitality, their interest and encouragement, for their many kindnesses, I am grateful and have dedicated the book to them.

I wish to express my gratitude for the assistance that was provided by the Research Board of the University of Illinois and by the Department of Economics of the Chicago campus, by the Hoover Institution and the Earhart Foundation with research grants, and by the Liberty Fund, which sponsored two colloquia on the economics of the arts, each an occasion for learning that while I was mistaken about some things, I was not about others.

Some of these ideas have appeared in periodicals. The dissection of the arguments made for government subsidies to the arts, the subject of the last chapter, appeared first in German in *Zeitschrift für Wirtschaftspolitik,* the publication of the Institute of Economic Policy of the University of Cologne. The *Zeitschrift* also published a prevue, or overture, to this book under the alliterative title "Kunst, Künstler, und Kapital." The leading ideas of chapter six, on why government supports the arts, are summarized in "Rent-Seeking in Arts Policy," which appeared in *Public Choice.* I thank the editors for being quite agreeable to my saying here what I first said in their journals.

Pricing the Priceless

INTRODUCTION

A View of the Horizon

THIS IS a study of art from the viewpoint of economic theory—how art comes into being, how it passes from the artist to those who value it, and what determines the value they place on it: three matters that are, respectively, supply, exchange, and demand. Economics should help to explain them as they apply to art (and explain why they do so apply) just as it explains them as they apply to other things. It also should have something to say about how art is paid for, how it could be paid for, and how it should not be.

An economic view of art does not replace aesthetics, criticism, or art history. Rather, it complements them. It looks at the activity of art in a way that can be much different, hence it sees different things, and if used properly it can be informative. It does not tell us all we would like to know—nothing does that about anything—but it may be able to tell us more than we have been told about why artists do what they do in the way they do it, why the world values their work, or does not, or values it less than the artists themselves do, and why when they cannot get from the market what they believe is their due they turn to government to be supported.

The theory that is used here is neo-classicism, a set of ideas that explains how people conduct themselves in order to get as much as they can from what they have. Neo-classical economics is about sensible and self-interested behavior. It is not, as it is used in this book, particularly difficult. Its brute, irreducible elements, as William James could have called them, are self-evident. One is that if people do not have as much of something as they want and are offered more for nothing, they will take it.

Ideas like that, while they are simple, are not simple-minded. They can be informative. Why did John Frederick Lewis abandon his prominent position as a watercolorist in Britain and turn to oil painting? Some would look into the inner man for a psychological explanation, others to the outer world for possible transformations in Victorian society, still others for evidence of a new aesthetic (snipping off the "s" as they snip it off ethics). An economist will be satisfied with what Lewis himself said, humdrum but plausible, certainly intelligible: "I felt that work [watercolor] was destroying me. And for what? To get by water-colour art £500 a year, and this too, when I know that as an oil painter I could with less labour get my thousand." Admittedly, Lewis is not a familiar figure in the history of art, but he was not unusual. Luca della Robbia acted on the same principle (opportunity cost) when he turned from one form of sculpture to another, and the principle has directed many others, on both sides of the market, collectors as well as artists, and within it dealers and auctioneers.

ECONOMICS AND THE ACTIVITY OF ART

The reader may wonder if I intend to bring still another field of study within the scope of economics, a thing that has happened so often in recent years that economics has come to be called the Imperial Science. Psychology, sociology, biology, political science, international relations, ethics, and law—all have come within the domain of economics or have been affected by it in an important way. I would like to do just that with the visual arts and in particular with painting. There is no necessary reason why they cannot be studied with the aid of the analytical methods of economics, especially the leading ideas in the theory of utility and of cost. Much of my book attempts to do that. How well it is done is for readers to decide. If they should decide it has not been done well, they will, I trust, blame me and not economics. The activity of art—the making, the acquiring, and the using of it—is a certain kind of behavior. Behavior of all kinds entails choices, and all choices entail returns and costs. The two are what economics is about.

But in the world at large, there is the feeling that certain kinds of behavior do not belong in the domain of economics, hence it should not presume to study them. This is behavior that is touched by the higher values, as they are called. To ask if truth, beauty, and goodness are worth what they cost seems to debase them. "High Heaven rejects the lore/Of nicely-calculated less or more," Wordsworth said, and it has been said by any number of others, although not as well. Actually, if economics has no relevance to the higher values, it is a poor thing. But it has. They are the values that call for the most searching thought, the most careful comparisons, and the most nicely calculated choices—they call for the rationality that economics attributes to people in everything they do, whether they address themselves to the lower values or the higher. About the former, about mankind in the ordinary business of life, the critics of economics have said it is unrealistic; about the latter, mankind in the extraordinary business of life, they have said it has no application. If they were right, economics would be useless. But they are not.

Wordsworth himself made a nice calculation. After the *Lyrical Ballads,* he became a celebrated figure, and his home was a mecca for tourists. He provided them with refreshments—at a price. In doing so he implicitly acknowledged that poetry and tea are what economists call complementary goods and that an increase in the demand for one increases the demand for the other. Did he thereby debase his poetry (or his tea)? Today those who read it probably are not aware of its connection with a snack bar, and if they were they would be no more than amused.

My purpose, then, is to employ microeconomics to help to understand certain features of the visual arts, some reaching into history, some having to do with the present. The most I claim is that it can be helpful.

HOW THE ARGUMENT IS CONDUCTED

Economics can offer reasons why the styles of painting have changed throughout the history of art and predicts they will continue to do so. It cannot explain the choice of subject matter (or the choice of none at all), but often it can explain the direction of the change and usually can explain the limits of change.

One reason for change is that novelty is interesting while repetition is monotonous. This should reassure people who have been told and believe that the multiplicity of styles of modern painting reflects the disappearance of values, standards, and criteria, or the bewilderment of the alienated artist in a hostile world. The economist's explanation is, by contrast, prosaic—not a frisson in it—but it is intelligible and in principle can be judged empirically. It is an obvious implication of the idea of diminishing marginal utility, which is the idea that the more we have of a thing the less satisfying is still more of it. If this were not so, Andy Warhol need not have done anything more than have multiples made of a single drawing of Marilyn Monroe. The millionth or trillionth would have been as interesting as the first, and it would have been no more or less interesting than the last or first of the seventy-five copies Gilbert Stuart made of his portrait of George Washington.

Another implication, which is not obvious, though in no way difficult to understand, is that the satisfaction we get from anything we get only at a cost. The cost is not just the price paid for the object. It is also what we must do or have done in order to understand, apprehend, enjoy, or appreciate it; and that cost is the consequence of what we have learned, have experienced, and have worked to achieve. It is our accumulated investment in taste. All investment, whatever its form or purpose, has a cost and is made when the return it yields is worth the cost. Only a few people ever have found the investment in a taste for art to be worthwhile. They have not found it to be worthwhile in the past, not in the present, and probably will not in the future. Just why is a question that leads one to the distribution of income (art is a luxury) and to the distribution of occupations (art is useful information in some jobs). An implication is that the surest and quickest way to bring the masses to art is to pay them to notice it. Such topics have to do with the demand for art, and it is the subject of chapter two.

The making and creating of art is what chapter three is about. It describes the similarity of painters in their studios to businessmen in their enterprises. Painters have been directed by self-interest and have tried to do the best they could with their own, that is, they have been maximizers. When they placed their work on the market they took account of the price of work done by other painters. Joshua Reynolds, when he began to paint portraits, asked less for them than his teacher asked for his, and Reynolds as he became better known raised his prices until they equaled those of his teacher. Painters have not been able to set prices on their work, but have had to take what the market offered, because what each did was to some extent in competition with what others did. Their works did not sell at the same price at any one time in any one place because they were not perfect substitutes. On the other hand, none was unique in the sense that at no price would another work be preferred to it, not even when the works were quite different. Bramante thought he would not get the architectural commission for St. Peter's if the pope decided to spend money on a tomb for himself done by Michelangelo. Bramante got the commission but first had to frighten Michelangelo into fleeing Rome.

Painters also have been aware of costs, including the subtle notion of opportunity cost as Lewis and della Robbia testified by their decisions. They also have been aware of cost in the familiar, money, sense and have tried to minimize it by using assistants, collaborating with each other, subcontracting commissions, copying themselves, economizing on the use of materials, and employing their families, apprenticing their sons, or making sons-in-law of their apprentices.

A remarkable fact about works of art is that most of them, including those that in their day were highly valued, have not survived, some because they have deteriorated physically, but most because the world has lost interest in them. They have become worthless in an aesthetic and in a monetary sense. This does not mean works of art when newly created are systematically overvalued (if that were true there would be a futures market), but that they are subject to obsolescence. Collectors should know that the value of most art falls to zero in a fairly short time, just as other things do when the desire for them passes away. They also should know that studies of the rate of return to art do not all report the same results, which makes art a chancy investment and a still chancier speculation, suitable for risk lovers, whether or not they are art lovers, but not for people who don't care for risk or who want even odds however they may feel about art. The wise collector buys what he likes, pays no more than he must, and does so because he acts with reputable dealers.

Dealers and auctions conduct the market for art, and it is the subject of chapter four. The salient features of the market are the high cost and the uncertainty of information. They do not set the art market apart from that for other things or make undue demands on economic theory. They do call for close attention. It discloses the ways in which the market tries to reduce the cost of information and uncertainty. Buyers, in ascertaining the authenticity of a work and the correct attribution, seek out the provenance or previous owners. Dealers and auction houses have an interest in providing it. They and collectors want another kind of information. They would like to know where the art they want to sell or own is located and to know what the price is. An important part of the work of dealers consists of finding art to sell. What appears to be an enormous markup is the cost of doing business. If the markup were more than the cost, there would be an increase in the number of dealers until it was no more than the cost.

The market for art, like other markets, is a magnet for misconceptions, invites detractors, and elicits schemes for reform by means of regulation. Auction houses are said to misrepresent their actual sales by the practice of reserve prices. Dealers are said to pay artists very little for their work and to resell it at a great profit. Buyers are said to alter what they buy, hence to reduce its value and the value of other work by the artist. For each of these transgressions, a regulation of one kind or another has been proposed and in some places has been enacted. That the regulation can work to the disadvantage of those it is meant to protect as well as those it is meant to punish makes the regulation of the market for art like that of other markets.

Each of these chapters—on the demand, the supply, and the market—rests on the same assumption, and it is indispensable. It is that works of art are economic goods, that their value can be measured by the market, that the sellers and buyers of art—the people who create and benefit from it—are people who try to get as much as they can from what they have. In a word or two, the activity of art is a maximizing activity. Without that assumption, economics has no place in the study of art or of anything else.

The assumption does not mean art is no different from anything else. Of course it is, and so is each thing different from every other thing. If it were not, there would be no word "each," there would be no more than one noun, no more than one object in the world, and entropy would reign. Folk wisdom has it that apples and oranges cannot be compared, but the folks whose wisdom that is compare them every time they go to the fruit stand and choose one or the other. If they choose neither they are comparing each of them with everything else including art. Differences among goods do not determine which come within the scope of economics and which do not. That is determined by whether the activity entailed by the good—its production, distribution, and consumption—is a maximizing activity.

That, in turn, depends on whether the good is scarce. It is scarce if, at a zero price, people want more of it than is available. Art is scarce. Even though few people value it, they would want more than they now have if it were free. Because it is not, it must be created, made available, and held carefully, which is to say, economically. That means as much utility as possible must be gotten from it, in the form of enjoyment, pleasure, instruction, enlightenment, inspiration, and so on, and, what is just as important, must be gotten at the lowest possible cost. That is what maximizing activity is.

Throughout this book art is treated as a maximizing activity. The assumption has to be justified. Chapter one sets out to do that. It is closely reasoned, abstract in places, and while not long or particularly difficult may seem to be. Certainly it is not reading for the beach or material for a Walkman. I have tried to make it interesting with examples of economic calculation in the world of art and to make it convincing by explaining the property of art that brings it within the scope of economics. A necessary condition of doing so is to demonstrate that aesthetic values and economic values are consistent. In support of that claim I have marshaled information of various kinds. One is an empirical study which shows that the price of the work of the principal living artists of the world is consistent with the critical judgment that has been made of them.

To prove that people in art are people who maximize is not difficult, but to make the idea convincing is uphill work. The idea is so simple that if it is applied to farming or laying bricks or choosing a share of stock it might be thought trivial. People who maximize are simply people who prefer more to less and will try to get it if they expect the additional return to be worth the additional effort. But when the idea is applied to art, it seems to go against the grain—the grain being the anti-market mentality, a subdivision of the anti-materialist view of how people ought to behave. A noticeable part of this book is about the anti-materialist view because it has affected much of what has been said about art. The view has had much less effect, if any at all, on what most painters, collectors, dealers, museologists, and government functionaries actually have done and continue to do than it has had on what they say. The features of the anti-market mentality are first described in chapter one, and they appear and reappear in their protean forms in other chapters. Some are unintentionally amusing, as in one of Vasari's *Lives,* that of the excellent but diffident Andrea de Feltrini, a painter of Florence, who

had no taste for the hurly-burly of the marketplace and so formed a
partnership with a painter who did have the taste.

The disdain for the market is noticeable in what museums, the
subject of chapter five, say they would like to do and are not always
able to do because they haven't enough money to do it. They are
nonprofit organizations, and there is an economic theory at hand for
analyzing them. It is informative. One of the things it helps to explain
is why they exhibit only a part of their collection (about one-half in
the U.S.), yet want to collect more and want to build more storage
space. The reason is that they act as if their principal form of capital,
which is their art, were free. They also want to use more of their
resources for administration, research, education, and conservation
and to use relatively less for exhibiting their art. At present about
one-third of the space of new or newly enlarged museums is used for
exhibition, a proportion that is less than it once was. One reason for
the declining importance of exhibition is that museums have taken on
functions they did not have in the past or were less important than
they now are. The explanation is in what economists call the agency
relation, which is the relation between those who provide the resources for an organization and those who administer their use. In
organizations of all kinds, the administrators ideally should fulfill the
intention of the providers. That does not always happen and happens
less in a nonprofit organization than in an organization conducted for
profit. The agency problem in art museums is disclosed, for example,
in the way their purposes have changed, in the increasing importance
of research expenditure, in the declining importance of exhibition,
and in the controversy over popular exhibitions, which is a controversy over how important attendance is, and that in turn is the issue
of whose interest a museum is supposed to serve. Some museum
people seem to believe their professional standing—which affects
their present and future income, of course—does not depend so much
on how the public at large likes what they do as it depends on the
critical and historical value of what they exhibit as that value is
judged by their fellow professionals.

The distress museologists feel about attendance has become
more noticeable now that "blockbuster" exhibitions are being enlarged into "megashows" that include the performing arts, so that
along with painting and sculpture the public is offered theater, film,
music, and dance. The distress is a kind that can be felt only by a
nonprofit organization. One cannot imagine the management of Dis-

neyland feeling the same distress. Museums, to be sure, do not wish to be placed alongside theme parks. But they can hardly disassociate themselves from the enterprise of Charles Willson Peale, a painter himself and father of several others, the owner of one of the first museums in the United States, one of the few museums ever conducted as a private enterprise for profit. He certainly had his eye on the box office.

The nonprofit status of museums, although it does not entirely remove them from the market, does temper the market's harsh wind. It also does that for organizations in the performing arts: in music, dance, and theater. It is not the only shelter they have. They are subsidized in different ways in varying amounts by private benefactors and by government. In the United States, until a generation ago, the assistance was mainly private. Now government provides a significant amount, the federal government itself in more than 300 programs, and the governments of the states, cities, counties, districts, tax catchments, spending regions, and so on also give some help. The arts say they do not get as much as they deserve, not as much (they say) as the arts of Europe get from their governments (which in Spain and France importuned the Disney people to establish a Land within their borders). Nevertheless, in the United States, the place of government in the arts has become important. The arts would like it to become more so, in a relative as well as absolute sense.

Why people in the arts prefer government to private assistance, whether they are entitled to one or the other or either, whether (*quelle horreur*) they should justify themselves on the market—these are questions that draw art into the area of public policy. That area is the subject of chapters six and seven, which conclude the book. The aspect of policy that most often has engaged the interest of economists is why the arts cannot support themselves and should not be expected to do so. That is, most economists have believed and continue to believe government should assist the arts.

I am an exception, because I am not convinced by the arguments that have been made in favor of assistance, some eight of them by my count. In chapter seven they are described as fairly as I can describe them, and my objections to them are stated as plainly as they can be stated. The chapter brings one to the question ("overwhelming," to the people who value the arts, and less important to the greater number who do not): Should the arts support themselves? For readers who would like an immediate answer, it is that a strong argument can be made that they should. For readers who would like a brief as well as immediate answer, it is yes.

The issue is important, but so is another. Why *does* (not why *should*) the government assist the arts? That interesting matter is the subject of chapter six. It has gotten almost no attention, possibly because the reasons that have been advanced to justify government assistance have been thought to explain why it is given. But they do not stand up under scrutiny. Could there, then, be other reasons?

One might be what Burke called "the prolific imbecilities of reform." The National Endowment for the Arts in 1975 gave money to forty public schools in San Francisco to conduct an "art activity" that included teaching pupils and their parents farming and animal husbandry on vacant lots near the school buildings, the purpose being "to train people to address the critical problem of food shortages and in fact future survival." This seems to be as silly as government can get but was not as expensive as what another part of the government, the Department of Agriculture, was doing at the same time, which was to spend $25 billion to reduce food production.

But folly is an expletive, not an explanation. Looking closely at what government does usually uncovers a reason for its doing this, that, or the other thing for people in one group or another—in the arts, the schools, on the farms growing sugar beets, in Michigan making automobiles, or in the wilderness watching birds. The reason is often to protect people from the market, which means to provide them with a higher income than they could earn there. The government does not provide the protection out of a sense of benevolence or because it is infinitely wise. It does so because it is importuned to do so by the people who benefit. The importuning is rent-seeking (called that for reasons explained in chapter six). One finds that what the government provides the world of art in subsidies, tax advantages, and direct services (*a*) is sought by people in that world (who create, perform, produce, and enjoy art), (*b*) is mainly to their benefit and not that of the population at large which must finance the benefit by higher taxes or fewer public services, and (*c*) is obtained the more easily because the economic circumstances of the arts facilitate rent-seeking.

In the course of making my argument, I shall try to be convincing, of course; or if not that, to be plausible; or if not even that, then at least to be interesting. I shall try to be that by explaining that the economic characteristics of the arts are similar to those of the goods and services that are exchanged on the market and support themselves on it. Those goods and services mean different things to different people, yet have one feature in common: their value can be expressed in money as well as in other ways. The same can be said of works of art. Moreover, the values that are stated on the market are, some of them, values of goods that are as important as works of art, and some are more important. People in the world of art, and those outside it as well, would agree with this observation if they reflected on the field of wheat that the elder Pieter Bruegel painted and the actual wheat he saw.

THE PUBLIC ADDRESSED

This study is not meant for economists alone or even mainly for them, and its primary purpose is not to put forward a new application of microeconomics. The study does that, to be sure, and there are economists who may be interested in it for that reason. But the people to whom I want most to speak are outside of economics. They are interested in art because it is a part of our culture or because they collect it or because it is a practical affair in their lives 'as it is to artists themselves, to dealers, teachers, museologists, and people having to do with the cultural activities of government or simply because they like to visit museums.

The study is written in ordinary language as much as possible, and where the language of economics is used it is defined in the explanation of the idea it conveys. From time to time, when I wish to be as clear as possible to other economists and to myself, I have put things in the special vocabulary of economics and set them in brackets. The general reader who wishes to eavesdrop can note what they enclose; the reader who doesn't can ignore them. Parentheses, on the other hand, do not mark off the territory of economics or of anything else but are used in the conventional way (for parenthetical expressions of course).

The words "art" and "visual arts" are almost always used to mean painting, occasionally to mean drawing, prints, and sculpture, never to mean the decorative arts or architecture except if expressly stated. The term "the arts" has a general meaning that describes those objects and activities which provide an aesthetic experience (with a suitable exception for such things as sunsets, nightingales, and daffodils). The "performing arts" are a class of such activities, such as ballet, and are alluded to occasionally in order to make a distinction or to show a similarity to painting, painters, or museums. But the allusions are few, and the performing arts have only a small place here. There have been many inquiries into them, and they have gotten quite the attention they merit from economists.

About the visual arts, little has been written by economists. Some of that small amount has been of exceptional quality, like the work by J. M. Montias on the art and artisans of Delft in the seventeenth century, and the empirical studies of the prices of painting made by John Picard Stein and Robert Anderson. About museums, economists have written even less. There are the thoughtful papers of Alan T. Peacock, and they have an illustrious precedent: "The Use and Abuse of Museums" by W. Stanley Jevons, one of the great figures in the history of economics. He was not, however, at his best in this paper. It touches on many of the topics that museologists say are important—the scholarship or scientific inquiry of museums, their place in the education and improvement of the common people, the importance of how objects are exhibited, and the proper method of administering museums. Yet he said nothing about how they should be financed, a curious omission by an economist but understandable in a Victorian. "I find it very disagreeable to talk about money," a Trollope heroine says in *The Belton Estate*. Her suitor reflects it would be more disagreeable to have none to talk about but keeps the thought to himself.

The subject of money is not omitted in this study. Whatever faults it has, that is not one. Let us, then, get to it.

1

Art and Economics Reconciled

Get this into your head, no one really knows anything about it. There's only one indicator for telling the value of paintings, and that is the sale room.
—RENOIR

THE SUBJECT is the value of art: how it is described in economics and how people in art describe it differently when they talk about it, but not when they create, collect, and exhibit it, on which occasions they act like economists. The main question of this chapter is whether the value the market puts on works of art is consistent with their aesthetic value. I believe they are, and Renoir did too. His remark was reported by François Duret-Robert who added, "When he says 'value' he really does mean aesthetic value, not value in monetary terms."[1] Actually, what Renoir meant is that the two values are consistent.

The consistency makes economic calculation possible. That too is argued in this chapter and throughout the book. Because people in art calculate, their behavior lends itself to economic analysis. They do acknowledge there is a dollar-and-cents side to what they do, indeed lament the fact. Pictures have a price, so do violins and violinists; painters want an income; theaters and museums must be heated and lighted; guards, ticket sellers, and curators must be paid. Yet these facts, one is told, have nothing to do, really, with art as an object or experience having aesthetic value. The economic side of art is said to be necessary or inescapable. What is denied is that it has anything to do with art itself—the goal, purpose, objective, or end sought by people who provide it. An economist would say the costs they incur have a great deal to do with the value or quality of what they produce. If that were not so, all paintings would have the same price and so would all violins, and the incomes of all painters and violinists would be the same, or differ from each other for reasons that could not be explained or for no reason at all. The argument of this chapter is that the prices differ according to the aesthetic value attached to the objects.

The consistency of values is shown most clearly when an important painting is auctioned. The seller is as well informed as he can be about the importance of the work, and the buyers are also. Each of the latter has his reasons for wanting the picture, and the reasons are all related to aesthetic value in one way or another. The highest bid will be made by the buyer for whom that value is greatest. What is said about painting that is on the market can also be said about painting that is not (and it comprises a much greater part of the total stock). Its measured value must be consistent with its importance or simply with the care that is taken of it.

THE VALUED AND THE VALUABLE

By "the aesthetic value of art" I mean nothing more (or less) than the qualities that make it desired by someone. The definition casts a wide net, I admit. It seems to say the aesthetic value of an object is that which makes it aesthetically valuable. When the theory on which the idea of ecomonic value rests—the theory of marginal utility—was stated by Stanley Jevons in 1870, a contemporary remarked, Mr. Jevons seems to say the value of a good depends on its utility and its utility is what gives it value. Actually, the theory, although it may seem to be, is not circular. It says things are valued according to the utility they yield and utility is any kind of satisfaction an individual experiences from what he has. It can be one or a number of things, and it can differ among people. A painting can be desired for one or many reasons by one person or by many.

The reason can be beauty, yet to say that is not to say much, because the word means different things to different people and to any one of them when it is used about different objects. However, there is one thing beauty cannot mean. It is not an explicit property that everyone agrees is a necessary and sufficient condition of a work of art, a property that is clearly definable in professional or ordinary language, and that by observation can be said to be present or absent in a particular work. To be brief, by aesthetic value I do not mean an objective property.

Does anyone? Probably not. But people in the arts are known to express an opinion in a way that makes it sound like a demonstrable truth. Aesthetic value cannot be, and at most it can only suggest a limit or segment of a periphery within which a judgment of value can be made. It may not even do that. Consider the celebrated principle of Berenson, that a painting must have tactile values (its touch-stone?). Could that have been what Renoir meant when he said he knew he had finished painting a nude when he felt like patting her on the bottom? Some museums post signs, "Don't Touch." But not all do. Does that mean not all collections have tactile values?

Berenson's principle is not much heard of these days, and he himself made less of it as time went on. Actually, aesthetic judgments, or statements about aesthetic value, do not have the place they once had in art history, criticism, and reporting. They now are so unusual that they come as a surprise. In 1988, there was a grand exhibition of the works of Degas, and it must have included about everything he ever did including his photography. The ballet paintings were present of course, and they were described in one report as "breathtakingly beautiful."[2] Not everyone would have said just that, or would have said that at all. Some would have said they are pretty, others that they are beautiful but not breathtakingly so. Still others would sigh at still another exhibition of Impressionism and reflect that of the making of Impressionist exhibits there is no end and in the seeing of them there is endless delight, apparently.

In 1986, when the Helga paintings of Andrew Wyeth were made known to the world at large, a news magazine asked a number of knowledgeable people for their opinion of him. He has for years been one of the most popular painters in the United States, as indicated by the attendance at exhibitions of his work, and by the prices he receives for it. The knowledgeable people who were consulted were not of a single opinion about him. They did not even agree about whether he was to be taken seriously, whether he was an "artist" in the way knowledgeable people define "artist." Admittedly, Wyeth is difficult to place; but hard cases should not make bad aesthetics. If it laid down clear, certain, and universal principles, the difficulty would be overcome.

Aesthetics does not do this and has not in the past if one infers its content from the judgments that knowledgeable people have made about paintings. Ruskin said things about Turner that came to be believed and still are. He said things about Murillo and Teniers that if remembered would be an embarrassment (that Murillo was immoral and Teniers simply vulgar).[3] Jacques Maritain said religious painting must be judged by its power to enhance the belief of the viewer, the belief being not just Catholicism but Maritain's version of it.[4] In Naples in the seventeenth century, the Board of Deputies of the Capella del Tesoro did not believe the local artists were qualified to decorate it and called on artists from other parts of Italy. Today the excluded painters (Ribera was one) are in the museums of the cities that exported their talent to Naples.[5]

From the sixteenth to the nineteenth centuries, the mosaics of St. Marks in Venice when they became worn were not restored, nor was the original subject matter retained. They were replaced by new subject matter from new designs by artists of the day. In the great period of Venetian painting, Veronese, Titian, and Tintoretto made cartoons that craftsmen then set in the ceiling and walls in mosaic form. If today their work, or what is left of it, were to be replaced by that of living artists, for example, Enrico Baj, there would be a hue and cry and all right-thinking citizens would be expected to berate the vandals. Actually, there was controversy at the time, but it had nothing to do with the artistic heritage. An action was brought against the craftsmen who were to execute the cartoons in mosaic form. They were accused of painting over the old tesserae instead of using new. The episode touches on three parts of applied economics: property rights, cost-minimizing, and the principal–agent relation. Today there happens to be another controversy over a celebrated ceiling, that of the Sistine Chapel in the Vatican, and the controversy is another indication of the diffuse character of aesthetic judgments. The people engaged in the restoration insist that all they are doing is removing dirt from the surface and removing the overpainting done by previous restorers. Their principal critic says that whatever they are doing they shouldn't be doing it because Michelangelo's colors could not have looked the way the cleaned portion of the ceiling now does. (They certainly are different from the colors of the uncleaned portion and surprise one by their pastel shades.) The issue seems only to be authenticity: Is the cleaned or uncleaned portion nearer to the original? But if that actually were the issue, the history of art would have to be done over because innumerable paintings have been altered, a few by the artist himself. On looking at any of them, one cannot be certain whose work it is. There is not even agreement among recognized experts about whether a painting in poor condition is more true to the artist's intention than a painting that has been restored with fidelity to his intention. If things stood so in literature, we would not know whether Shakespeare or someone else wanted Hamlet to soliloquize. (Of this, more in chapter four.)

Impressionism and Postimpressionism provide another example of the caprice of aesthetic opinion. These painters are especially interesting because their merit is said not to have been recognized in their time. Admittedly, they were not popular. Meissonier spoke contemptuously about "the gang of *jeunes,*" and Daumier when he saw a painting by Monet in a gallery window urged the dealer to remove it. Puvis de Chavannes disliked the work of Cézanne. Moreover, the Impressionists and Postimpressionists didn't care for each other. Manet urged Monet who knew Renoir well to advise his young friend to give up painting while there was time. Years later Renoir said the work of Manet, who didn't want to be associated with Impressionism, suffered from the association. It made him give up black, Renoir said, and he should not have done that. Degas also regretted that Manet had given up his "magnificent prune juice" for the sake of light. Cézanne and Renoir disliked van Gogh's paintings intensely.[6]

Yet the fact that people disagree about aesthetic value does not mean the judgments they make have no foundation, hence no content, and thus no meaning. The judgments have a firm foundation in the preferences of the person who makes them, and his or her preferences have their origin in what economists call a utility schedule or (when they want to bring things to a high finish) the arguments in it. It is the collection of wants, needs, desires, likes, dislikes, propensities, aversions, etc., to goods and services which when acquired or avoided satisfy those wants, aversions, etc. To state the point simply, a painting has aesthetic value to a person if it gives him the satisfaction he calls aesthetic. And a liquid is thirst-quenching if it quenches his thirst.

This could be taken to mean there are no standards of any kind, not even in the sense of common preferences that are revealed by the choices people are observed to make. The idea then implies that choices do not show a central tendency, that likes and dislikes are scattered evenly over all of art such that if there are 100 people and 100 pictures each person will like only one of them and he alone will like it. The fact is otherwise, as every museum visitor knows. There are more people looking, or trying to look, at the Mona Lisa than at any of the other paintings by Leonardo a few feet away from it in the Louvre, and downstairs there are more Japanese being photographed with the Venus de Milo—full frontal, both—than in front of any or all of the sculptures nearby. The fact that people have preferences in common makes their behavior predictable. I once was standing at the head of the Grand Gallerie wondering if I should have coffee before making the long journey down it to see Cimabue's *Madonna in Majesty* (a picture that is an example of cost-minimizing as explained in chapter three). An American girl walked by uncertainly, paused, returned, and asked, "Do you work here?" The question was understandable since I was wearing a jacket similar to those worn by the guards and I was standing by in the idle fashion of a guard. "No," I said, "but are you looking for the Mona Lisa?" "Yes." "Second door to the right." A year or so later I was standing in the same place, wearing the same jacket, when two Germans came briskly forward and briskly demanded, *"Wo ist die—*?" Before they finished the question I waved them along to the second door on the right.

Taste is another name for preference, and, contrary to the wisdom of the ages, it can be described, analyzed, and to a certain extent can be explained (as it is in the next chapter). It can even be disputed, not (need I say?) by an absolute standard of aesthetic value, but for its consistency. If a man says he likes both *Greyed Rainbow* by Jackson Pollock in the Art Institute of Chicago and the *Assumption* by Titian in the Church of the Frari in Venice and wonders why, he might be told the Venetian painting of that period is distinctive for its high color along with the sense of movement just as some Abstract Expressionism is and that if, movement apart, he likes the high color of that Titian, he might also like the work of Mark Rothko.

Enough for the time, then, about aesthetic value.

Economic value, strictly speaking, is the general form of all value, including that which is aesthetic and that which is not aesthetic but is value of another kind. An object—good, service, or whatever—has economic value if it yields utility. If it is a work of art, the utility is aesthetic. If it is something else, it yields another kind of utility, and that utility is its economic value. To say that aesthetic value is "consistent" with economic value is to say no more than that the particular comes within the general, or that aesthetic value is a form of economic value just as every other form of value is.

That statement is, in effect, the proof of what this chapter claims. But I shall not leave the matter there. A consequence of the relation of the values is that the price of a work of art is proportional to its aesthetic utility. That, in turn, means the price of work A is to its aesthetic utility as the price of B is to its aesthetic utility. This is another way of saying the prices of things are proportional to their [marginal] utilities. In ordinary language that means when we buy something we believe it is worth its price; otherwise we would not buy it.

THE PRESENCE OF PRICES

To ask if something is worth its price is to ask if it is worth the other things that could be had for the same price. People in the arts ask this question—if they think at all of what they are doing, and they do seem to as much as anyone else does. When they ask it they are making an economic calculation. They ask it even though they are given to saying—are fond of saying, delight in saying, insist on saying—that considerations of money should not interfere with considerations of artistic merit.

The National Gallery of Art in Washington has a "Special Exhibition Policy for Corporate Contributors." The statement, after explaining that Congress provides money for special exhibitions but requires the Gallery to solicit private contributions, and after acknowledging that corporations have been generous, goes on to specify what they may and may not expect for their money. They may not, among other things, use trademarks inside the Gallery but may use them outside. They are to understand that special exhibitions open with a social event at which the lenders of works on exhibit are publicly thanked, and that the cost of the event is borne by the corporate sponsor. The sponsor may have a social event of its own and may serve liquor if that is done "in a manner consistent with normal practice" as described by the Gallery. How the corporation advertises the exhibition "must have prior approval" of the Gallery. The statement goes on for nearly a thousand words in this vein. A corporate executive of any sensitivity might just think he was being hectored, might even wonder if the Gallery wished him to believe that by accepting his money it was raising him from the netherworld of commerce into the realm of art with a way station in the purgatory of the policy statement. Also to be wondered is whether the statement was meant to show the world of art what a high moral line the National Gallery can take, higher even than the Metropolitan, its arch-rival, can take because the Met cannot rely on as much money from the government. Nevertheless, the National Gallery lives in the same world, the world where resources are scarce, wants are abundant, hence where choices have to be made, thus where economics obtrudes. When it bought Leonardo's *Ginevra Benci,* it must have asked whether the $12 million or so (the rumored price) could have been used to better advantage on other acquisitions, and the fact that it was not so used, the fact that the Leonardo was acquired instead of another work, means the Gallery believed the painting paid for itself. There is also the delicate matter of where the $12 million came from. Had it come from the government, it would have been a transfer from the public that does not visit the museum to the public that does. The question then would have been whether the people whose taxes paid for the painting received as much benefit from it as they would have gotten had they spent the money themselves on things of their own choosing (including gifts). Since most people prefer to spend their income as they wish rather than to pay taxes with it, may one not say the picture bought with their taxes would have been worth less than what they had to give up? Hence may not one say that in those circumstances the Leonardo was not worth its price? I believe one may say just that. There are others who emphatically declare that one may not say that at all.

The disagreement is examined in chapter seven, on subsidies. It happens not to have been an issue when the Leonardo was acquired, which was with money from private sources. As the gift was voluntary, the giver or givers must have gotten more satisfaction from doing what they did than from not doing it. In a word, *Ginevra*

Benci paid for itself, and the principle of economic efficiency ruled.

The Cleveland Museum of Art provides another example. In 1974, it bought a painting, *St. Catherine,* by Matthias Grünewald whose work was in only one other American museum, then learned the painting was not authentic, returned it to the dealer, and was refunded the million or so paid for it, while the dealer was left to reflect on the relation between value and cost, specifically that the value of a work of art, or what it is worth, is measured in money, just as its cost is measured that way; that there is a right and a wrong relation between them; and that when it is wrong someone loses, in this instance the seller.

The director of the National Museum of Wales must have reflected on the same question when in 1979, at a cost of about one million pounds, it acquired four cartoons that British experts said were the work of Rubens. An American expert said they were the work of a lesser artist of the same period. Each side attracted partisans, and a transatlantic row ensued. Meanwhile, the director could have taken note of the interest the money would have yielded had it been in bonds while the attribution of the art was being decided. There would have been no uncertainty about whether the bonds were really bonds and what was their price and yield. Of course, the bonds could have become worthless by the debtor's defaulting, hence the difference between them and the art is their being less risky, hence for a given return they are more expensive (all of which will be made clear in due course).

The Museum of Fine Arts in Dahlem, West Berlin, learned that the portrait of *The Man with the Golden Helmet* was not by Rembrandt as had been thought. The Metropolitan in New York is of the opinion that two paintings which for a long while were said to be by Rembrandt now are believed not to be (*Pilate Washing His Hands* and *Woman Paring Her Nails*). Surely these new attributions have not only lessened the importance of the paintings from an aesthetic and historical point of view but their money value as well, as indicated, for example, by the insurance provisions made for them. By the same reasoning, there must have been an increase in the money as well as artistic value of particular objects in the Vatican collection that the curators at the Metropolitan discovered were historically related when they were being prepared for exhibition there in 1983. In the Fine Arts Museum of Indianapolis, at the entrance to a small gallery that contains works attributed to Rembrandt and Titian, a guard was heard to say, "Ah—if 'attributed to' could be changed to 'by,' how much more the gallery would be worth!" (as art and in money).

What these examples signify is that people who buy and sell paintings make an economic calculation, just as people who buy and sell anything else do. What is calculated or decided is whether the object is worth what must be given up in order to get it.

THE ANTI-MARKET MENTALITY

This would not have to be said about art any more than about wheat were people in art and most of those outside of it not given to denying that the money value of art is consistent with its aesthetic value. They often go further and denounce the very idea of assigning a money value to it.

"To attempt an estimate of the money value of the contents of our museums would be an intellectual [sic] vulgarism. . . . A great collection is a service to society as free from the rules of demand and supply as the service of the law." This was said by T. R. Adam some fifty years ago.[7] About twenty-five years ago the National Bureau of Economic Research wanted to know the value of the collections of museums when it was making an estimate of the capital stock of the United States. The Bureau was told by museum authorities that such an inquiry was out of the question because the collections consisted of objects that were "priceless and irreplaceable." Later the authorities relented but no doubt held to their initial view that art should not be valued on the market. The view is centuries old and is honored in the present. In a conversation with the director of an American museum that is highly respected and rich, I asked why the value of the collection was not on the balance sheet. "Because it is not for sale," he said firmly. I then asked, not innocently, if the building was for sale since its value was reported. He then said that what is most wrong about the art world today is the attention it pays to money values. I thought again of Trollope's heroine to whom the mention of money was distressing and reflected that the museum director, like her suitor, would be even more distressed if there were none to talk about.

The museums themselves have been charged with fostering the very attitude that the director deplored. The charge was made by Robert Hughes in the first Harold Rosenberg Memorial Lecture at the University of Chicago.[8] They do this, he said, by calling attention to the price paid for their acquisitions. They are in fact not so inclined at all, as the National Bureau learned. Yet Mr. Hughes believes they are not silent enough and believes they invite visitors to think about money by the way pictures are exhibited, such as looping a velvet cord before a prized acquisition, which the Metropolitan did when it first hung Rembrandt's *Aristotle Contemplating a Bust of Homer,* acquired in 1961 at the then record price of $2.3 million, when the purchasing power of the dollar was about four times what it was in 1989. Is a guard always present where *Ginevra Benci* is exhibited because the National Gallery wants visitors to know it was costly or is he there because it is valuable? (On my first visit, he was staring intently at the painting—so I thought until he straightened his tie and combed his hair in the reflecting glass, using the picture as the most expensive mirror in the world.) The price of the picture is one of the very few a museum has come near to boasting about. "The cost per square inch of paint of the portrait . . . is the greatest in the history of collecting," John Walker stated in the catalogue of the National Gallery of Washington, of which he was director when the painting was acquired. That seems to warrant the objection of Mr. Hughes, at least for amateurs of the same disposition as Trollope's young lady. So also does Mr. Walker's remark about Rogier van der Weyden's *St. George and the Dragon* that, "It was bought at auction, and the final bid represented a price of $26,552 per square inch." He provides the dimensions of the picture, from which the spectator can compute the total price. However, this may be read as badinage. What is usual is for museums to keep a solemn silence about the value of their collections. Mr. Walker himself, in his autobiography, describes how the Leonardo was acquired, and does so in great detail, yet never mentions the price, nor does he offer any clue to it.[9]

If museums were as far removed from the market as Mr. Hughes would have them be and ignored the money value of paintings as well as disdained it, they would not know where to place their guards, if they had any at all. Art thieves, however, know the value of pictures and would not be misled by which were protected and which were not. Insurance companies and police details are also informed, and each in their own way and for their own reasons believes the money value of paintings is relevant.

Not so, however, was an outraged Englishman, L. J. Olivier, who wrote to the *Times* of London about its index number of art prices. The very height (depth, really) of commercialism and vulgarity (intellectual and other), he called it, and went on to say why. His objections are typical, even commonplace, but are stated with a brio that makes his letter noteworthy. His fervent hope is that in due time the "philistine businessmen . . . and wretched art journalists will be stoned to death with fake Etruscan bronzes." His Parthian shot is at the editor: "In the meantime, a curse on your loathsome percentages and despicable graphs, and shame on you, Sir."[10]

The fulminations of Mr. Olivier are in my notes under the rubric "Art Mentality," which comes within the larger class "Anti-Market Mentality," and that in turn is within the still broader class known to Neo-Austrians and others as the "Anti-capitalist Mentality." As this book continues, it will give other examples, more often of the species, Art Mentality, than of the genera, Anti-capitalist. I leave the latter to the followers of von Mises, as they are better suited than I to detect it, and from the former I turn for a time, yet not forgetting, as James Jeffrey Roche said, that "all love Art in a seemly way/With an earnest soul and a capital A."

Consider now what economics can say about what art is worth, or its value, specifically, whether the price of a painting is related to or determined or influenced by its intrinsic quality, merit, or aesthetic value. The question stated still more specifically is whether the prices of paintings are proportional (at least ordinally) to their aesthetic value. For example, if for any reason the world of art believes painting A is superior to painting B, is the price of A likely to be higher than the price of B? The answer in my opinion is likely to be yes. That opinion rests on several kinds of evidence, namely, (*a*) private collectors are reasonably well informed about what they buy and sell, dealers are well informed, and major museums are very well informed; (*b*) while the market is not perfectly competitive—since works of art are not homogeneous—there is reason to believe the range within which prices are set defines the limits of aesthetic value; (*c*) prices set at auction and values given in tax inquiries are consistent with the aesthetic quality of the works; and (*d*) the prices received by the major artists of the present are consistent with the professional judgment that is made of their work.

Each of these kinds of evidence will be described in turn, that related to (c) and (d) in detail in this chapter, while that related to (a) and (b) will be summarized here and described in detail in chapter four which is about the market. I must first say that none is conclusive and at best is no more than strongly suggestive. The information that is available does not allow one to say with certainty that the prices of paintings are proportional to their merit as art. With one possible exception (the prices received by living artists), the information is not the kind that would be admitted to a workshop in econometrics. However, it is quite the equal of the information which the art world presents to support its conclusions—the conclusions of art historians, curators, collectors, connoisseurs, art administrators, critics, journalists, and others who write about art.

Many of these people—although, significantly, not all of them—believe the judgment of the market and their judgment have nothing to do with each other. "The enormously high prices that works of art now bring . . . bear absolutely no relation to the quality of the object, but then prices rarely do," said Hilton Kramer, a principal in New York art circles, in his contribution to the *Arts Review,* which the National Endowment for the Arts published in 1987. "The market value of a painting?" a curator at the Louvre said, repeating my question. "Poof—what does that mean!" she shrugged, as if no thinking person would ask such a question. Nonetheless she explained. The market value depends on whether the painting is hung in the Louvre or in a lesser museum, where it is hung and how often, what is its condition, if it has been repainted or otherwise restored or has been altered, where it was before it came into its present ownership, how certain the attribution is and if it ever has been changed, whether the painting is interesting at present to art historians or whether the painter is, whether other works of his have been at auction and what price they brought, in whose private collections the painter is represented, whether he is being spoken of in the popular as distinct from the professional art journals (*ARTnews* as distinct from *The Burlington*), and if dealers are promoting or disregarding him.

These considerations were not every one of them named by the French curator, but all have been mentioned by people in art who have spoken about the price of paintings. What is interesting is that these considerations do not remove art from the scope of economics. What is said about the factors that affect the demand for art can be and are said about the demand for other goods and assets. For the painting, substitute a common stock, and for museums substitute portfolio, or mutual fund, then ask which are holding IBM, in what amount, what is being said about it by Value Line and Merrill Lynch, what has its price been and what has been the volume of trading, are the services advising buy, sell, or hold? The only question asked about paintings that is not asked about securities has to do with attribution. There is no danger that what is represented as a share of IBM will turn out to have been issued by General Motors.

Yet there is also a form of uncertainty about securities—it is indeed the single and the great uncertainty—which is analogous to the uncertainty about the attribution of a painting. What is analogous is the yield, or return, or satisfaction, that each provides or fails to provide, and there is no certainty about what that will be from either. The earnings per share of IBM can fall or rise, and the satisfaction from a painting will change if there is a change in its place among all paintings, say, because its attribution changes. The collector who bought a Flinck which later is discovered to have been painted by his teacher, Rembrandt, will get more pleasure from the painting than he originally did, and if he doesn't, he can sell it for much more than he paid and take pleasure in the profit.

The people in art, then, are not completely outside of economics. But they have some way to go before they reason entirely within it.

BUYERS AND SELLERS MISCONCEIVED

Among the more egregious misconceptions held by people in art is their notion of how the market operates (a misconception they share with much of the human race, unfortunately). They believe buyers do not know what they are doing, or do not know as much as they ought to know, and that sellers take advantage of the ignorance. That, on the face of it, is a solecism. Most collectors of art are on both sides of the market because they sell as well as buy. If when they are buying they do not know enough to avoid paying an excessive price, they cannot when they are selling know enough to charge an excessive price. The same person cannot be an ignorant buyer and a shrewd seller. Of course there are the dealers, the middlemen, the hobgoblins of misconceived economics. But they cannot, like a deus ex machina, be brought in to dispel the solecism. If one dealer can profit from the ignorance of collectors (and it would have to be ignorance about selling as well as buying), so can another dealer and another and another. They would be driven, regretfully but necessarily, to lower the price of what they sell, and raise that of what they buy. The result is that the collector, whether ignorant or knowing, pays no more than he need and receives no less than he must. In order for the outcome to be so happy there must be competition among dealers (and collectors). To believe there is competition certainly is plausible. There are hundreds of dealers and thousands of collectors. On either side, but not on both, there is profit to be made from conspiring to turn prices to the advantage of one or the other. There is, however, no evidence that any one has more price power than another has.

There is considerable evidence that the market in art is reasonably well informed, meaning by "reasonable" that the people who buy and sell spend time and money to inform themselves to the extent that the expenditure is worthwhile. A collector who had an eye on Rembrandt would not spend as much as a museum, and a museum would not spend as much as the Amsterdam research project, which itself does not have unlimited resources to invest in information. Major collectors usually are knowledgeable about their particular interests—knowledgeable about aesthetic considerations, about considerations of an art-historical nature, and of course about prices. Moreover, they often seek expert opinion about what they mean to do. How they go about doing it is described in chapter four. An interesting feature of American collecting is that much has been done by businessmen who have gone about it with the efficiency and dispatch that made their enterprises profitable and enabled them to become collectors.

Museums are the other component of the art market. No one would deny that considerations of aesthetics and art history govern their decisions to buy and sell. This does not mean each museum would assign the same value, economic or aesthetic, to a given work. To some it would be worth less than to others, because they have different goals, some are nearer than others to realizing them, and given the goals and the extent to which they have been realized, there are differences among museums in the value of information.

AESTHETICS AND ECONOMICS AT AUCTIONS

There is another kind of evidence of the consistency of economic and aesthetic value. It is that information about auctions is widely reported. That is in keeping with a standard proposition in economics according to which the more informed buyers and sellers are about a market the more efficient it is likely to be. The market for art is not efficient in the way the market for securities is efficient. There is no reason to believe it should be, because the cost of making it so would probably be greater than the gain. However, it is a market where bids and offers reflect the merit or esteem in which a work of art is held by critics, museologists, art historians, and connoisseurs.

About auctions there is abundant information, although, to be candid, an economist would like still more, and that is a statement or classification of the prices at which given works have been sold at different dates. What is available and is especially interesting is the classification of the works of an artist according to their authenticity: whether a given work was done entirely by him or very probably was done by him alone, whether it was partly done by him, whether by his students, by assistants in his workshop, or under his influence, or whether it is a work done in his style while he was living or later. In addition, there is information about where the work was before it came to the given sale together with the names of the buyer and of the auctioneer, the place and date of the sale, the material of which the work is made and what it is about (for example, painting on copper of two figures, landscape in background, dog lower left corner). In addition, there is of course the price, yet that, *mirabile dictu,* is not clear. Sellers may set a minimum or reserve price, and if the bidding does not reach it a bid is made at the reserve price by an agent of the auctioneer, and the work is returned to the owner. The fact may be reported later or discovered or may never be known. How many prices are real and how many are fictitious, the auctioneer and seller alone know. However, I would not be surprised to learn that most prices are actual prices; that is because sellers must pay the auction house a commission whether the work is actually sold or only seems to be.

The information about the market has a cost, and it is paid by the people who use, buy, and sell art. The information would not be collected, distributed, and paid for if the market was indifferent to aesthetic quality. The art market is not indifferent, no more than is the museum world. There is, in fact, a striking resemblance between the way museologists classify art according to its authenticity and the way the market classifies it. The similarity is interesting to an economist and should also be interesting to people in art. I do not mean the market and the museums always agree on attribution or authenticity but that both attend to it closely. An instructive comparison can be made between *Art Prices Current,* a kind of trade publication, and the *Census of Pre-19th Century Italian Paintings in North American Collections* by Burton B. Frederickson and Federico Zeri (1972). *Art Prices Current* lists the sales of the work of any one painter in descending order of the probability of their being autograph (done entirely by the painter named), with those most probably so at the head of the list and at the bottom those not done by him at all but only in his style. Not surprisingly, the prices drop as one goes down the list. The *Census* reports whether the painting is autograph, if it is a copy, has been done by a follower of the painter, has been done in his manner, is of the school of the painter, whether the attribution is uncertain, whether the attribution is to more than one painter, or if the painting is an "imitation" which implies it is a forgery.

If the classification of a painting is changed, whether by the market or by expert opinion, the price is almost certain to change simply because (as I have been at pains to explain) the opinion of experts is the principal determinant of price. As this is written, the museums and collectors who own paintings by Rembrandt must be on edge because the Rembrandt Research Project of Amsterdam has been re-examining the paintings that have been attributed to him. Proceeding chronologically, it has studied ninety-three paintings he was said to have done between 1625 and 1631, and concluded that forty-two of them actually were, forty-four were not (of which eleven are in the United States), with the remaining seven in an undecided status. The study is continuing, and the final volumes, to be published after 1988, will report the findings about the work of the last twenty-five years of Rembrandt's life.[11] The economic effect of removing a painting from autograph status is to reduce its value by as much as $1.5 million.

In view of the consistency of values, one would expect this effect to be noticed in the reports that are made about auctions. It rarely is. It was noticed in the report of the sale of the Rubenstein and Thompson collections in 1966. "Despite all of the intangibles of auction sales the prices reached prove a good yardstick for judging the quality of the material," the report stated.[12] Another rare notice, and one that stated the consistency as clearly as it can be stated, is a report of the brisk trade of the eighties in nineteenth- and twentieth-century American art. "Indeed, said Carl Jorgenson [a dealer] in Washington, D.C., 'The market really revolves around experts and expert opinion.' It works both ways, said Roger Howlett of Boston's Childs Gallery. 'They feed on each other,' he said, with museums' attention sparking interest in the market place and market excitement generating scholarly monographs."[13]

The consistency of values is also indicated by a practice of the Internal Revenue Service, a surprising source of information about aesthetics, but one to be noticed. It has an Art Advisory Panel of twenty-five members who are dealers, museum officials, scholars, and people from auction houses. They meet periodically to advise the IRS about what it calls the "fair market value" of works of art that appear on tax returns as bequests, gifts, or charitable donations. An unsurprising feature of the practice is that the panel finds the value of many of the works is overstated (in 1984, 71 percent of those that appeared on personal income tax returns).[14] What is more interesting and may be surprising to the art world, although not to an economist, is that the estimates which members of the panel make are similar. That is, the scholars and museologists concur with the dealers and auctioneers (not, in all likelihood, to the last dollar, however). Of course they could all of them be wrong, or their estimates may have nothing to do with how a historian or curator would judge a painting from a purely aesthetic point of view. Conceivably they could, when they estimate the proper price of a painting, imagine they were dealers and wonder what they would do if they were not who they are, but were someone else. Hume also could have been wrong when he said a miracle is to be believed if to disbelieve it constitutes a greater miracle.

VALUE AND PRICE IN CONTEMPORARY ART

The last kind of evidence that bears on the consistency of values has to do with living artists: with the standing they have in the art world and the prices of their work. This information was brought together from time to time in the 1970s by the late Willi Bongard of Cologne, an economist, art journalist, teacher, and man of parts. He made a judgment of the standing of an artist by noting the recognition the artist received in such ways as being in the permanent collections of museums, by one-man shows, group shows, by the notice received in periodicals and television, and by other marks of esteem. Dr. Bongard boldly assigned numerical values to each mark according to his esti- mate of its importance. Thus an artist was assigned 300 points for each work in a major museum like the Metropolitan and 200 for each in a museum not quite as major like the Art Institute of Chicago or the Stedelijk of Amsterdam; if the artist was mentioned in *Art Actual* he received 50 points and in *Connaissance des Artes* 10 points. This was done for a large number of artists, and the 100 having the greatest number of points were ranked according to their totals. Dr. Bongard then obtained the current price of a representative work of each of the 100 and added it to his compilation. The two numbers invite a statistical analysis because the point value of each artist is an indica- tion of the aesthetic value of his work, and the price of a representa- tive work is of course its economic value.

With the help of a colleague, I did a regression analysis of the information in order to see if the price of a painter's work was con- sistent with the points assigned to him and I found it was. The corre- lation was far from perfect; but the results did show that as the number of points increased 10 percent, the price of the representative work increased 8 percent. [The coefficient of aesthetic value was .59 with t $= 4.2$, and $R^2 = .25$.]

The purpose of Dr. Bongard's investigation was quite different from what I made of it. He did, to be sure, want to see if the market correctly measured the value of an artist's work, yet not in order to make a judgment about the artists or the market but to discover if any were underpriced. He was looking for bargains. For each artist, the price of a representative work was divided by the number of points assigned to him, the result being the price per point. In 1976, the American Rauschenberg was first among the 100 with 20,490 points, and the price of a representative work of his was 17,000 West German marks (about $6,000 at the exchange rate then). Dividing 17,000 by 20,490 gives .83 or a price of 83 pfennigs per point. There were differ- ences in prices per point among the artists (the average was 1.8) which follows from the fact that the correlation between total points

and prices was not perfect. The German Becher was at the bottom of
the list with 5,170 points, a representative price of 500 marks, and a
price per point of .09. That made his work a bargain since his price–
point ratio was only 5 percent of the average of 1.8. Rauschenberg's
work was also said to be low priced because his ratio was less than
half of the average. The work of artists whose ratio was above the
average was said to be expensive, such as that of the American
sculptor T. Smith whose ratio was 2.7.

Those in the world of art who took notice of Dr. Bongard did
not care for his inquiry. The artists themselves affected indifference but kept an eye on the periodic lists. An American who said
he didn't care where he ranked fired off a lengthy cable after slip-
ping down the list one year, Dr. Bongard related with amusement.
Critics objected to his presuming to measure aesthetic standing or
alternatively objected to the way he did it. Their main objection
was to his relating the standing of the artists to their prices and to
classifying artists according to whom among them gave buyers the
most for their money. If Mr. Olivier was incensed by the mere reporting of prices, he would, had he seen Dr. Bongard's information,
have been apoplectic.

To tell collectors where to get the most for their money is just
what he meant to do. His "price-per-point" for an artist is analogous
to the earnings–price ratio of a share of stock. He called his list of 100
artists the *Kunst Kompass,* and reported it from time to time in
Capital, a business magazine published in Cologne. It was translated
and republished elsewhere, including the Italian design magazine
Domus, [15] where the greatest bargains were described as *convenien-
tissimo.* Dr. Bongard compounded his offense by offering collectors,
at a price, a monthly letter about the state of the market for contemporary art. The letter was suspended after his death in 1985 in an
automobile accident but will be resumed if the plans of his widow
materialize.

Willi Bongard advised people how to maximize their return from
art, or how to get the most for their money. Value for money, indeed!
How irrelevant, Louise Lippincott said in *Selling Art in Georgian
London.* She examined "how dealing and collecting advanced or
detracted from the formation of the English school of painting," and
she did so by "looking beyond the irrelevant question of whether the
collectors received value for money." [16] Actually she didn't ignore the
question, and had she done so she would not have had much of a

book. It is about Arthur Pond, who was a painter as well as a dealer, and the collectors he dealt with surely thought the question was relevant. They could hardly have thought otherwise. Can one imagine the following conversation?

"Tell me, Mr. Pond, what is the price of that landscape?" "Price, Sir? The question is quite irrelevant, you know." "Irrelevant, Mr. P.? I say!" "Indeed, it is. What is relevant is how your purchase will advance or detract from the formation of the English school of painting. You must think of that, you know." "Just so, Mr. Pond, and I shall leave such thinking to you while I pop down the road to a chap who will tell me the price of what I fancy."

ART AS A COMMODITY

The "value for money" that buyers then wanted and still do (whether or not historians want them to want it) is simply the satisfaction the ownership of art provides—not simple in the sense that it is simple to describe but in the sense in which satisfaction was defined a few pages back. Art provides satisfaction, or utility, in the same sense that any object that is desired provides it. It is not the same for all objects, obviously, or does any one of them provide the same utility to everyone. What they all have in common is that they yield utility of some kind in some amount. That (again, as explained above) is what gives them value.

A painting can be regarded as a capital good if it is expected to yield utility, hence is expected to be desired for as long as it endures physically. Old Masters are of this category. An example is a self-portrait of Rembrandt. He did more than fifty, and all are esteemed. Are they an exception to the principle of diminishing marginal utility? No. Any one of them would be esteemed even more if the others did not exist or were found not to have been painted by Rembrandt. If a painting is not likely to be desired—to yield utility—for as long as it can survive physically, it can be regarded as a durable consumer good that is subject to obsolescence. That is a good which is discarded before it is worn out. Most art is in this category, and the reason is explained in the next chapter. An example is scarcely possible because hardly anyone would know anything about it. A few will know there was a painter named Ambrosius Holbein, the son of Hans and elder brother of the younger Hans. If any of his work has survived, it is not well remembered.

Whichever a painting is—a capital or a consumer good—it is an object that in and of itself yields utility. It is valued for the satisfaction it provides *someone*. All consumer and capital goods are of this nature, for example, a house and the furniture in it, the paintings on the walls, and the land on which it is situated. They are called real assets. They are distinct from financial assets, such as a bank account or a share of stock. What the owner of a financial asset receives is interest or dividends or access to ready money (liquidity). What the owner of a painting receives is the satisfaction of owning it, which may be the pleasure of looking at it, of inviting others to look at it, of knowing it belongs to him, or knowing others know it belongs to him, of its being part of a collection that expresses the taste, knowledge, effort, and character of the owner, of its being something that will perpetuate his memory, or the satisfaction there is in some other consequence of ownership. Ultimately the satisfaction that is gotten from the visual arts is the visual experience they provide *someone,* whether or not he is the owner. If the satisfied person is not the owner, the owner nevertheless derives satisfaction from knowing that what he has is valued by others. What is not included in the satisfaction of owning art is an explicit money return, and that is what is provided by a financial asset. If a man buys a picture, he hangs it on the wall, and the return it yields is the pleasure he gets from its being there. If he buys a bond he puts it in a safe place, and the interest he collects is the return it yields.

The market value of both the painting and the bond may increase, and if they do they will yield an additional return. But the additional return cannot have been expected by the market, that is, by other sellers and buyers. If it had been, the price of the painting and bond would each have been higher than it was: the collector would have paid more for his picture, and the bond holder more for his bond. This does not mean there can be no profit in buying and selling art or securities. There can be, and there also can be losses; and both are uncertain. If a painting or share of stock was certain to be worth twice as much tomorrow as today, the price would double today.

The distinction between real and financial assets is useful, as useful in the world of art as in other worlds. It is at the center of the explanation of why art is not a superior investment, as claimed, and why as a speculation it is even less attractive. It also explains why people who do not care for games of chance acquire art for its own sake and not for profit. The explanation, set forth in chapter four on the market, rests on economic theory and observation, not on morality.

SUMMARY: BEAUTY, TRUTH, AND THE MARKET

The argument of this chapter is that the value which the market places on works of art is consistent with the judgment which is made of their aesthetic quality, a term I use to mean beauty, historical importance, or any attribute other than price. In saying that economic and aesthetic values are consistent, I mean that if outside the market painting A is said to be superior to painting B then on the market the price of A will be higher than B.

In support of the argument there is evidence of several kinds. What museums offer to pay for a work is (given their means) determined by the judgment made of its artistic merit, which of course would include the suitability of the work for the collection of the museum. This fact would be acknowledged by people in art, certainly by museologists, but possibly not by living artists since they are in competition with the dead.

What is not readily acknowledged, or acknowledged at all, is that collectors are well informed. The stories are legion of how they indulge their bad taste with good money that ought to be spent on something the storyteller favors. However, a detached view of the information about collectors (a view detached from the anti-market mentality) indicates their choices too are governed by artistic merit (again, given what they have to spend). Their choices are naturally more personal than those of a museum, and that is explained by what each is trying to do as well as by how ably each can do it. A curator who makes a recommendation no doubt thinks of what others in his profession will say about it. A collector of course may wonder what other collectors think of his pictures. But his standing in the world where he makes his income is not likely to be affected by their opinion.

Just who painted a picture is considered when a judgment is made about its aesthetic value. That the value is consistent with economic value is indicated by the fact that when the attribution of a painting changes its price usually changes. There is additional evidence of the consistency in the close attention paid both by the market and by people in art to the question of how nearly autograph a work is (done entirely by the artist, done in part by assistants, by students, and so on).

That does not complete the evidence. There is also the fact, minor but not insignificant, that when museologists and historians are called on to estimate the value of a work that figures in a tax return, their estimates are similar. Then there are the findings of Willi Bongard about the standing of living artists on the market and in the art world. They indicate that the price of a representative work is higher for artists who have received greater recognition (by being in permanent collections of major museums, for example). The prices are not perfectly proportional to recognition, as Dr. Bongard measured it, but close enough to show a statistically significant correlation.

Whether or not the argument is granted—that the market recognizes aesthetic value as much as the art world does—everyone will agree that when works of art are bought and sold they have a price. The price represents the value of an object that provides something or other to those who pay it; if they got nothing from the object, they would not pay anything for it. What people do receive from the art they pay for is pleasure, pride, instruction, enlightenment, inspiration, or any other kind of utility as economists use the word, to mean a return of one kind or another. That return is the yield from art, and in principle it is measurable. If a collector spends $10,000 on a painting instead of buying bonds that yield 7 percent, he is giving up $700 a year. If he believes the painting is worth what he gave up in order to get it, as he must if he buys it, the yield from the painting is at least $700.

If one does not grant the argument, that is, if one denies the market recognizes aesthetic value, one nevertheless must grant that people who buy art get something from it, including aesthetic pleasure, even if it is not related to what is paid for the art. Art, then, is acknowledged to yield a return. What yields a return is either a capital good or a consumer good. A work of art is capital if it yields utility as long as it endures physically, that is, until it deteriorates if it ever does. If before it deteriorates the interest in it passes away, it no longer yields utility to anyone and it is a consumer good that is subject to obsolescence. Most art has been of this kind. The world lost interest in it sometime after it was made, let it fall into neglect, then discarded it. Whichever a work of art is—capital or consumer good—it is a real asset. That is an object which is valuable in and of itself. It is distinct from a financial asset, like a share of stock, which is a claim against a real asset and is valuable for the dividends it yields.

The distinction between real and financial is the distinction between an object and the claims against it. Art, as explained in chapter four, is a lackluster investment, and as a speculation is not attractive except to people who relish risks, as many seem to do considering the popularity of lotteries. For others, the "gain," "profit," or "return" from art is the satisfaction it offers as an object. The satisfaction can be aesthetic in the narrowest or in the widest sense; it can be moral or didactic or heuristic; it can be of the earth or the heavens, subjective or objective, calling people to action or turning them in upon themselves. Its essential feature is that it comes from the object itself and not from the money income of a claim against an object.

Put simply, the most certain value of art is art itself. That has long been urged on grounds of morality. Here it is urged on economic grounds.

2

The Acquisition of Art

If you buy a work of art because you
like it, then that is the best form of
patronage.

—SIR ROBERT SAINSBURY

AS THERE IS for anything that is desired, there is a demand for painting; and as there is for anything that is scarce, it has a price. And like all other things, the price is determined by demand and supply. The demand is explained in this chapter (the supply in the next), and it is about such questions as:

What determines the interest people have in all forms of art and why are so few interested in any form of it? What determines the amount they spend on art? How is the demand for the visual arts related to the demand for other art forms, such as music? Does the principle of freedom of art apply to people who buy it as well as to those who create it? Just how does a patron of art differ from a purchaser? This chapter also considers how income affects the demand for art and is affected by it but leaves to the next chapter the important subject of how art is affected by who is spending whose money to buy it.

I am not, I hasten to say, able to answer all of these questions even to my own satisfaction. What I shall do is to use certain ideas in economic theory in order to throw some light on the questions—a prudent ambiguity that means to offer a tentative answer, a partial answer, a suggestion, or a guess.

ABOUT PATRONAGE

The most important of the questions is what determines the demand for art. It is also the most laborious to answer and is best postponed while we warm to the labor by considering a less complicated and more engaging question: What has patronage of the arts meant? This question is related to the issue of the freedom of art.

The first observation is that what art historians call "patronage" usually turns out on closer view to be simply buying, that is, a market transaction. Cosimo de' Medici I patronized Cellini in the way I once patronized General Motors. A second observation is that historians attribute great ages of art to patronage or at least associate great ages with it, hence patronage is presumed to be good for art and non-patronage to be bad. But since patronage usually has meant no more than purchasing, what follows is that many buyers are good for art and not as many buyers are not as good. That makes a great age of art like a good year for automobile sales. Do the people who write about art mean no more than that?

A third observation is that the first two must be qualified. Collectors have at times paid more for a painting than the least the artist was willing to accept and have done so knowingly in order to encourage him or to promote the visual arts as an activity. In this sense the collectors have been like the patrons of the opera or of a performing artist. They have given assistance and have not expected a return other than that the assistance be used for artistic purposes. Caillebotte, himself a painter, came near to being a literal patron. He was, Renoir told the dealer Vollard, "the first protector of the Impressionists. He did not buy our pictures as a speculation. His sole idea was to help his friends as much as possible, and this he did admirably, for he took only the things which were unsalable."[1]

The other qualification is that art historians have not always implied that an age when much art was bought was an age of great art; and if they were asked if more has always meant better, they no doubt would say no. In support of their answer they could cite the fact that in the 1960s there were more painters in New York City alone than in all of Italy in any decade of the Renaissance,[2] or that in the 1970s the number of art students in the state colleges of California (25,000) was many times greater than the number of apprentices during the great age of Florentine painting.[3]

This leads to an observation on the observations. What has been written about patronage is not as clear and careful as the writers could have made it. So while they do not expressly say the great ages of art have been those when there was a great demand for it, they say less than they should to warn the reader against making that inference. They come near to inviting the mistake when they write, as they have written, of the generosity, the understanding, the enlightenment, the exquisite taste, the magnificence no less, of certain patrons, and of the great services they rendered to art. Historians are even more culpable for failing to distinguish between patronage and a market transaction, and they leave the reader to discover for himself when a patron was a benefactor and when he was a customer.

BENEFACTORS AND CUSTOMERS

These observations can be illustrated from numerous accounts of the relation of artists to (*a*) people who have been their benefactors, which is the way I would use the word "patron"; and (*b*) people who have been customers.

One account is the *Autobiography* of Benvenuto Cellini. There may be reason to wonder if he told the whole truth about his derring-do, since he was given to bawling out praises of himself. However, there is the sound of truth in what he says about his business transactions because he does not come out of them covered with credit (in a moral, not accounting, sense). Cellini had dealings with Cosimo de' Medici I, who was duke of Florence as his uncle had been and like him was a collector, although not on as grand a scale. There is one sense in which he was a patron of Cellini (though not the sense in which I would use the word, to mean an intentional benefactor). For some of his art Cosimo paid more than it was worth to him, not because he meant to but because he received less than he expected. He might be called, as the American taxpayer has been called with respect to the arts, a patron despite himself.[4] Or he could be described as a dissatisfied customer. He was known to ask about the price of a work before he commissioned it, which is also more the way of a customer. The fortunes of the Medici family came from business ventures of various kinds. They probably also got something out of their commanding position in the public sector. They certainly did well from their activities in the private sector. One was banking, which of course includes money lending. The coat of arms of the family was the three brass balls that have come down the centuries as the insignia of a pawnshop. In time—so an English pamphleteer of the nineteenth century wrote in the manner expressive of the anti-market mentality—"the family of the Medici mounted from the counter to the throne [and] had the wisdom to sink the qualities of the merchant in the nobler attributes of the prince."

That was not Cellini's opinion. He was promised an annual stipend from the duke who sometimes paid it and sometimes did not. A stipend was not unusual and was not necessarily a gift or subsidy to the artist. It could mean a gift, but it also could mean he was obliged to provide something in return. The obligation could be to offer to the person making the stipend the first choice of what the artist did and to offer it at the market price. This was similar to the arrangement a magazine today has with contributors by which it makes regular payments to them in return for the right of "first refusal" of what they do and by which the contributor is paid an additional amount if the work is accepted. Cellini was to be paid for what became, along with the *Saltcellar,* his most celebrated work, the statue of Perseus. It was commissioned by the duke, and the price was to be determined in due course. Cellini claimed he left it to the generosity of the duke, as was fitting, he said, when dealing with a noble person. He came to regret he did so, because he discovered Cosimo "was more a merchant than a duke, [not] a prince but a commercial man" from whom he should have gotten a written contract.

What happened, one gathers from the *Autobiography,* is that the duke stopped making payments fifteen months after the commission had been given and the statue was not finished. Whether the payments were a part of the stipend or partial payments for the statue is not clear. The duke sent his man of business to ask when it would be finished and what the price would be. "I quickly replied that it was not my custom to put prices on my work," Cellini recounted and expressed his contempt for the man of business "with those spidery hands of his [and] shrill gnat's voice."

Cellini did not mean what he said about prices. Elsewhere he says he had hoped to get upwards of 5,000 crowns for the Perseus. The duke would not agree, and an acrimonious dispute ensued, followed by the two of them calling in an arbitrator who set the price at 3,500, which, Cellini avowed, was never fully paid. The duchess chided Cellini for not having put the matter in her hands and said she could have gotten him 5,000.

In his account of his business dealing, Cellini cut anything but a *bella figura.* That is odd, because in what he wrote he was at pains to do just that. For an income, he did not rely entirely on his art, as highly esteemed as it was in his day and as it continues to be. He speculated in land and did a little in the way of money lending. He writes of a merchant in Rome for whom he made a bust and who never paid for it. Cellini was outraged, although he had lived in the merchant's house and had paid no rent. He also left money with the merchant on the understanding it was to be loaned at 15 percent. The borrower was none other than Cosimo. The transaction is equivalent to Cellini's selling art to the duke on credit with a carrying charge of 15 percent on the unpaid balance.

What Cellini recounted is not given here as evidence that most patrons of art have been purchasers, but it is a signal illustration of my argument to that effect and is a suitable beginning to it. More persuasive evidence, although not as vivid, is what is said by Francis Haskell in his book on patronage in Italy during the period of the baroque.[5] It is about a period after Cellini's but a time when, there is reason to believe, the relation between artists and patrons had not changed substantially. Haskell states that a painter in the seventeenth century in Rome would begin his career by doing pieces for a few clergymen and continue in this way until he was known and obtained commissions from other buyers. Often he would be given a start by a bishop or cardinal who came from his region. The young painter's situation was uncertain ("precarious," in the language used outside of economics), and he would consider himself fortunate if he could become a *servitu particolare.* He then would live in the patron's house as a kind of upper servant, would receive a monthly allowance, and in addition would be paid for his paintings. Haskell says he would receive the market price, but that is improbable. Had he received as much from the patron as he could have received from someone else, he would have gotten more than the market price by the value of his food, lodging, and allowance. If in fact this did occur in a household, the patron was truly a benefactor—not a buyer of art, or an employer of the artist at a market wage paid partly in food and lodging and partly in an allowance—and there must have been a queue of young painters who aspired to become his upper servant. If there were any such desirable posts or soft touches, they were rare.

In northern Europe also there were painters who were household servants, one of them a very great artist, Pieter de Hooch. J. M. Montias relates that de Hooch was an employee of a burgher in whose household he rendered personal services in addition to painting pictures. The pictures when completed became the property of the burgher.[6] The arrangement appears to have been less favorable than that in Italy but was not necessarily so. The northern artists may have been paid more for their services, and that would have compensated them for not having been paid separately for their paintings.

Haskell states painters found the upper servant arrangement to be suitable only at the beginning of their careers which thereafter were best pursued by the artists leaving their patrons and opening a studio. Once established, an artist would obtain commissions, hence paint to the order of particular buyers, or would do a work independently of any particular buyer and sell it through a dealer, or would sell his work from his studio. Some painters had a stock of partly finished pictures which they showed to prospective customers who if they were interested could specify how they wanted to have them finished.

About placing their work on the market to be sold to no-one-knows-whom, Haskell writes, "Artists usually disliked the freedom of working for unknown admirers, and with a few notable exceptions exhibitions were assumed to be the last resort of the unemployed." The dislike could be explained as behavioral scientists today explain it and as it was explained in the nineteenth century by the young Marx and before him by Carlyle: as alienation, cash nexus, separation of worker from his product, dreadful freedom, etc., etc. Or the reason could have been that they preferred to paint a picture they were likely to be paid for because it had been commissioned rather than to paint one for a dealer who might or might not be able to sell it. In between the two practices in degree of risk the painter could add to his stock of unfinished pictures. In whatever way the painter worked—whether for a known customer, an unknown customer, or an in-between customer—the painter was supported by the market and not by a benefactor. His relation to the collector was an exchange relation, not a gift relation.

The fact can escape notice in the accounts we read of the close relation there has been between artists and the people who have asked them to do a painting or piece of sculpture—who have "given" them a commission. The relation is what one associates with a benefactor and his beneficiary, and the impression is deepened by the fact that the artist is almost always in an inferior position while the manner of the person who orders his work is the manner of lord and master. The duchess asks Cellini to help her wheedle money out of the duke as if Cellini were a member of the household, and at another time tells him if he had come to her she could have gotten more money for him from the duke, as if Cellini were a lesser member of the family. Yet on closer view the relation is seen to be that of buyer to seller or employer to employee. The artist was more likely to be in an inferior position if he did a commission than if he made a painting for the market, and his inferiority was the inferiority of working men. They have their way of getting back at the boss. Cellini in his *Autobiography* gave Cosimo several of the best. Giotto, whose fame was great and his commissions many, was more like an employee than a seller. He made his feelings known in the way a jester does. "Giotto, if I were you, this hot day, I would leave off painting for a while," King Robert of Naples once said to him. "So I should certainly, if I were you," Giotto answered. Michelangelo, who towered even higher and had a fierce temper, was nevertheless capable of abasing himself before the popes who engaged him for the Sistine Chapel. The commission for the ceiling was given by Julius II, whose successor, Paul III, commissioned him to do *The Last Judgment*. Before each he humbled himself, but not before Paul's master of ceremonies who objected to the nudes and later found himself depicted as Minos in hell with a serpent coiled around his nude middle. Louis XIII, after inveigling Poussin into returning to France, said to him, as if he were a runaway, "I've caught you!" He was unable to keep him, actually.

CONSUMER SOVEREIGNTY

Nevertheless, patrons were more often purchasers than benefactors. As purchasers, they expected what a historian referred to disdainfully as value for their money. What is reported about the means they used to get their money's worth indicates that in the market for art as for other things consumers have been a force to reckon with. They have not been sovereign in the sense that the artist has always done as he has been told and accepted what he was offered; but consumers have been sovereign in the sense of being able to decide for themselves what to buy and what not to buy. Artists on their part have done what they could to satisfy their customers while of course keeping within the bounds of their consciences, which do not seem to have been unduly narrow. The anonymous Master of the Sforza Palace in the last half of the fifteenth century painted the *Madonna and Child with Doctors of the Church and the Family of Ludwig the Moor*. Ludwig was the duke of Sforza, known as the patron of Bramante and Leonardo. He appears in this painting with his wife and two children, all smaller than the principals and kneeling in prayer beneath them. The Christ Child looks toward the duke and extends His hand in benediction. Surely the patron has been compensated for his patronage. This anonymous painting is not a rare instance of an artist seeking to please his buyer by placing him in the painting the buyer commissioned. In the same museum (the Brera in Milan where the Sforzas were the first family) is a greater picture, this by Bernardino Luini, and in addition to the Madonna and Child there are, suitably reduced in size, the buyer and his two daughters. Even Leonardo deferred to the taste of Ludovico when he painted "the court beauties of that subtle sensualist," according to Berenson who regretted that Leonardo did so.

The Lombard painters were not alone in dispensing compliments in this way, or (if the expression may be allowed) of thanking their patrons for their patronage. Or they may have been doing neither but simply pleasing the buyer. Perugino was commissioned by Pope Sixtus IV to have a part in the decorating of the Sistine Chapel. He did an *Assumption of the Madonna* that included a portrait of the pope kneeling before Her. Palma Giovane painted *Doge Renier Zen Blessed by the Redeemer* (Accademia, Venice). Christ is shown in the sky surrounded by a nimbus with putti, His hand raised in benediction over the doge who in the thirteenth century founded the Ospedaletto dei Crociferi. The painting was made for the building when it was renovated in the sixteenth century, and the artist surrounded the doge with dignitaries of the day, some clerical, some lay, who (one guesses) paid for the work. There is scarcely a museum in Italy which does not have a biblical scene that includes a portrait of the donors, usually clerics, depicted in the lower foreground, right and left, in an attitude of devotion.

The Italians are known the world over for their desire to please. They are not unique when they express it on the market. In England in the eighteenth century, George Stubbs, revered for his pictures of horses, did not always place them against a complete background. The buyer might ask for a building or a landscape or perhaps his dog, and Stubbs would add it. Or the buyer might want it just as it was. Benjamin Marshall, a follower of Stubbs, began as a portraitist, and turned to horses when he found there were buyers who were willing to pay fifty guineas for a picture of their horse but not ten for a portrait of their wife.[7] Stubbs was commissioned to do a portrait of a husband and wife on their horses. The husband later believed his wife was unfaithful and had Stubbs paint her out. When the painting was restored years later, she reappeared.

In the nineteenth century in France, Boudin (the pride of Honfleur) said his object was "to please the sovereign public. . . . My little ladies on the seashore are very popular. Some people even think there is a vein of gold in these subjects ready to be exploited." There was, and he exploited it. But he disliked doing so and turned to painting workingmen and sailors. His income fell, and so did the quality of his art, according to John Walker. "The treasure he had found, though he did not know it, had been aesthetic as well as commercial. . . . Boudin was a victim of social consciousness, perhaps the first but certainly not the last in the history of art." Who the others were—they who replaced the acquisitive with the aesthetic instinct— Mr. Walker does not say. He relates a charming episode in the career of George Inness of the Hudson River School. Needing money, Inness agreed to paint *The Lackawanna Valley* for the Delaware, Lackawanna, and Western Railroad which specified that there be four rails, a roundhouse, and the letters "D. L. & W." on the tender of the locomotive. Inness was offended but did as he was asked. Mr. Walker continues: "Out of the actual scene he was compelled to paint he has created a vision of ordered beauty. Today *The Lackawanna Valley* is more highly prized than the misty landscapes he painted at the end of his life when he had no patron to dictate."[8]

The doors of the Baptistery in Florence are another example of the authority of buyers. Antal says the first of the two that were done by Ghiberti "in every respect was exactly prescribed."[9] Vasari, however, says it was the outcome of a competition which Ghiberti won.[10] In either event, he tried to please the counsels of the Guild of Merchants who extended the commission and he did not try to please himself. He succeeded admirably, and they commissioned him to make a second door and "to make it as he pleased" (in Vasari's account). It is the more celebrated of the two, the door that Michelangelo said was worthy to be the gate to Paradise and is now the door around which so many tourists gather that most of them cannot see it. What the experience of Ghiberti indicates is that like many others he acquired the freedom to please himself by first pleasing others. The freedom which an artist acquires he does not always keep. The paintings Picasso did in his blue period, between 1898 and 1905, pleased buyers and commanded high prices, but the pictures he did in the thirties in a different style were almost unsalable.

The power of demand—the revealed preference of buyers—has been felt even by the romantics (small "r"), the free spirits who act on inspiration, to whom art is all and the world is nothing. Salvator Rosa in the seventeenth century is a letter-perfect example. Yet he kept a stock of finished paintings in his studio, just as the unromantics did, so that he would have something to show prospective buyers when they called.[11] Unlike his fellow painters, he would become angry with the visitors when they chose something other than what he wanted them to buy. But he sold when he could and he kept his inventory in order.

More examples could be given. Rubens offered to replace a hunting scene because the buyer said the lions were too ferocious and because the artist's assistants had done some of the picture. Rubens said he would replace it with a "hunting piece less terrible than that of the lions" and would paint the entire picture himself, that "on the word of a gentleman."[12] Raeburn did a portrait of John Tait, and later when Tait became a grandfather the family asked Raeburn to add the grandson, which he did. Marie Laurencin did a portrait of Chanel, the *couturière,* who didn't like it and refused to pay for it. "Yet I pay her for my dresses," the artist observed and went on to say she would "pretty up" the picture and sell it to the dealer Rosenberg, who, she knew, was making a collection of her work to give to his children. Gilbert Stuart was heavily in debt and put off his creditors by telling them, "I hope to make a fortune by Washington alone." He did a portrait of him on commission from Martha Washington and although he never finished it he made seventy-five replicas that he sold for $100 each—"Stuart's one hundred dollar bills"—one of which went to Mrs. Washington in place of the original she commissioned.[13]

Renoir told Vollard that most of the people whose portrait he painted had one thing or another to say about how it should be done. In 1868 he was down on his luck and did portraits to order. One was of "the cobbler's wife, which I painted in exchange for a pair of shoes. Every time I thought the picture was finished and saw myself wearing the shoes, along came the aunt, the daughter, or even the old servant to criticize." A few years later, during the Commune when he was poor again, he providentially was asked to do a portrait of a lady and her daughter. "I will say to her credit that she refrained from all comment on either my painting or my draughtsmanship. It was quite a new experience to find a sitter who never once remarked, 'Couldn't you bring out the eye just a little more!' "[14]

There have been artists who would not. They tempered the power of the buyer with their own temper or obstinacy. Carlo Saraceni, a Venetian who was in Rome early in the seventeenth century, was commissioned by the Carmelites of Santa Maria della Scala to do an altar piece, which he did, *Death of the Virgin* (now in the Art Institute, Chicago). Columns surrounded the head of the Virgin, and he was asked to replace them with angels. He refused, but there is a halo about Her head. Saraceni was a contemporary and admirer of Caravaggio who was commissioned by the same church to paint the same subject. The friars found his *Death of the Virgin* unsatisfactory also (Louvre). His *Madonna of the Rosary* (Kunsthistorische, Vienna) was also found objectionable, possibly because he gave prominence to the dusty soles of bare feet (which really do seem irrelevant as does the figure, perhaps the donor, in the lower left, of a man dressed in clothes of a period other than that of the religious figures). Caravaggio did *St. Matthew* for the church of San Luigi dei Francesi in Rome and again rendered bare feet and dusty soles in a way that offended. The church authorities refused the painting (now lost). He made a second painting, with the saint more saintly although not saintly enough to satisfy everyone. It did, however, satisfy the church and is still on the altar. The late David Smith, the American sculptor, is a recent example of the defiant artist (or semi-defiant, as Caravaggio was). "I don't price my work to sell it. I price it based on its worth," he said. Dealers wished he hadn't because few of his works could be sold. But within a few years after his death in 1965, the price of his work increased very much (from $15 for something the original buyer later sold to a dealer to $10,000).[15] That, as the next chapter explains, is a most unusual occurrence; the price of the work of most artists falls after their death.

To defy the market is laudable by the standards the art world today professes but does not always practice, indeed rarely does. To ask an artist to reduce his prices is thought to be demeaning, and to alter his work is an assault on his rights. The reason is partly art-historical; it interferes with the work of art historians. Another and more important reason is that there can be considerable economic value in the property rights of an artist (as explained in chapters three and four). But the reason most often given, even though it may not be the most important, is that to interfere with the judgment of an artist is to assault the conception he has of his creative efforts. Whether or not anyone else is interested in it, the artist is and is entitled to it. So the reasoning goes. It has multiple roots: in self-interest, in custom, in law, and in Locke's argument for private property. All are described in chapter four, on the market.

Alterations in works of art are restrained by still another factor. It is the opinion of people in the art world. While they agree restoration is not objectionable in principle and that conservation is in principle an obligation of museums and collectors, they may disagree about how these things should be done, and the disagreement can be intense. Consider the acrimony generated by the work (restoration/conservation/neither/both?) done on the ceiling of the Sistine Chapel in the 1980s. What would be said if the painting itself was to be altered, say, by concealing the nudity of the figures, or making it more obvious? Art historians will not be tricked into answering because they know Paul IV had da Volterra put loincloths on thirty figures in *The Last Judgment* and told Michelangelo it was to be done.

ART, AN ECONOMIC GOOD

From these engaging but not, I trust, trivial matters, we go to the stern stuff of economic theory and consider the principal subject of the chapter. It is the demand for art. To be examined is what determines the amount of art that people will buy at a particular price and how the amount changes when the price changes. If art can be treated as an object that is bought and sold—as I believe it can be, as in fact it has been for centuries—then the demand for it can be analyzed in the same way as the demand for goods and services of all kinds: food, clothing and lodging, the protection of life and limb (insurance and medical care), the care of the mind and the cure of the soul (education and religion).

Art is not demeaned by treating it in this way any more than religion is demeaned by noticing it requires the materials of the earth as well as those above. The Church for centuries obtained material support by asking its communicants to pay a portion of their income in return for what it provided them. In the church of the Gesuati in Venice is the celebrated ceiling by G. B. Tiepolo of the *Institution of the Rosary*. The Virgin is in glory with the Child, and they are surrounded by clouds of angels; below is St. Dominic who, having driven out heresy is distributing rosaries. "In this fresco [to cite the indispensable Lorenzetti], with its daring foreshortening, and movement of masses and lines, the superb conception quivers with a faith which finds vivid expression in the very delicate, almost evanescent tones of grey, green and rose of the group with the Virgin, which contrast with the strong and decisive colours below symbolizing the Fiend and Heresy." A visitor who happens by in the morning may hear the organist practicing in a loft above the high altar, which is decorated in lapis lazuli and a brocade of red and gold. The church is on the Zattere and faces the broad Giudecca Canal that sparkles when there is sun and glows when there is not. Is not the Gesuati a perfect example of what Justus Dahinden meant when he said a church "leads away from the profane to the transcendental"?[16]

Yes and no. That is not all there is to be seen. From time to time deliverymen arrive with boxes and stack them before the chapel in which there is the *Crucifixion* by Tintoretto. They contain candles that will be lighted and placed in candelabras about the chapels by believers who will have left 100 lire or more, depending on the size of the candles, in payment for them. This materialism seems not to trouble the communicants. If they were told that religion is demeaned by attending so plainly to money matters, they might reply it would be even more demeaned if it did not have the resources it needs to do what it is called on to do. They are scarce, hence have a price.

The same is to be said of the resources used in art—that is why it is not free. Whether it is worth its price depends on the value it has to the people to whom it is offered, the public. The value they place on it depends mainly on four considerations. One is the aesthetic judgment they make of works of art, and that was considered in the preceding chapter. There a passing reference was made to the fact that the amount of art people acquire is also influenced by their income, by their capital, and by the prices of other goods. In the language of economics, the position of the demand curve, denoting the quantity demanded at each price, is a function of family income, net worth, the prices of goods related to the given good as substitutes and complements, and utility which itself incorporates the aesthetic judgment. This last is removed below and replaced with indicators of utility: education, other "investments in taste," and age.

How the amount of a good that is bought at a particular price is affected by the income of the buyer, his capital, and the prices of other goods depends on how important the good is among all of the goods that can satisfy his desires, wants, or needs, that is, depends on the total utility of the *initial* dollar's worth of art relative to that of the *initial* dollar's worth of something else, or what Menger called the importance of the need as distinct from the intensity with which it is satisfied.

Goods obviously differ in their importance, and not everyone assigns the same importance to any one of them. This would not have to be said if it was not so often ignored. In the scale of human needs, the need for beauty does not rank as high as the need for food, not even for those who worship beauty. We do not have to be told that or to look at the world around us for evidence of its being so. Yet the fact seems to be overlooked by the people who want to generate public interest in the arts, by such means as "exposing" the young to it, which means rounding up schoolchildren and driving them in herds through the galleries on the supposition that when they grow up they will choose to spend Sunday afternoon in a museum.

I may not go so far as to say the young are urged to place art before eating. I have, however, seen them called away from the snack bar where they had slipped off to have a Coke while others were looking at pictures. In the Hirshhorn in Washington there is a monitory notice that reads:

In the Museum . . .
Please . . .
Muse, Converse, Smoke
Study, Stroll, Touch, Enjoy, Litter

Relax, E̶a̶t̶, Look, Learn
Take notes with P̶e̶n̶, Pencil . . .

Such are the devices of outreach, uplift, and downspeak.

What I am permitted to say is that those who promote art would like to change the preferences of the public so that art will ascend the scale of needs. This means—since income and time are scarce—that food, clothing, lodging, transportation, and the like must descend the scale.

ART, A LESSER GOOD

Actually, people do not have to be told what the art world believes is good for them. When asked in opinion polls, they answer in the way that world wants them to—that art is good and there should be more of it. What they do not do is behave as if they believe what they say. In an Australian poll, people were asked if the country benefited from the government's subsidizing of symphony orchestras, and two-thirds said yes. Yet 80 percent said they had not been to a concert in two or three years. In another poll they were asked what they would do with more free time if they had it. Less than 1 percent said they would attend arts performances, and 15 percent said they would use it for sports.[17]

In an American poll taken in 1973, 90 percent said they believe art museums are important, 66 percent that they are interesting, 62 percent that they should be visited often, 50 percent that they did not make one visit each year, 48 percent that they did visit at least once a year, and 2 percent were "not sure" they had made a visit (which could mean they were unsure that what they saw was art, and who, including the knowledgeable, has not been?). The 48 percent who said they made one visit a year were not all of them telling the truth. If they had been, the total number of visitors would have been 75 million, assuming there were that year 150 million people old enough to visit a museum. Since some people made more than one visit, the total number of visits (as distinct from visitors) would have been more than 75 million. But, according to the art museums, the number of visits was only 43 million.[18] Yet again, the museums are given to inflating their attendance, according to the former director of the National Gallery in Washington—by as much as 100 percent. That brings the number of visits down to about 22 million and the number of visitors to less than that, say, 15 million on the assumption that the average number of visits per visitor was one-and-a-half (which is probably low). These adjustments reduce the number of visitors by 80 percent (from 75 million to 15 million) and suggest that four out of five people didn't want to tell the poll-taker the truth.

Two facts emerge from the surveys. One is that a relatively small number of people obtain satisfaction, or utility, from art, quite apart from income, capital, and related prices that affect the demand for it. What is reported here about art museums is similar to what is known about the interest of the public in the performing arts. Their audiences too are a small part of the population. Many of the people in them are the people who visit art museums. The museum audiences since 1973, when the poll reported above was taken, are very likely what they were then. The National Endowment for the Arts in 1982 reported that 22 percent of the population over eighteen had visited a museum at least once during the preceding year. That would have been 36 million, more than twice my estimated 15 million for 1973. However, included in the definition of "museum" were "monuments, buildings or neighborhoods of historic or design value." How many of the 36 million saw the Washington Monument and how many the National Gallery also or instead? *Museum News* in April 1983 published an article entitled "Staying Away. Why People Choose Not to Visit Museums," and it said "hundreds" of surveys made over the preceding fifty years had all reported that museum audiences came from a small part of the population. To be noted is that the article was about museums of all kinds—history, science, technology as well as art— and that art museums are the least popular. Museologists, however, are unwilling to accept their small audience as a permanent condition. A study made in 1969 for the International Commission on Museums was of the opinion that "people stay away from museums for many reasons, but principally because of ignorance, apathy or indifference, compounded in some cases by poor experience." An impartial observer would take that to mean people are not interested in them, and that may have been what the study meant to say. But it certainly did not leave the matter there, because it went on to aver that the "potential public" for museums was growing "faster than was thought." Just what the rate of growth was thought to be, what it actually was, and why the two were different were not reported or were the grounds for optimism. Actually, there is no evidence that the increase between 1959 and 1988 in the proportion of the population having an interest in art was any greater than could be accounted for by the increase of purchasing power and the average number of years of education.

The other fact emerging from the surveys is that many people believe art is what economists call a "merit good." It is something people profess to believe they should have more of, something they say is good for themselves, and moreover is something they can afford, but for numerous reasons—habit, procrastination, weakness of will, but not cost—they decline to buy or have or do to the extent they say they should. They say they ought to read more Great Books, get eight hours sleep each night, eat fresh vegetables, attend a concert, visit a museum, buy a reproduction, rent a picture, get to know it, and buy it. Merit goods have their opposites in demerit goods: cigarettes, liquor, too much rich food, not enough sleep, too much television, too little exercise. These notions seem to be jejune, as in fact some (but not all) are, and to be the chimeras of social psychology which also is true. Nevertheless, they are professed, and while they have no great effect on the behavior of those who profess them they do have an effect on what government does and, in a small and oblique way, on what is done by those who profess them. If New Yorkers were asked whether the Met, the museum, deserved money from the city more than the Mets, the baseball team, they undoubtedly would say yes. If they were asked to make a donation so that a teenager could be brought in from the suburbs to see a baseball game, they would be less likely to give than if he was to be brought in to visit the museum. On the other hand, if they were offered a free ticket to one or the other, which would they choose—which, indeed?

INVESTMENT IN TASTE

There is more to be said about merit goods, and it will be said in subsequent chapters, including seven, which is about subsidies. Merit goods provide what (in my opinion) is the strongest argument that can be made for subsidies. That is not to say the argument is convincing. In this chapter what is more to the point is why art is a merit good. The question, restated, is why are so few people interested in art even though they believe they should be?

One reason, I suggest, is that an interest in art is the consequence of experience, training, and learning. In the language of economics, the appreciation of art requires an investment in taste, and that in turn requires time and education. The idea is commonplace when stated in ordinary language, namely, that to value painting one must look at pictures, and knowing something about how they are made adds to one's understanding, to which still more is added by reading art history and criticism. An understanding of art or anything else can be acquired only at a cost, and the cost is the other goods and time that must be given up in order to acquire the understanding. Whether the cost is incurred at all, and if so how much is incurred, depends on the value the individual places on the understanding. Or how much is invested in the understanding of art depends on the marginal effort that must be made in relation to the marginal value of the understanding.

Some people value art more than others do, and understanding it is easier to some than to others. Who are these people? Audience studies report they have more education than the population at large. Among art museum visitors, according to a 1978 report, 84 percent have attended college compared to 26 percent of the entire population.[19] That is what one would expect. A taste for the arts is acquired, and one way it is acquired is by education. Not everyone who has attended college has taken a course in the appreciation of music or the history of art, but almost everyone who has been enrolled in a liberal arts curriculum has been required to take courses in the field of the humanities. If anything that is studied ("taken" or endured) will instill an interest in the arts, a course in the humanities will.

One also would expect that the people who teach these courses are to be found in arts audiences more often than people who teach other courses (materials engineering or economics). That must be a conjecture until another survey is made. But we do know that when audiences are surveyed for the occupations that are represented in them and the results are compared to the occupational composition of the labor force, teachers come to the fore as the predominant group. In the language of the surveyors, teachers are "heavy attenders among heavy attenders." They comprise 4 percent of the labor force and 22 percent of the arts audiences. People in managerial positions comprise 11 percent of the labor force and 15 percent of the arts audiences. Blue-collar and service workers are scarcely to be seen, only 7 percent of the audience, but they are a large part of the labor force, 47 percent. Also "under-represented"—more survey-speak—are blacks (about .5 percent of the audiences and about 12 percent of the population).[20]

The presence of so many teachers in concert halls, theaters, and art museums I would not attribute to their being able to understand the arts with less effort (at a lower cost) or to their taste being superior, although both may be true, but to their obtaining a greater return (more satisfaction, pleasure, benefit) from a given effort. This again is a conjecture, because it assumes that the teachers in the art audiences are in the main the teachers of the humanities. A teacher of drama should get more benefit from an evening at the theater than is gotten by someone who does not teach drama (economically speaking). The same can be said about a teacher of music and the concert he hears, and about the art historian and the museum he visits. The additional benefit is that each may use in the classroom some of what he hears or sees—"may," not "can," as its value depends on the quality of the paintings or the music or the play. If there are more musicologists than materials engineers in the audience of the Chicago Symphony—as one would guess there are—this is the explanation. To call one under-represented and the other over-represented is an odd use of language and ethics.

In summary, one of the reasons why an interest in the arts is limited to a relatively few people is that only a few have made the investment in taste or learning which the interest requires, and that is because the investment is worthwhile for only a few. They are not only teachers. Yet teachers, as indicated by their predominance in the audiences, apparently find investing in taste to be more worthwhile than other people find it. The explanation, I suggest, is that the return adds to their knowledge of their subject as well as being a satisfaction in itself. Of course, another reason may be that the cost to them is less. There are differences in the ability to learn and in the interests which people initially have. Those who study and teach the humanities may do so because they have greater facility and more interest in them than others have. In either case—whether the return from a given investment is greater or the cost is less—a part of what they obtain from art is of value in earning an income.

EXPLAINING TASTE

If the effort an individual makes in order to enjoy or obtain utility from art has an effect on *how much* of a demand he has for it, the effort should also have an effect on the particular *kinds* of art he prefers. That is, if investment in human capital is a determinant of an individual's demand for art of all kinds (his "aggregate demand"), it should also have an effect on the composition of his demand. So that if economics can help to explain how much interest there is in art, it ought also help to explain what kind of art is preferred. In saying this I am venturing to explain taste, not in its entirety, I hasten to say, but in part. To attempt even that was out-of-bounds in modern economics until a few years ago. Taste was a "given." If anyone wanted to account for it, he had to do so outside of economics. Today he need not, indeed had better not.

What I venture to suggest is simple. A man who cannot read has no interest in John Donne and a man who has never seen anything more graphic than a chewing gum poster does not care for Duccio, at least at first sight. The venture moves taste from the status of a given to that of a variable. Instead of its being accepted for whatever it happens to be—as economists of this century, but not earlier, took it to be—it is itself something to be explained. My explanation is that it is related to investment, and that it also can be made a variable by relating it to cost and return. There are differences in what people invest in the understanding of art, hence differences in which art forms interest them, and within each form which styles they prefer. One reason for the differences is that the investment can increase the income of some people, as well as provide satisfaction from the understanding of art. That would help account for the interest teachers have in it. There is another reason, and it applies to everyone whether or not an understanding of art has an effect on his or her income. It is that the cost of investment is not the same for all people. This difference can be taken back to the circumstances in which people acquire the capital they have in themselves, what economists call initial endowments. A child in a household where there are pictures on the wall (even Impressionist reproductions) will have more visual sensibility than a child in a household where there are no pictures, and the greater sensibility of the one will enable him to acquire still more sensibility at a lower cost or less effort than otherwise would be needed.

If this seems stilted or unduly abstract, it can be made obvious by noticing it simply means that the child of parents with a large vocabulary will himself probably have a larger vocabulary than will a child of parents with a small vocabulary. Or children born in France speak French better than children born in Chicago.

Putting the idea this way can lead the reader to think, True, perhaps, but trivial—whereas his earlier reaction may have been, Not trivial, but probably not true either. To persuade him to think better of it, I submit two considerations. One is that it has implications which are informative and are also interesting. The other is that he may find it a more plausible explanation of taste than explanations made by people in art.

One implication is that it predicts the subject matter of painting will change if there is a change in the kind of people who buy it (hardly surprising) and the change will be toward simpler or more complex subjects according to whether the new buyers are more or less informed (not altogether expected, perhaps). For example, if the new buyers are less learned than those who preceded them, the new pictures will depict what is familiar (flowers, animals, loaf of bread, bowl of fruit, lemon with peel unwinding, drops of juice sparkling) or what is exotic (monkey, satyr, unicorn) or improper (gambling, boozing, and wenching in the tavern) or catches the eye (the fly at the edge of the picture: Is it painted or is it real?). What I am describing is the subject matter of pictures that were painted in Holland after it secured its independence from Spain and the influence of the Catholic Church declined. The religious subject matter that was characteristic of painting when the church was the principal buyer was replaced by subject matter of interest to people who had less education than the clerics who had decided what was to be bought.

Churches do appear in Dutch pictures. Ever so many show architectural details: a massive pillar, a Gothic window behind it, and, in the foreground, the fine figure of a blade in greatcoat, boots, one hand on his hip, the other on the hilt of his sword, and on his head a feathered hat he has not bothered to remove in a house of worship. The point can be made obvious by recalling that a century earlier in Flanders, not far to the south, the Master of Bruges painted in full and exquisite detail *Our Lady in a Church* (Royal Museum of Fine Art, Antwerp).

INCOME AND TASTE

Another implication of the idea is that the way a change of income affects the demand for and subject matter of painting depends on how the change of income affects the investment people care to make in taste. This is related to the preceding implication but is more extensive.

There is evidence that an increase of income brings with it an increase in the demand for art in many of its forms. The effect on the performing arts in the United States has been measured. In the 1960s, a 10 percent increase of income induced a 10 percent increase in spending on theater tickets [an income elasticity of one with ticket prices constant] according to Thomas Moore's study of the American theater. For all of the performing arts (music and dance as well as theater) the effect of income appears to be smaller, .81 percent, Dick Netzer stated in his work on the performing arts in America.[21] That indicates spending on the performing arts, while it increases when income increases, does not increase in as large a proportion. One is tempted to say the difference between the two estimates may be accounted for by the fact that the theater is the most popular of the performing arts and the ballet, which is not included in Moore's estimate but is in Netzer's, is the least popular.

I do not know of an estimate of the relation between changes of income and purchases of painting. However, one is permitted to believe that as income rises people spend more on paintings. People interested in the visual arts are similar to those interested in the performing arts (often the same people), according to studies made of the income, occupation, education, and age of the two audiences. In addition, one has the impression that income and the buying of pictures moved together in the past, especially in the nineteenth century. It was a time when the amount of painting done increased substantially; so it is reported by people who have looked closely into the matter. That can be set alongside what is more than an impression: It is information, drawn from historical statistics, that there was an increase in real income per person.

Harrison and Cynthia White, in their informative study, estimate that in the last half of the nineteenth century in France there were 20,000 pictures painted each year by "reputable," i.e., professional, established, artists.[22] The studios in Britain were also busy. The painter William Buchanan introduced his *Memoirs* in 1824 by saying, "At a period when a taste for the Fine Arts is rapidly spreading through every part of the British Dominions . . . and a desire to cultivate these Arts increases with the growing prosperity of the country; some details concerning those works which are now objects of general regard may not be unacceptable to the amateurs of painting." One notes in passing he used "amateur" in the sense of one who loves art, as Redon used it when he said he always put aside a few copies of his lithographs to sell to his amateurs at a reduced price (until he discovered they were being resold at a higher price).

A detail which may not be unacceptable to amateurs of economics as well as of painting is that the connection Buchanan saw between art and prosperity was explained not long after by another Englishman, T. C. Banfield, who said in *Four Lectures on the Organization of Industry* (1845), "The first proposition of the theory of consumption is, that the satisfaction of every lower want in the scale creates the desire of a higher character. . . . The highest grade in the scale of wants, that of pleasure derived from the beauties of nature or of art, is usually confined to men who are exempted from all the lower privations."

What Mr. Banfield said (or would have had he expressed the same idea 100 years later) is that the demand for art is income elastic. It is something people buy more of as they get richer—a "superior good," it is called in economics, as are foreign travel, the theater, second and third cars, and homes. What he did not say or have others said is why the greater demand for art brings about a change in its subject matter, in styles, in the very definition of art or what comes within the word. Does it include the baseball bat, eighty or so feet high, designed by Claes Oldenberg, and placed before an office of the Social Security Administration? Or the 1985 ballet *Arien,* "a stunning example of Pina Bausch's theatricality—the entire stage surface is transformed into a pool of ankle-deep water while the dancers perform in the company of a hippopotamus"? So the *New York Times* described it.

There is a possible explanation for this in still another implication of the idea of investment in taste. When income increases, investment in taste may not increase as much, at least in the sense of having an immediate effect on what is consumed. That is why people who are newly rich do not buy the same kinds of goods as are bought by people who have been rich a longer time. (I use the term "newly rich" because it is convenient and not as a pejorative.)

From this it follows that the more rapid is the increase of income in a country—hence the more rapid is the increase in the number of the newly rich, and the greater is the proportion of them in the population—the more rapidly will the styles of painting change, and also the greater will be the number of styles to be seen at any one time. Britain and France in the nineteenth century offer illustrations of this, and the United States since 1945 does also.

Within Britain and France there were different styles of painting in the nineteenth century—some sequential, some concurrent—and the same can be said about Italy and Germany at that time. In France the predominant style early in the century was classical, exemplified by David and Ingres, and it was succeeded by the painting done in that tradition by members of the Academy. The Academy, in addition to being a means of perpetuating the production of a particular style, was a means of selling work that was done in that style. Alongside Academic painting there were new styles: that of the Barbizon painters; of the mystics and symbolists Moreau and Redon; of independents like Manet; of the Romanites, the Impressionists, the Postimpressionists, the Nabis, down into the twentieth century and its still greater variety.

The French painters who were not in the Academy are said to have been treated shamefully and have been cited over and over as an example of genius unnoticed and merit unrewarded. If the painters outside of the Academy did in fact merit more attention than they got, they are among the few in the history of painting who did not receive their due. What is common is that artists have been treated better during their lifetime than their works have been after the artists' death. That subject is considered later in this chapter and in the next. Here I shall say only that if the French painters outside of the Academy did live in neglect, they must have thrived on it. There were so many of them, and they so persistently plied their craft.

About England in the nineteenth century, there is no legend of neglect and harsh treatment. As the taste for art extended through the country, just as Buchanan predicted it would, new styles of painting developed to satisfy it. There was anecdotal painting (*Uncle Toby and the Widow Wadham* or *Puss Runs Off With the Yarn*), and it surely can be said not to have made demands on those who looked at it. There also was Constable; his popularity may possibly be attributed less to his anticipating Impressionism, as he is said to have done, than to the English fondness for the country, also a sign of rising income. Turner, on the other hand, could not have appealed to many when he moved toward abstract painting. The Pre-Raphaelites did not make demands on the viewing public, and there probably is significance in their being most popular in the industrial areas of the north where investment in human capital took the form of managerial skill rather than cultivating the humanities.

About American painting since 1945, less need be said to illustrate the propositions that (*a*) the demand for pictures increases when income does and (*b*) styles multiply when investment in taste does not increase as much as income. Less need be said because Americans are more familiar with contemporary American art than they are with French and British art of the nineteenth century. They are so not only because the present is more familiar than the past and because it is all the more familiar if it is near and not far away. Contemporary painting has less competition from the past in the United States than it has in Europe, which also means Americans see more of what their artists now are doing than Europeans see of the work which theirs are now doing. American museums do not have as much art of the past as European museums have, especially art before the nineteenth century. Our museums treat the public well, as well as any I have visited anywhere and better than most, but they simply have not as much to show us.

That there has been an increase in the number of people who own art is reported by dealers, auction houses, the professional periodicals, and the popular press. That income has increased is a matter of record, the real gross national product at about 2 percent per person each year since 1950.

With this increase has come a change in the styles of painting, compared, say, to the representational work of the pre-war period, and also a large increase in the number of styles that flourish together or at least coexist. The abstract expressionism for which the fifties were celebrated was not the only style of the time, and in the years that followed the styles increased so rapidly and abundantly that none was preeminent, with the possible exception of Pop. Thick and fast they came, and though not at last, yet certainly more and more.

A guide to this embarrassment of riches, or simply embarrassment, was published early in the seventies: *Glossary of Art, Architecture and Design Since 1945*. It is peppered with the sharp opinions of the compiler, John A. Walker (*not* the John Walker of the National Gallery), and they could be used as a buyer's or viewer's guide, for example, *acceptable, not acceptable, best buy, tasteless.* A sampling suggests there are about one-and-a-half styles described on each of the 200 or so pages, which means the amateur of modern art has about 300 kinds at his disposal. Actually, he has more because since the glossary was published in 1973 still others have made an appearance, although, to be accurate, one must note that some also have vanished. At any rate, a new edition is in order, perhaps in loose-leaf form with periodic supplements.

What the art of the present demands from the public—from those who would understand, appreciate, or obtain satisfaction from it— seems best described as tolerance, a willingness to believe that the visual arts can take surprising forms. Whether this makes the present different from the past is a question I leave to others. While waiting for an answer, I shall go on believing that novelty in art has a long history and that artists have indulged in it even at the risk of offending the public or possibly in order to do so.

The art of the present does not require a large investment in taste in order to be valued and bought. Of course something more than the income of the buyer influences his choice. He must have a taste for novelty. But that is acquired at less cost than the taste which values the art of the past. A Campbell's soup can is recognized by people who wouldn't know Catherine's Wheel from any other, but one also must say that people who know the legend of St. Catherine of Alexandria probably could not find the concepts in Conceptual Art. In justice to the moderns one can say the appreciation of them may be heightened by Sociology 101. In the Minneapolis Institute of Art there is Jonathan Borofsky's *Hammering Man,* a figure twenty-four feet high, in black silhouette, its arm in continuous motion (after closing hours as well?). The label explains the figure "restates the forced engagement in regulated monotony that is part of everyone's life [and] reflects the strain and impersonality of late twentieth-century life." (As a factual statement it could hardly contain more mistakes.)

The fact that income is continually rising is not the only idea that economics can offer to help explain the character of art today. After all, income has all been rising for a long time. That is shown by historical statistics of the nineteenth century, and for earlier periods there are indications, such as increasing population, that income rose then also. During all of this time, the amount of art created has also increased. But the present does seem to be different in that new styles appear in more rapid succession and in the large number of them present at any one time.

CHANGES IN TASTE

The explanation for this is, I suggest, that the income of people who buy paintings is so high that in order to get the most out of it they must alter their preferences and seek novelty more often than they would if their income was lower. This is a conjecture, and if the reader is kind he will tolerate it just as he does the arts of the present.

It is derived from the idea that as the real income of an individual increases, the satisfaction diminishes that he gets from still more—not the satisfaction from his *entire* income but from an *additional* amount. For each person there is an income at which still more goods are worth no more than the effort needed to get them [at which the marginal utility of income is equal to that of leisure]. There are limits to the amount of everything one wants if more is to be had only by spending more time to get it. Stated another way, each person asks how much effort he should make to increase his income, and some (who are not necessarily rich) ask whether any effort at all is worthwhile. That question entails their making a comparison, whether explicitly or not, between the satisfaction they would obtain from the additional goods which the higher income would buy and on the other hand the satisfaction they would obtain from the additional leisure they would have if they did not make the greater effort. No one works twenty-four hours a day or would if he could. Just how much less depends on the return from working relative to the return from doing something else.

The return from working would decline more than it does if, when income increases, the additional goods purchased were identical with what had been purchased before. But that is not done. If a woman has ten pairs of shoes they will not be identical. If her husband has thirty identical ties, he would be odd, and if when his income increased he bought ten more just like them he would be very odd. As his wife, when she adds to her stock of shoes, adds something different from what she has, so he, if he is like his fellow men, will have an assortment of clothing.

The point is that as income increases, the decrease in the satisfaction from still more can be retarded by buying something different. The decline cannot be prevented, but it can be reduced. [By diversifying one's stock of consumer goods, one can retard, though not arrest, the declining marginal utility of income.]

Disposing of goods while they are still usable is one of the ways people diversify their holdings or is one of the consequences of diversifying. Most goods are replaced before they are entirely worn out— clothes, furniture, appliances, automobiles. They do lose some of their value because they depreciate in a physical sense and some lose value because they become obsolete. The higher is the income of a family the more rapidly does the family replace its consumer goods. The same is true of nations: the higher is their average income, the greater is the diversification of their aggregate stock of consumer goods, and the higher is the rate at which they become obsolete. As rich Americans change cars more often than Americans who are not rich, so all Americans change cars more often than all French. Clothing is an obvious example of a consumer good that becomes obsolete, which simply means out of fashion, and furniture is another.

Are works of art an example? Decidedly not, Kenneth Clark once said: "The fact remains that in a godless age and in what we call a free society, art is the only escape from materialism which is not subject to the law of diminishing returns, and one of the few which is not damaging to health."[23] My conjecture is that works of art are subject to diminishing returns. Whether they are damaging to the health is a question that is outside of economics (and, one would have thought, also outside of art history).

Consider their relation to other goods. Pictures are a part of the furnishings of a house, and thought is given to how they will harmonize with other things in it. That may bring disapproving clucks. Yet curators give much thought to which paintings are to be placed in a room that contains furniture, ceramics, rugs, and decorative works that complement the pictures (along with how well the paintings go with each other).

I offer this as one kind of evidence that art is subject to obsolescence and that it is what economists call a complementary good, one which enhances the satisfaction derived from other goods and becomes more satisfying when placed among them. When the complements of a work become obsolete, it does also. This is not the only evidence that paintings are subject to obsolescence. The change of style and manner is another and is probably more important because it can be interpreted as the result of the continual increase of real income, of the declining value of still more income, and of the consequent and quite sensible desire to arrest the decline by acquiring what is different, unfamiliar, or novel. But what is new, if it is to satisfy, must not be so *recherché* as to bewilder the beholder or so distant from the familiar center of art as not to be a visual experience at all. [The product must not be so differentiated as to reduce its cross elasticity with art works to zero, as it would be if it was of no interest whatever to the "median amateur."]

THE OBSOLESCENCE OF ART

There is other evidence. Most of the art that has been made since the beginning of time has not survived. What has become of it? Not all of it can have completely deteriorated physically or have been destroyed against the owners' wishes. Where are the 20,000 pictures that were done each year in France in the latter nineteenth century? G. E. Burcaw declared that 1 in 10,000 done at that time was worth preserving.[24] Mr. Burcaw was the director of a historical museum, and there are those who will say he was biased. He did say art museums get too much money and he may have believed (just possibly) that history museums should get more. Let us suppose he was *parti pris* and in error by a factor of 10. Then more paintings have been worth keeping: 1 in 1,000. What became of the other 999?

They were thrown away, discarded, neglected, forgotten, lost, burned, willfully destroyed, sold for the frames, the canvas put in the trash or scraped to become another picture that had the same fate. That is what my conjecture implies. Lest it be misunderstood, let me say it does not mean that most art has proved to be worthless (except what the artist could not sell or give away or want to keep himself). What he sold must have been worth at least as much as was paid for it or the buyer would not have bought it. Also, the conjecture does not mean that what the buyer paid for and later discarded represents a mistake of judgment. People buy goods they know will mean less to them as time goes on and eventually will mean nothing at all and will be thrown away. Certainly that is true of clothing. I believe most buyers of art would say, if pressed, they do not expect it to keep its value forever. There is comfort in the obsolescence of art for people who dislike what is modern. Let them be patient. In time the offensive, and most else, will be thrown away. There is no comfort to be gleaned from this for people who dislike older art, because it is going to be here indefinitely. Moreover, the modern art that is discarded may be replaced by what is disliked even more.

Not only do collectors lose interest in their possessions but museums do also. *The Song of the Lark* was once a prized possession of the Art Institute. It is said to have been reproduced more than any other painting, though that is doubtful in view of the competitive power of *La Gioconda*. The Art Institute still owns the painting but as time went on gave it less and less place. It had hardly a place at all in 1985 when it was hung high on a wall in a corridor where there were other mementos of the Institute's history, none of them, as Baedeker would say, of a kind to detain the hurried visitor. Later it returned to a visible place on the wall of a gallery of nineteenth-century gallimaufry, hardly a compliment to Jules Breton.

Another observation is in order. If the obsolescence of art were not so and works of art were in danger of being discarded while they still had value—instead of being discarded because no one valued them—the market would rescue them. Dealers would buy what some people no longer want and sell it to other people who do want it, which in fact is just what dealers now do with art that is not subject to obsolescence (or they think is not).

It has been said that the private sector cannot be relied on to maintain the cultural heritage of a country. That may only mean that if a collector can sell a painting for more to a foreigner than to a fellow countryman, he will do it—which is true but omits the fact that the foreign exchange received by the collector replaces the art the country no longer has and may be used to buy other art. But another inference is sometimes drawn. It is that individuals do not conserve their art as well as they should. I am as ready to believe this as to believe that a man who owns a share of stock is careless about it even while it has value. If he does discard it, the reason is that it has become worthless on the market. If he discards a picture, the reason is that it no longer has any value to him or to anyone else. If he is mistaken and it is worth something to others, a dealer will correct his mistake. If such mistakes were common, there would be a futures market in undervalued art. Dealers would contract to deliver it in the future to people who correctly value it. The owners who undervalued it would willingly sell it to the dealers for less than what the futures contract assured the dealers of receiving.

What all this signifies, or is meant to, is that the numerous changes in the styles of art since 1945 can be explained, at least in part, by the fact that the higher is the income of people the more will they diversify the kinds of goods they buy and the more quickly will the goods become obsolete. To believe that this applies to works of art one must believe the demand for them is affected by income and believe also that they are subject to obsolescence. That income affects the demand for works of art is rarely doubted. That they become obsolete, I have done my best to make plausible and can do no more. To those who are not persuaded, I leave a question: What became of the other 999?

Many observers have said the styles of art have changed with unusual rapidity since the end of the Second World War, hence one of my factual assumptions, the less important, is acknowledged. The more important is that the change is related to American income being high (in an absolute sense) and to its continuing to increase. Even that is acknowledged in a roundabout way by people who believe the present condition of art—described as serious or critical—can be attributed to the institutions of modern society, for which read capitalism. In *Museums in Crisis,* an anthology published in 1972, Bryan Robertson deplored the growing practice of museums staging spectacular exhibitions, the blockbusters, and went on to say, "but producer–consumer societies involve conspicuous waste, as well as voracious consumption of style which now demands constant revivals; so perhaps this lavish expendability, this reduction to theatricality, is understandable."[25]

What he did not say is that it has ever been so. Museologists surely agree that art is subject to obsolescence. If they did not they would want to conserve everything—a stunning prospect that would have fascinated Malthus, had he been alarmed by pictures as well as by people. Will the number of museums, he would have asked, increase as much, more, or less, than the number of pictures drawn into them?

COUNTER-EXPLANATIONS

Mr. Robertson is one of many who have seen a connection between the subject matter of art, the taste of buyers, and the social environment. Edward B. Henning, a philosopher, maintained the difference among styles expresses the differences among the tastes of patrons or buyers, which hardly can be denied. He continued that differences among patrons issues from different ideologies, social positions, and psychological desires, which is not self-evident. Among his examples is the conflict between the aristocratic Ghibellines and the middle-class Guelphs during the Renaissance. The conflict, he said, was concurrent with the transition of Italian painting from the Byzantine (and Gothic) style to the realism of the fourteenth century.[26] The explanation is ingenious as well as interesting. But could not the change perhaps be more easily explained by saying the Ghibellines, being the older dynasty, were more familiar with the earlier style of painting than the Guelphs, who achieved eminence later and acquired a taste for a later style? The families, we may suppose, invested in different tastes because they began to accumulate their fortunes at different times. Of course, the Guelphs could have adopted the taste of their rivals, yet does not rivalry take the form of differentiation of taste as well as of products? My explanation necessarily assumes that it does.

Thus does economics confront the philosophy of Mr. Henning and offer the reader a choice. The choice is not plain when economics confronts the explanation of Frederick Antal. He claimed the emergence of Florentine painting expressed (reflected, was caused by, related to?) the decline of the medieval idea of beauty—the Neoplatonist conception of it as an ideal construction—to something different which allowed nature onto the canvas as well as allowing religion and imagination.[27] This explanation is not of the kind from which some can be accepted and some refused. It must be taken altogether or not at all. Economics can say no more about Mr. Antal than that he asserts what happened did happen for reasons that may or may not explain why it happened.

Economics is able to say something more about two explanations of taste that were put forward in articles in *ARTnews*. Fairfield Porter explained what he called the "anomaly" of Maurice Prendergast (the American pointillist of the early twentieth century). The anomaly, he said, is the outcome of the Industrial Revolution, which brought to the world standardization, interchangeable parts, and a literal or literate approach to reality. They militate against art, which by its nature is about particulars—"specific experience," not uniformity—and is to be apprehended, not understood.[28]

An economist could inform Mr. Porter that the Industrial Revolution began some time before the age of Prendergast, so long ago actually that historians dispute about just when it did begin. It may have been when Henry VIII appropriated the monasteries and made them available to entrepreneurs as workplaces. The standardization that ensued conceivably had an effect on the position of the painter or on the content of art. If it did, it placed innumerable painters in an anomalous position and placed Prendergast within a grand succession of anomalies. It invites a question about the unknown painter—possibly English, possibly not—of the Wilton Diptych (National Gallery, London). Had he witnessed machine production and for that reason placed against a metallic ground of fine crosshatching a large number of angels who are rendered with the precision a gunsmith brings to his work? Of course the painting antedates Henry VIII by a century. Yet could that indicate the Industrial Revolution began even earlier? Here art history may be of service to economics.

The other explanation was offered by Horst C. Gerson and is about Dutch art (on which I have commented above). He said, quite agreeably, that "the heroic and spiritual values which had once received expression under the influence of royal and ecclesiastical patrons—these were essentially absent from Dutch art of the 17th century." He noted the merchants of Holland wanted Catholics and Jews to be tolerated by the ruling class of Calvinists and continued that the tolerance of the merchants "helps to account for their permissive attitude to different styles and schools of art." Yet, Mr. Gerson said, they were not "permissive about 'adventurous art.' "[29] The explanation, an economist could say, is that their investment in taste was limited, hence they preferred the familiar to the unfamiliar which the adventurous by definition always is.

They would have seen, had they lived 300 years later, the familiar in *Falling Shoe String Potatoes,* a piece of soft sculpture by Claes Oldenberg (Minneapolis Institute of Arts). Their counterparts of the present day are informed that while it is familiar it transcends the familiar (and so is familiar in an unfamiliar way). The label (possibly prepared by the curator and sociologist *manqué* who explained *Ham-*

mering Man) states: "On a vastly altered scale, in a different material and in the context of the art gallery rather than the fast food restaurant, the potatoes become a cultural commentary [on] American ideals of bounty and speed."

Sociology, while it is the most fertile source of explanations of taste and style, is not the only source. Gerald Reitlinger, in *The Economics of Taste,* took most of his explanations from outside of sociology (and of economics). He drew on literary history and observed that late in the eighteenth century when the gothic *Mysteries of Udolpho* by Mrs. Radcliffe was popular, there was a concurrent rise in the prices paid for the paintings done a century earlier by Salvator Rosa who was alleged to have been a bandit (as well as the irascible businessman described earlier in this chapter). Mr. Reitlinger also found reason to say that during the reign of Victoria the highest price paid for a Rubens was for a fully draped figure, which suggests moral history as a guide to taste.[30]

Denys Sutton, the writer, editor, and guardian of British holdings of foreign art, said the popularity of some painters can be attributed to their association with their homeland (Krieghoff with Canada) or a region (the Englishman Ferry with Greenwich)—which suggests social history as a source.[31] Social psychology may be another, as it is as good a place as any to file the numerous allegations that buyers are malleable in the hands of dealers, are unduly receptive to what is said in the press, and are given to following the lead of prominent collectors (like the Saatchi's of the 1980s).[32]

Then there is psychology proper. It has much more to say about why people buy art than about what kind they buy. Anthony Storr, a psychoanalyst, has said that collecting "is one expression of the human need for order . . . to comprehend, to predict, and finally to master what had previously seemed beyond control." He does say that the objects we collect may "act as mirrors, reflecting ourselves to ourselves, and thus affirming our identities"[33]—which may be a clue to taste and certainly explains why people have their portraits painted (and buy mirrors). The most arcane use of psychology I have come across is in *Art on the Market* by Maurice Rheims, a title that does not lead one to expect the arcane. One infers from what Mr. Rheims says, if I understand it, that the creation of art is an act of propitiation and the person acquiring it is the power that is propitiated. The collector, then, responds to beauty in the degree to which he believes he is propitiated, and the offer of art to him is an acknowledgment of his power. Mr. Rheims wrote this about product design and why some is more successful than others—because being aesthetically more pleasing, it serves the end of propitiation more effectively or the other way around.[34] The idea, if it is relevant to the applied arts, should be relevant also to the fine arts. Whether it is relevant to either, whether indeed it is an idea, is the issue.

So ends this report on how taste has been explained. If the purpose has not been clear, let it be made so. It is to support my belief that what economics has to say about taste, while less than one would like to know, is more complete and more plausible than what has been said elsewhere.

SUMMARY: THE DEMAND FOR ART

Works of art are most of them goods that become obsolete. They do not depreciate fully or get lost or destroyed but are discarded after a time. What is preserved is what subsequent generations have believed is worth keeping and is not representative of the visual arts in their entirety. The making of art—what painters and sculptors do and what is done in the decorative arts—is directed principally to the time in which it is undertaken. The time can be brief because what buyers want and what artists offer to satisfy them can change rapidly. This is true whether art is looked at from the viewpoint of economics or in some other way.

From an economic point of view, most paintings have been durable consumer goods subject to obsolescence. The painters may have hoped that what they were doing would be cherished down the ages, and what a few did actually has been. But the pictures done by the great majority were acquired by buyers, held for a time, then replaced by other pictures which were held for a time and themselves replaced, and on and on. The evidence for this is, first of all, the fact that so little art has survived. The change in the subject matter, the way it is rendered, and the very methods of painting are also evidence. In addition, art is a good which complements other goods—is used with them—and when the other goods become obsolete art does also. Then there is the fact that dealers do not find any reason to rescue art about to be discarded, which they would do if what was discarded was of value.

The rate at which art becomes obsolete depends on the income of the buyers, on the rate at which it is increasing, and what they have invested in taste, that is, in acquiring satisfaction from art.

The higher is the income of a person, and the more goods he has, the less do a still higher income and still more goods add to his satisfaction. This is true of people who are not rich as well as of those who are. All of them, in order to get as much satisfaction as they can from their spending, distribute it among as many different kinds of goods as practicable, instead of confining it to a few. This is simply because variety is more satisfying than uniformity. When they add to their stock of consumer goods (as distinct from replacing what is used up), they choose the novel over the familiar or the less familiar over the more familiar. If they have an interest in art, they will choose it in the way they choose other goods. Hence, as income rises, the choices of buyers of art change, and artists respond to the change by offering works in a different style.

There are, to be sure, people who do not act this way. They prefer the familiar to the unfamiliar, the tried-and-true to the untried because it may be untrue. They seem to be a minority, however, because obsolescence is observable in markets for many kinds of goods. What is unusual is a market where it is not observable.

Obsolescence is not the only reason why styles change when income increases. The increase brings art within the reach of people who previously could not afford it, meaning that when their income was lower, art did not provide as much satisfaction as other things that cost as much as art. Their tastes usually are different from those of people who for some time have had an income that makes art affordable. The newly rich in addition to buying art also buy other things they previously did not buy or did not buy as much of. Among them are education, travel, and other services that have an effect on taste. But since these things affect taste slowly there is a noticeable difference between the choices made by those who eventually become able to afford art and those who for some time could afford it. The latter can be said to be people whose stock of human capital is large relative to their income and the former group to be people whose accumulated investment in human capital is small relative to their income.

Changes in the styles of painting are evidence that what artists do is affected by what buyers of art would like them to do. Of course, it could be evidence of the opposite—that buyers buy what artists choose to paint and take what they can get. But what is known of the conduct of collectors and painters in the past and what is reported today allow one to conclude that the relation between demander and supplier in the market for art is similar to that relation in the market for other things. In none, or hardly any, is the consumer an absolute sovereign. But in all markets his choices affect what producers do, and what they can and are willing to do also affect him. There is a division of authority: a dual sovereignty, if you will.

The buyers of the present appear to stand in much the same relation to artists as did the buyers of the past. This needs to be said because the past is associated with patronage, and patronage is misunderstood to be benefaction. When one looks into the details of patronage, they show that patrons more often than not were customers, that their relation to the artist was an exchange relation, and that instances are rare of a painter being subsidized in a disinterested way by a benefactor who had only the good of the artist and of art as his motive. This is not meant to disparage the people who are remembered as the great patrons of art. It is meant to explain that the great ages of patronage were periods when there was a substantial demand for art, hence a large amount of it came into being.

The preferences which people have among styles of art depend on what they bring to it: their sensibility, understanding, knowledge, what tolerance they have for the unusual and the novel, how willing they are to risk disappointment, etc. These properties come together to form taste, and they are the product of intentional effort combined with the circumstances in which the effort is made. It is what I have called investment in taste. Taste governs the choices the individual makes, once prices and his income are given. But investment in taste is affected by income and prices, and taste changes when they change.

Like any other investment, it is made at a cost, in time as well as money, and the cost is incurred in the belief that the investment will yield a return. The return is the satisfaction art provides. It can be no more than the pleasure of looking at a sunflower or no less than the spiritual elation that comes from a Madonna and Child. To the majority of people who have an interest in art (and they are a minority of the population) the return is closer to the first than to the second. So it is, if we may (as indeed we can and should) infer their utility from their preferences and their preferences from the rooms they visit in a museum, from the art books in their personal libraries, and from the reproductions on their walls. And from the price of a Postimpressionist painting relative to the price of a pre-Mannerist painting.

In addition to providing satisfaction—a subjective experience— the return from art can take an objective form because to some people it is a source of information that affects their income. A concert is useful to a musician, a ballet to dancers, a theatrical performance to teachers of drama, and an exhibition of pictures is of particular inter- est to painters, art historians, architects, and others whose occupa- tion is related to the visual arts. This return from the arts can raise the income of those who experience them. It helps to explain why in the audiences of the arts the proportion of teachers is much higher than it is in the population.

It does not explain the presence of the other people in the audi- ence, the non-teachers, and there are more of them. Or does it explain why the arts audiences in their entirety are such a small part of the population (about 10 percent visit art museums).

These questions can be answered by what seems to be a truism. People have an interest in the arts if they make the effort to acquire it. Most people do not make the effort either because it is too costly or because the return is too small. Why either should be so is a question that in principle can be answered if taste can be accounted for, as I believe it can. There are circumstances in which the effort has an unusually high return or an unusually low cost, and most people are not in these circumstances. One such circumstance is to be in an occupation where art is a source of information that in- creases one's income. Another is having parents with a taste for art and who want their children to acquire it. This throws the question back in time but also calls attention to the fact that the interest which the parents transmit to their children is a bequest of capital which by its nature cannot be accumulated quickly.

Not everyone who is interested in art is so because of being in either of these circumstances. Many become interested while in col- lege and study subjects that instill the interest. They too are in a minority, not just because most people do not go to college but be- cause not all who do have a taste for art. Those who have acquired it in this way have acquired it at a cost to themselves which is less than its full cost. Their investment in taste has been subsidized in part because colleges themselves are subsidized by gifts, grants, and tax expenditure.

Not all of the families on whom the cost of government assistance falls benefit from it, because not all families send their children to college. Among those who do not, there are some who would like to escape the cost, but they cannot, hence their contribution to the investment in taste is involuntary. Those who make gifts do so voluntarily, of course, in order that higher education can perform its functions. One function is to instill an interest in art; this is done by directing some of the subsidy to investment in taste. The people who contribute voluntarily to the subsidy are people who truly are patrons because they expect no monetary return from their giving.

What emerges is that the patronage of art yields a greater benefit to the demand side of the market than to the side where the art is produced. The people for whom it is made—the buyers, users, collectors, museum visitors—receive more support than the artists themselves. A public choice economist will quickly explain the reason: the median voter is more likely to be a user of art than a creator. Or (very roughly) collectors and museum visitors have more votes than painters but not so many more that they are unable to organize to secure a benefit.

Nevertheless, the fact does invert the way the moral order is supposed to be, because the less deserving seem to receive more and the more deserving, less. An Italian proverb says that when the poor give to the rich the devil laughs. It would be pertinent if artists have usually been poor. Whether or not they have been is considered in the next chapter.

3

The Art of Painters and the Craft

Andrea was the best man who ever took up the brush. His diffidence made him unwilling to take up any work, as he dared not ask for his pay. . . . He associated with Mariotto di Francesco Mettidoro, one of the most skillful masters of his profession and a good man of business. They also took Raffaello di Biagio Mettidoro into partnership, sharing the gains between them.
—VASARI
Lives

THIS IS about the supply of painting and how painters have conducted their business affairs. My purpose is twofold, as it has been in the preceding chapters and will be in those that follow.

One part is to explain why works of art can be regarded as a part of the stock of goods that are produced and purchased, supplied and demanded, just as the familiar goods of life are. This is not meant to disparage art and artists or is it meant to disparage the goods other than art and the people who make them. It is meant to show that when we ask how art should be supported, whether on the market or in some other way, we may—indeed should—think about it in the way we think about other goods and use the principles we use when we ask how they should be supported and how provision can be made for an adequate supply of them. The explanation is necessary because the world has been told for ever so long that art has a special place in the works of man and should not be judged by the market, although in fact it has been judged by it for ever so long. The special position that is assigned to art is extended to artists, and they too are placed in a world apart, although like their works they also have been a part of the market. Being so, they invite the attention of economists.

The other part of my purpose is to explain how the activity of art—here, the work of the artist—lends itself to economic analysis. The inquiry is not an exercise in applied economics, or is it meant to clarify economic theory. It is an account of some of the things artists have done, why they have acted in certain ways and why they have not acted in others. It is economics for art's sake.

THE ARTIST AS ECONOMIC MAN

Painters have tried to maximize their net returns, that is, have tried to do the best they could with what they have had. This is thrust upon one by what has been written about them. There is much that I have not read, and it may tell of painters who while they dedicated themselves to perfecting their art were indifferent to the price at which they sold it, if they sold it at all, who didn't give a thought to the cost of materials and the value of their time, and who managed to have a roof over their head, bread on the table, a model on the dias, and lapus lazuli on their palette. A selfless artist seems about to emerge from the account of Andrea de Feltrini that is given by Vasari, but as it develops it becomes an account of the division of labor in an artistic enterprise. Mariotto, having a good head for business, spends some of his time on the market while Andrea, having no taste for it, spends all of his time painting.

One is not allowed to say there is not a single example of a selfless painter. (There is one example of everything including an exception to the statement that there is.) But until we have an account of such a person, we shall have to do with painters who simply were poor, possibly because they were selfless, more likely for other reasons. Of them there are many examples, just as there are in other occupations. Much has been written about painters who were dedicated to their art. But no account I have read claims the painter was indifferent to the return from his effort or that he was indifferent to whom received it. Painters have not been an exception to the principle that all of us would like to do the best we can with what we have in order to get the most of what we want from it. We may want to be altruistic—and are more likely to be, the higher is our income—but that want is no more noticeable among artists than among others.

In trying to be efficient we ask if what we are doing with our own is as sensible as something else we could do with it. We apply the principle of opportunity cost. It is that the cost of anything—anything at all—is what must be given up in order to get it. An inspired example is in Butler's *Lives of the Saints* where he writes about Saints Columba and Gall who were drawn from Ireland to Switzerland: "The people did not receive their new teachers gladly, and they soon left that stiff-necked and thankless crowd, lest in trying to fertilize these sterile hearts they should waste efforts that might be beneficial to well-disposed minds."

Luca della Robbia employed the principle when he turned from stone and metal to terra cotta for the material of his sculpture. Vasari relates: "But since, on reckoning up after these works how much there had come to his hand and how much time he had spent making them, he recognized that he had gained very little and that the labor had been very great; he resolved to abandon marble and bronze and to see whether he could gather better fruits from another method."

The "other method" was to place a glaze on terra cotta. To make sculpture in this way—Vasari implied and others have expressly said—had never been done before. Della Robbia had to find the proper way to prepare the material so that it could be worked into a bas-relief, and before he succeeded he had made a substantial investment, considerably more than is needed in order to get pleasure from an experiment. The effort turned out to be profitable to the sculptor-*cum*-inventor-*cum*-venture capitalist who then became an entrepreneur as well. He kept to himself what he learned and was the only sculptor who could do work of that kind. In order to increase the amount he did, he taught his nephew who taught his own five sons, and together they operated a family enterprise that prospered and continued after the death of Luca. Vasari concluded the account by stating that what was good for the self-interested artist was good for the world because (as certain Scottish philosophers were to say later) Nature will have it that way: "Thus Luca, in passing from one thing to another . . . did not do so from slothfulness or because he was capricious, unstable and discontented with his art, as many are, but because Nature led him on to new things, and because of his need for employment suited to his taste, which should cause him less fatigue and bring him more profit. Thus it was that he came to enrich the world and the art of design with a new art, both useful and beautiful, while he won glory and immortal fame for himself."

Artists have denied they were seeking after profit and have denied it when that was just what they were doing. This is another way in which they resemble the rest of the world. Businessmen when asked in surveys if their purpose is to maximize profit say no (at least 90 percent of them). Some in fact do not make a profit, but that is not their intention if it may be inferred from their behavior as distinct from what they say. Nevertheless, they do deny they are self-interested whether they are in art or in some other business.

Artists and others are likely to be as Redon was, to feel they must apologize for their success while nevertheless enjoying it. He once set aside ten copies of each of his prints and sold them to his amateurs for 200 francs, but stopped doing so when he saw one of the copies at a dealer's for 3,000; thereafter, he sold his entire runs at the market price. He was constrained to apologize and to explain: "They are offering me such sums now that I hardly feel it honest to accept them. . . . I feel homesick for my old amateurs. . . . Still, if she wants to buy carnations, my wife isn't obliged to skimp on something else now."[1]

The French artist Louis Tocqué, the pupil and son-in-law of Nattier, was offered a commission in 1754 to paint the Empress Elizabeth of Russia. He told the Russian and French functionaries who were to arrange the affair that (a) he would need eighteen months to paint the portrait, (b) he would be foregoing between 27,000 and 30,000 livres, which he could earn in Paris in that time "without stepping outside of my studio," (c) he would by his absence from Paris interrupt his business, and (d) place his health and very life in jeopardy by making the journey to Russia and living in its harsh climate. Despite all of this—in which (b) and (c) constituted double counting—he said he would accept the commission if in addition to being paid for the portrait there would be set aside the sum of 25,000 livres which in the event of anything happening to him would be paid to his family.[2] (He went.)

A final example of artistic opportunism, in a cost sense, is in a letter from Rubens to the agent of a collector who protested the price of a painting was excessive in view of Rubens not having painted it entirely himself. Rubens answered, "If the picture had been painted entirely by my own hand, it would be well worth twice that much."[3]

What makes these artists interesting is that in trying to increase their incomes they explicitly compared what they were doing with what they could do, that is, they compared alternative opportunities.

There are many more examples of artists who simply said they wanted to increase their income or did things that said it for them (which, however, does not mean they overlooked the importance of alternative opportunities). "Sodoma said that his brush danced according to the tune of money," Vasari relates, and when he comes to Perugino he says, after deploring the painter's want of belief in the immortality of the soul, that: "He relied entirely upon his good gifts of fortune and would have gone to any lengths for money." The acquisitive instinct is not confined to celebrated Italians or to all Italians or to the artists or the non-artists of any one nation. Edward Burne-Jones, a leading figure among the Pre-Raphaelites, said to his studio assistant when the preparations were being made for Victoria's Diamond Jubilee: "Do you hear that 30 million is to be spent over the Jubilee and none of that comes to us?"[4] His countryman Turner seems to have been extraordinarily alert to each opportunity to increase his income. He was once a guest at a country house where the host was an amateur painter. There was a partially finished landscape on an easel in the drawing room, and Turner gave it a touch here and there. He later sent his host a bill for instruction in painting.[5] Picasso's manner was different. When in the south of France he would take his friends to a superior restaurant and pay the bill with a quickly made sketch. The waiter is said to have paid the bills himself, kept the sketches, and later sold them at a handsome profit. If that is so, Picasso did not do as well as he might have.

Those who did, or wanted to—and they were many—make one believe Jonathan Routh was right when he said, "It's my theory that inside every artist there's a sensitive financier striving to get out and express himself in the hardest, the most beautiful, the most rewarding art form of all, the making of money." But that is not really so, although one does understand why he said it and is grateful to *Punch* for publishing it. It is wrong because artists have tried to do more than increase their money income. That they wanted to do more emerges from a reading of the lives of painters, including Vasari, of course.

ABOUT THE INCOME OF PAINTERS

Few people want only as large a money income as possible, not even people whose work gives them much less satisfaction than art gives an artist. What they want is a number of desirable things among which a good money income is important, perhaps the most important. But (to repeat), it is not all that is important. Many people enjoy the work they do, not enough to do it for nothing but enough to work for less than they could get from doing something else. There are teachers of art who could earn more if they did commercial art, but they do not choose to do it; and there are painters who would have a higher income if they were teachers. The difference between what a man or a woman actually earns and what he or she could earn in the best alternative employment is a measure of the other, the non-monetary, returns which there are in what a person is actually doing. One of the nonmonetary returns is the satisfaction in the work itself. An argument can be made that the satisfaction a person finds in his work is a form of consumption. Painting is that if it is a hobby.

Taken all together, the nonmonetary returns must be relatively high in the arts—in painting, sculpture, architecture, and the other visual arts, and in the performing arts also. The evidence is of two sorts. One is the low money income of people in the arts, and the other is the high unemployment which indicates that incomes, as low as they are, are not low enough to give everyone the amount of work they want to do.

There is information about the income of painters in an inquiry made in New York City between 1950 and 1954.[6] Like other information about art, it is at most suggestive; nevertheless it merits notice. About 130 painters were queried, half of them over thirty-five years old, all of them having exhibited or having been classified for exhibition by one or more of five recognized arts organizations including the National Academy of Design and the Museum of Modern Art. The gross income of 95 percent of them was under $3,000 (which would be about $13,700 at the 1988 value of the dollar), and the average net income was about $600 ($2,700 in 1988 dollars). At the time the inquiry was made the yearly income of a factory worker in the East was $3,300 ($14,900 in 1988 dollars). Not all of the difference can be attributed to the pleasure of painting. Some of the artists supplemented their income by additional work, some supplemented it by being married to working wives—which means, respectively, that for some the average income of $600 was received for less than a year's work and for others the pleasures of painting were shared by their wives. But even these adjustments leave the income of painters low which implies they received a substantial return in the form of the satisfaction painting itself gave them.

The low income of painters is of course related to the low price of their pictures. Yet even at that low price they cannot sell everything they paint, and as they go on painting they accumulate more and more canvases. The unsold pictures could be called evidence of unemployment. If we learned a brickmaker did not sell all of the bricks he made, yet continued to make them and to accumulate more and more of them, we could conclude that the time represented by the unsold bricks was as unproductive as if it had not been used to make bricks at all and had been a time of unemployment. Or more plausibly we could conclude that the brickmaker liked to make bricks. During the time he was in effect unemployed, his unemployment was voluntary, and the time it made available he used to indulge in the pleasure of making bricks. Painters have an advantage over brickmakers because pictures, unlike bricks, are not alike, hence painters can increase their income by exchanging pictures with each other. Their collecting can be traced to their money income being low and their nonmonetary returns being high. By bartering they convert some of the latter into real assets (the pictures of others) having a higher value than the real assets they produce (their own pictures) which they do not sell and do not wish to keep.

At times artists have been able to barter their pictures for something other than pictures done by others. In China during the Ming Dynasty, painters and calligraphers along with members of the literati exchanged their work for goods and services. Dutch artists did the same in the golden age of Delft, according to Professor Montias.[7] He reports that so much art was exchanged for so much else that it was a "relatively" liquid asset. Centuries later, in the golden days of the New York School, an unidentified Abstract Expressionist was reported to have paid his dentist (also unidentified) in pictures, which if the IRS did not object made what each produced buy more than it otherwise would have done. A Chicago artist of the representational school made a similar arrangement with his Chicago dentist in the 1930s when, however, tax avoidance was less profitable.

The low income of painters rarely is explained as it is here. The usual explanation is that their merit is not acknowledged because the public is unduly slow in appreciating contemporary art. The implication is that their work will be justly valued in time while alas in time the artists will not be alive to benefit from the recognition. The implication is contradicted by the fact that the work of most painters is valued less after their death than when they are alive.

Economists have given an account of why people in the arts have a low income, but it is not the account given here. What they have said is a variation of what Adam Smith said in *The Wealth of Nations*—that people overestimate the likelihood of their succeeding in the arts and in other occupations where the successful few become very rich and are celebrated by the public. His argument assumed that in making some kinds of choices people are not sensible, and that, he said, is because they are vain. Since Smith wrote, economists have learned, or ought to have, that a theory is on shaky ground if what appears to be inefficient behavior must be attributed to irrationality (or "institutional factors"). That is another way of saying there is no explanation; if there is none the fact should be admitted.

About the income of painters, there is an explanation. It could be enlarged by linking it to some ideas about how individuals make a choice that has an uncertain outcome. They can be perfectly sensible to decline to follow course A which has a desired outcome that is certain and instead to choose course B which has a desired but uncertain outcome. B is the more sensible choice if there is 1 chance in 100 of its yielding the desired outcome and if that outcome means more than 100 times as much as the desired outcome of A (forgetting that taking chances can fray the nerves).

Painters take chances, so do gypsies, and both are associated with bohemianism. Risk loving could be its differentia. However that may be, the risk was worth taking for some artists. In addition to the frisson, if it was desired, they have had the solid satisfaction of their work being valued by the market or by their peers or both. The returns can be very high indeed. Some artists have limited the number of pictures they do, or have kept some off the market, in order to reduce their taxes. Mark Rothko did. Picasso kept a large part of his work off the market in order to keep up the price of what he did offer for sale. Much of what he kept was used after his death to pay the estate duties and now is in the Picasso Museum in Paris. Rubens was a rich man, as his house in Antwerp and other evidence testify. It has only a few of his paintings, and they are not among the best or even the better of them. That Monet was a rich man is evident from his establishment at Giverny; it has no paintings at all, and tries to make amends with reproductions. Were these artists or their heirs of the opinion that the paintings were so valuable they could not afford to keep them? If so, that is a nice application of the principle of opportunity cost, as nice as what the dairy farmers of Denmark once did, which was to sell their butter and buy margarine in the town for their own use.

Rembrandt prospered as an artist, studio entrepreneur, and teacher, until at the age of thirty-six misfortunes befell him, first of a personal nature and within his family, then in the art trade, until at the age of fifty he was compelled to declare himself bankrupt. Within four years he had satisfied most of his creditors, of whom his son Titus was the largest, and thereafter settled his debts with paintings. His son and second wife formed an art dealership of which he was the adviser, and by the end of his life he was able to leave a modest estate.

GUILDS AND MARKET POWER

Gerrit Dou, a pupil of Rembrandt, became rich and successful in Leiden. A collector paid Dou a stipend in return for having the right of first refusal of his work. The prosperity of Dou attracted other painters to Leiden. He was himself attracted to it by there being fewer restrictions on the art market. The city authorities did not permit the formation of a guild, and Leiden was the only important city in Holland where this was so. However, after 1648 a guild was permitted, and its practices were like those of the guilds of other cities according to Ivan Gaskell.[8] He states that the work of painters everywhere was strictly regulated. Yet what the effect of the restrictions was, as well as how extensive they were, is unclear. These are questions an economist would ask, and they call for more information than Mr. Gaskell provides. Professor Montias provides information about the Guild of St. Lucas in Delft but does not expressly say it made the prices of pictures higher than they otherwise would have been.[9]

In what it *wanted* to do, the guild in Delft probably was no different from other guilds. It probably wanted to raise the income of its members by restricting the supply of what they produced or (what does not always come to the same thing) to engage in practices, such as preventing the membership from falling, that would operate to the benefit of the functionaries of the guild or the people who administered it. In what it wished to *appear* to be doing, the Delft guild again was probably like others. In Amsterdam, according to Professor Montias, the guild said its purpose was to keep shoddy goods off the market ("rubbish of poor boy apprentices"), to provide its members with a living wage, and to improve the quality of painting.

What is not known is whether the Delft guild (and others) did limit supply, and if so just what product or service was limited. The painters were not the only group in the guild. At its inception, the guild was also to include sculptors, engravers, embroiderers, art printers, the makers of glass, tapestry, faience (the familiar delftware), and merchants who sold these goods. The makers of them also were permitted to sell their own and the goods of others.

The number of pictures an artist painted was not limited directly by an output quota or similar device. But it was limited indirectly by the limit on the number of assistants a painter could employ, by the cost of becoming a member of the guild, by the period of his apprenticeship, and by the requirements he had to satisfy in order to complete it. Yet there seems to have been no effective control over the number of paintings that he could offer for sale in Delft. While all of the pictures painted and sold in Delft had to be the work of members of the Delft guild (no sales by non-members of the Guild were permitted), there was no effective restriction on the sale in Delft of pictures painted elsewhere. There were weekly and annual fairs at which paintings done elsewhere could be offered for sale. Whether paintings from outside of Holland were admitted, I do not know; I would guess they were not, because a purpose of all Dutch guilds was to limit (or prevent) competition from Flemish painting.

"The view of Delft" one gets by looking at the guild from the outside, while scarcely as becoming as the painting of that name by Vermeer, is not the sight of an art center that was harried, hobbled, and badly harmed by a cartel. Its restrictions were not as severe as they could have been and such as they were they were not always enforced; for example, outsiders sold art and other goods. The explanation may be that what the guild tried most to do was to collect tribute from craftsmen (including painters) and to do so for the benefit of the functionaries of the guild and of the city officials who shared the proceeds of the fines. If this was in fact the purpose, it was served by the very moderation the guild practiced because such moderation did not unduly limit the number of members.

A feature of the guild of interest to an economist is the fact that among the apprentices to the various occupations within it the boys who came from families with relatively high incomes were likely to be apprenticed to painters, yet the income of painters, while above the average income of all guild members, was lower than that of printers, booksellers, and (consistent with my hunch) of art dealers. The fact invites one to go beyond the nonmonetary returns from art, which returns can be considered a form of consumption as they are to a Sunday painter. They can explain why the weekday painters in Delft were paid less than the printers. Can they not also explain why the apprentices to painters came from the richer families? Consider that the pleasures of painting, however great, put no bread on the table, and if there is to be any it must, some of it, come from the capital of the family which the children inherit when they grow up and receive the relatively low income from painting. Conversely, one of the less attractive occupations in the guild was faience making, and the boys who were apprenticed to it came from poor families.

Another inference is invited. It is that within an occupation with high nonmonetary returns, those returns will be smaller relative to monetary returns for people who come from families that are not particularly rich or not rich at all. The reason is that those who do not inherit the bread on the table must work hard to buy it, which means they must please the market. Put simply, one would expect painters from families that are not rich to be more successful than those from rich families.

Vermeer can be brought forward, not as proof certainly but as an illustration. The circumstances of his family were modest. His father was an art dealer and innkeeper, his grandmother a dealer in inexpensive paintings, used furniture, and old clothes. Vermeer himself dealt in art, as well as creating it. In time he received the highest prices for his work of any painter in Delft, and they were equal to those received by Rubens.

Time has not diminished his art or has it that of Rubens. When Vermeer died he owed 617 gulden to a baker who accepted two pictures in payment. If the baker and his heirs were collectors, they did quite well. In 1959 when one of the most recent sales of a Vermeer was made (*Girl's Head,* 16" × 18"), the price was 4 million gulden.[10] If the baker's pictures were of like quality they would have been worth 8 million gulden. And of course he and his heirs would also have had pleasure of possession for 284 years. On the other hand, if they didn't care for the pictures and held them only for price appreciation, they did not do as well as they would have done had the baker been paid in money, had used it to buy a security yielding 3.5 percent (approximately the rate on Dutch government bonds at the time), and had reinvested the income. By 1959 the heirs would have had 10.8 million gulden. An economist who wished to put a high finish on this exercise would add that the baker and his heirs would not have done as well as they might even if they had gotten pleasure from the pictures for 284 years but not pleasure worth 2.3 million.

THE ACADEMY AND MARKET POWER

The guilds in France were troubled by the competition of Italy: by the paintings that came from there, by the Italian painters who came to France, and by the French and Flemish painters who were trained in Italy. The guild painters were unable to satisfy the taste of the collectors of France among whom the Valois kings were preeminent. Francis I brought Leonardo to France and treated him in the proprietary manner in which the English treat all of Italy. Leonardo died in France and as late as 1970 was identified as a French painter on the labels of his pictures in the Louvre.

The competition of Italian art was not brought under control until the Academy of Fine Arts was formed in 1648. It became a power in 1661 when Colbert extended the authority of the government over the economy. The arts were to be made a part of the economy, in which there was to be a place for everything and everything was to be in its place whether it wanted to be there or not. When Colbert called a group of merchants together and asked them what the state could do for them, one, Legendre, said, "You can leave us alone" (*"Laissons-nous faire, laissez faire!"*) He did not leave the arts alone (Colbert, not Legendre) and in due course gathered the Academy into his hands. It has been described, by Francis Henry Taylor in his learned history of collecting, as "an intellectual ideal, and . . . a program for the glorification of the French monarchy."[11] His observation has found favor with historians. They also note, however, that like the academies of Italy in the sixteenth century it was a rival of the guild for market power and in time replaced it. However, the last word is yet to be said about Colbert and his economic policy, mercantilism, and until it is one is permitted to ask how much of his Grand Design was a means of restricting the market for the benefit of some at the expense of others. Or as a great reformer said, "It makes a difference whose ox is to be gored." The ox was French in part and Italian in greater part. The Academy replaced the guild of French painters, reduced the demand for Italian art, and enlarged the market for the work of French Academicians. One way it did this was to learn from the art the Italians had created and was in French collections; another was to make use of French artists who had studied in Italy. Charles Le Brun had done so. He was made rector of the Academy and laid down the principles of painting. Among them the salient was, "Drawing is the probity of art." (Two hundred years later Renoir, after completing a portrait, was to be grateful to the subject for not having commented on his draftsmanship which Manet and others said was bad.[12]) The ukase of Le Brun probably had less to do with Italy or art than it had to do with giving the Academy power in the market. The paintings of its members had a favored position there by reason of the official position of the Academy and of the prominent place of Le Brun as a painter apart from that as an official of the government. The Academy's view of what constituted painting was inculcated on both supply and demand—on the former by the way the Academy instructed painters and on the latter by the taste it fostered among collectors.

One of its measures contributed to the notion that art should be above the market and is vulgarized by being associated with it. Members of the Academy were prohibited from selling their works directly to collectors. The Academy and its successors staged exhibitions periodically—the celebrated, or notorious, salons at which paintings were sold. They were in effect market days and served also to inform the public of the work, or current output, of the artists who had official standing. The salons were open to the public, were meant for it, and admission was charged.

By the middle of the nineteenth century, according to Harrison and Cynthia White, the daily attendance was as high as 10,000, and there were as many as 5,000 pictures at a single salon.[13] The walls were covered from floor to ceiling, and the pictures, hanging frame to frame, competed for notice in a way that was not altogether fair. So it was said by the Academicians whose work was hung out of sight or off in a corner. The pictures were selected by a jury except those of members who previously had exhibited. Prizes were awarded but were less than the prices at which the pictures so distinguished were sold. When the Academy prohibited its members from selling directly to the public, they had recourse to intermediaries, and the intermediaries were among the early art dealers of France. The stated purpose of the prohibition was to avoid "confounding" the status of Academicians with that of a person engaged in a mercenary activity.[14] What the actual purpose was is a matter of conjecture. It probably had a place in the designs of Mazarin, and of Colbert after him, to enlarge the economic authority of the state, and in order to do that privileges were granted to special interests in return for their cooperation. The prohibition could also have reduced the quantity supplied of painting by increasing its selling cost.

The Academy has been anathematized by historians because it did not allow the Impressionists to exhibit at its salons, which is true, hence for trying to stifle their genius, which is probably not true. Bouguereau, the archetypical Academician and *bête noire* of the avant-garde, was in fact more tolerant of Impressionism than it was of him (which was not tolerant at all). Long after he died, Picasso paid him homage, grudgingly, to be sure, but homage all the same.

That the Academy excluded non-members from its salons is no less or more reprehensible than a cartel excluding non-members from its marketing system. Indeed, the economic theory of cartels helps to understand the Academy, which was comprised of a large number of independent producers (the artists). It monopolized the most important method of selling paintings (the periodic salons). It reduced the supply of pictures by limiting the number of painters. It did that by limiting membership in the Academy and by conducting its own program of instruction. It tried to increase the demand for the paintings of its members by informing buyers that the work of its members satisfied the canons of taste, the source of which was the Academy itself. But because the Academy could not control the entire supply of painting, it was not a monopoly. Not all painters were in the Academy, and while it could advise a collector against buying non-members' works because they did not have its cachet it could not prevent them from being bought, as it would have been able to do had it, for example, secured a law that prohibited the sale of non-Academic painting (as non-guild paintings once could not be sold). Moreover, the Academy did not limit the number of pictures done by its members. It did limit the number that were exhibited at each salon because work submitted by members who had never exhibited had to be approved by a jury and also because space was limited. But that, while it affected the price a painter received, did not otherwise affect the number of pictures he painted. His being prohibited from selling directly to collectors could have reduced his output. The prohibition may have been imposed for that reason.

In the nineteenth century, the power of the Academy was lessened by the large amount of painting that was done. One reason for the large amount seems to have been several inventions that reduced the cost of painting (as will be explained in a few pages).

Guilds and academies are not the only ways in which artists have sought to reduce competition. The attraction of these methods was their legality, hence relatively low cost. The political authority to which they were subject did not interfere with their efforts and on occasion is known to have assisted them. The government of the city of Delft had a particular interest in doing so because it received a share of the fines levied on craftsmen and artists who violated guild regulations. The disadvantage of legal cartels, which is what the guilds and academies were, is that the results they seek can be slow in coming, the restrictions they impose on the market may be circumvented, the members of the cartel are tempted to cheat each other and often do. One of many examples is OPEC.

Hence there is a temptation for producers to employ direct methods against competitors. The painters resident in Naples early in the seventeenth century are said to have resisted the competition of painters who were invited there from other parts of Italy by the church and civil authorities. Bernardo de Dominici in his account written shortly after the event said that Ribera, Corenzio, and Caracciolo were *mafiosi* who controlled the market. (Ribera was Spanish, Corenzio was Greek, and only Caracciolo was Neapolitan.) The account has been made lurid by later writers who claim there is corroborative evidence for it.[15] Dominici is not always reliable, and what he said about the three is omitted from the abridged edition of his work published a few years ago.[16]

However, there is evidence that competition among the artists was not free. Francis Haskell, a reliable source, does not mention the *mafiosi,* but does say the effort to attract painters to Naples was met with hostility.[17] Nevertheless the effort was made. The decoration of the Capella del Tesoro, its Board of Deputies declared, was not to be entrusted to any Neapolitan or foreigner living in Naples. The board seems to have believed none of the local artists were good enough. Nevertheless, Ribera did receive a major commission, for the Carthusian Monastery, after the Spanish viceroy intervened on his behalf. One can believe political means were used to regulate the market because they are altogether familiar. Ribera was to have been paid 100 ducats for each of 14 figures which, his heirs declared after he died, was not done, and they went to law—which is also familiar, not as a way of interfering with competition but as the consequence of doing so.[18]

Even very great artists have had rivals who wanted to drive them out of the market. Michelangelo fled from Rome where he was the premier artist of the papacy. Among his commissions was the tomb Julius II wanted for himself. It was a massive affair, very costly, and troubled the architect who had been commissioned to do St. Peter's because he did not know just where to place it in the basilica. The architect was Bramante, and he was a rival of Michelangelo for the patronage of the pope, which is to say, for the money the pope had to spend on art. Bramante wanted to have his way about the construction of St. Peter's, and Michelangelo believed Bramante meant to have him murdered. He sped to Florence against the express wishes of the pope who ordered him to return to Rome. The *Signoria* (municipal authority) of Florence directed him to obey but Michelangelo would not. As a probable victim of Bramante, his expected income would have been zero.

Bramante like Ribera could invest his work with a spiritual quality that was transcendent. Art historians have noted Ribera's skill at depicting torture, martyrdom, and penitential saints. An amateur may also notice he could penetrate the character of a sitter to an extent that evokes Rembrandt, and that his lights and shades, while not as lucid, are harmonious enough to make one think of Caravaggio, for example, *The Apostle* (Städtiches Museum, Solothurn). Bramante was a painter as well as an architect. He did a series of frescoes, *Men at Arms,* who had they been encountered in life would strike one as people who were inclined to have their own way. Beyond this there seems to be no connection between the art of Bramante and Ribera and the business practices they employed to market it. In any event, their business practices did not ruin it.

The same can be said of the Delft painter Linschoten, who is mentioned by Professor Montias. Linschoten, after completing his apprenticeship in Delft, went to Naples and continued his studies under Ribera, who seems to have taught him more than art. He returned to Delft and did religious paintings that brought high prices. He too was given to violence and three times was banned from Delft and The Hague.[19]

PRODUCT DIFFERENTIATION

All of these painters tried to increase their income by reducing the supply of painting (and painters). There is another way to increase income, and it has been attempted more often. It is by an artist making his work a substitute for the work of others and their work no substitute for his. The practice is product differentiation and is to be observed in matters having to do with art and in matters having nothing at all to do with it, such as making automobiles.

Every painter who has tried to excel (and who has not?) has tried to set his work above that of others. That is what excelling means. If the efforts succeed, competition is lessened. Rarely is it eliminated. Although the work of an outstanding artist is distinctive, it is not unique in the sense of its value never being affected by the work of other artists, in particular by the work of other outstanding artists. In the language of economics, there is some cross elasticity of demand for even the greatest of artistic creations and there is even more for what is not great. In ordinary language this means that even the finest work has a substitute. This doesn't mean the work has no unique features (except if it is a multiple of some sort, and even they are usually not identical). What is meant is that for a given work at a particular price there are other works which at particular prices will be preferred to it, at lower prices will be even more preferred, and at higher prices will not be preferred at all. Did not Bramante show he believed the Michelangelo tomb for Julius II was a substitute for what he, Bramante, wanted to make of the basilica of St. Peter?

Most artists have not been distinguished, which is true by definition since art, like economics and most things, is not a caucus race. However, most artists have wanted to distinguish themselves—to do something that is valued and has not been done by anyone else. The effort to be singular seems to have been more noticeable since the end of the Second World War. The impression probably is correct in a quantitative sense, for the reasons put forward in the last chapter. An example of the present is a piece by the British sculptor Bill Woodrow. William Feaver, an art journalist, describes it: "The lid of the four-legged box standing on the world map has flipped open, releasing a glum head on the end of a long black coil made of sheet metal cut from the industrial shelving that frames the box and supports the inner spring. And that's not all. An overcoat hangs from the frame, a strolling player's coat adorned with cuttings from the map (mid-Atlantic mostly, and parts of Africa)."[20]

Such conceits are said—mistakenly—to be the distinguishing feature of the art of the present. Those who say it often do so with a long face and solemnly explain them as the consequence of the modern world having no standards of value (another factual mistake). Novelty always has had a place in the arts. It is another name for product differentiation. What is interesting is that it has limits, and the art that is valued at any time is that which comes within them. As there is a median voter whose views must be followed if a candidate is to be noticed, so there is a median amateur whose taste painters must respect if they are to be recognized. The limits of his taste, we reasonably can suppose, depend on what he has invested in acquiring it. The amount of the investment and the form it takes were explained in chapter two. At any particular time, the taste of each person has particular properties. They are not the same for all persons, hence there is a demand for more than one kind of art and there is more than one way in which an artist can work. But (to repeat) there are limits. One of de Kooning's women would have been off-limits in the seventeenth century when Reni painted the *Penitent*

Magdalen, and if anyone today painted the way Reni did, even if he were Jasper Johns, he too would be off-limits.

In about all periods of art (perhaps in *all*) there was a place for both solemnity and levity. Not every Old Master was always solemn, and not every member of the avant-garde has meant to shock the bourgeoisie. Today's painters can be earnest. Consider the Americans who exhibited in the Venice *Biennale* of 1984. "The work of these twenty-four artists [the brochure in the American pavilion stated] together represents a search for enduring values, which grows out of a sense of potential loss and destruction, and a deep belief in basic concerns which are not only indigenous to America, but to human beings everywhere." Who could ask for anything more in the way of values (and *fin de siècle* diction)?

Consider those who came before and how they sought novelty. There is caricature (or could it be mockery?) in *The Holy Family* by Joos van Cleve (Gemäldegalerie, Vienna). Joseph looks through a window at Mary and the Child. He seems to have had no part in the matter and simply is passing by, an itinerant scholar carrying a book, squinting through glasses, wearing an oversize hat that is about to flop over his eyes. In other paintings the *bizarrerie* is not obvious. But they invite conjecture. An example is Tintoretto's *Mercury and the Three Graces,* one of four related wall paintings by him in the ante-room of the Hall of the Collegio of the Ducal Palace in Venice. His first biographer, Ridolfi, writes about the picture in a way that doesn't hint at even impropriety. "One [Grace] is leaning on a die, for each of the Graces has an attribute. The other two hold the myrtle and the rose, both sacred to the amorous goddess, symbols of perpetual love. They are accompanied by Mercury to show that the Graces bestow themselves with good reason, just as favors are bestowed by the Senate on its deserving citizens."[21] That may be just what Tintoretto intended the painting to mean.

Yet might a senator have had other ideas, one who gave it his close attention. Mercury is most familiar as the god of commerce, and Venice certainly was commercial. So his appearance is *comme il faut.* But he is also the god of thieving. Was Tintoretto commenting on shady deals along the Rialto and could he have been showing his distaste for commerce? Even more interesting is that Mercury was also the god of gambling. (One can understand why polytheism declined with economic progress and the increasing value of time.) The die on which one Grace is resting is painted to show two sides, one with four spots and the other with three which brings us to seven. Was it lucky in sixteenth-century Italy? Gambling with dice is that old and in fact much older. Finally there is Mercury as still another god, of wrestling. The movement of the Graces may express nothing more than movement, a familiar feature of Venetian painting. Still, there is Mercury in the background who could be presiding over the start of a contest, at the moment only in the sinuous stage, later perhaps to become movement appropriate to gymnastics (of which he was also the god). One would not be surprised that the senators wanted a word with Little Dyer about his little jokes. There is no report that they did but there is of their possibly having objected to the price they had to pay. They called in arbitrators to set a fair value on the four pictures.

There are other paintings by Tintoretto that tempt one to ask if he sought novelty by using humor where it is not expected (or trying to be funny when he shouldn't). One is *The Last Supper* (St. Trovaso, Venice). The disciples look beyond Christ at two spectral figures in the distance. There is amazement, alarm, consternation, and one reaches frantically for the jug of wine behind him. In many paintings of *The Last Supper,* John, always seated next to Christ, is resting his head on the table in a manner that, were he a lesser mortal, would suggest he had been drinking too much. In the St. Trovaso picture, he alone among the Apostles is not agitated, is in fact resting peacefully.

This conjecture may be entirely wrong, may be silly. It is not the sort of thing one gets from art historians. One has written about the painting in St. Trovaso: "The tense counterpoint of spatial thrusts, moving with and against the divergent two-point perspective of the controlling table ... charges the entire picture with an instability that seems literally to extend at its nearest point into our space."[22] That could be just what the artist intended. Yet the communicants who for centuries have seen it might, some of them, just wonder if the Apostle reaching for the jug needed a drink to steady himself after he saw ghosts.

Secular humor there is in abundance. Frans Hals painted the *Banquet of Officers of the Civic Guard of St. George at Haarlem* (Frans Hals Museum, Haarlem). One of the eleven men is seated by a plate of oysters, his right hand placed over his stomach, his left reaching out with upturned palm as if in supplication, his head tilted sadly to one side. Did the oysters make him ill? The humor could be indelicate. The genre paintings of Steen, van Ostade, and Molenaer can be gross. Less known, and if not gross, certainly indelicate, is Watteau's *The Remedy* (Getty, Santa Monica), a nude reclining, bottom up, as a servant is about to apply a clyster. Then there is Hieronymus Bosch, claimed by the Surrealists as their forerunner, fascinating to psychologists of the present for his fantasy, especially the morbid side, and who now can be used by economists to illustrate the principle that there are limits to product differentiation. His work was outside most of that of his day. He was able to sell it and had some enthusiastic collectors, but he had next to no influence on his contemporaries. Pieter Bruegel the Elder was one of the few who tried his hand at the same kind of fantasy; he did not, however, confine himself to it or is he best remembered for it.

These interesting and curious particulars are offered for several reasons. They show that for a long while artists have engaged in *epater le bourgeois,* a fact known to anyone familiar with the history of art or who has visited enough museums. What is just as interesting is that shocking the bourgeois (read: people who buy art) is one way in which artists differentiate their work and try to excel. Even more interesting is that product differentiation is economic behavior and has its roots on both sides of the market. Artists engage in it in order to increase their income. Buyers choose a differentiated product because for a given expenditure it can add more to their utility than can an additional amount of a product with which they are familiar. So Flaubert's axiom ought to be rewritten: Observation (not hatred) of the bourgeois is the beginning of wisdom—understanding of course that the artist as much as the buyer is bourgeois.

We now may return to Mr. Woodrow and his jack-in-the-box. Can his juvenile high jinks be put in the same category as the witty allusions of Tintoretto? The market wants what it does, and does what it can. It is at present a market in which the income of buyers has risen faster than their investment in taste, and as a consequence taste has become simple. What could be simpler than a jack-in-the-box even when it is set in detritus that may or may not be "a political statement"? Such art is one of the simple pleasures of the poor in human capital. The artists alone are not responsible for it or are those who take pleasure in it. Both are, and economics explains why. It also explains why the probability of its being discarded in time is about 99 percent.

MINIMIZING COSTS

Reducing costs is another way artists have tried to increase their income. Of all of the enterprises of hand and mind, the painter's studio, one would think, is the last place to notice the division of labor, the substitution of machines for men, the use of prefabricated materials, the search for new materials and techniques, or to see a department of design, another for sales, and a chief executive officer. Yet that is what one does find, if not in every respect, at least in most.

An example from the present is the French sculptor, Daniel Buren whose leitmotif is stripes. He placed them on detruncated columns in the courtyard of the Palais Royal in Paris; he placed them on the grand staircase of the Art Institute of Chicago; and he placed them on the doors of the electric trains that pass by the Institute from where they were to be viewed as a significant visual experience. Whether or not the stripes really are significant is important, of course, but not here. What is relevant is that they are not made by Mr. Buren or by any other sculptor or by a painter. They are ordered from a factory and are made of cloth or paper. The sculptor is thereby relieved of "the mechanical necessity of painting the stripes himself," as one of his admirers states.[23]

An example from the past is the enterprise of a sixteenth-century painter of Antwerp known as the Master of Frankfurt because he did the altar of the Dominican monastery there. (He also provides an example of the high-jinks form of product differentiation. In the portrait of himself and his wife she is wearing a scarf, all stiff, white, starchy, and spotless except for an enormous fly on it.) He used a set of prepared pounced patterns to render the clothes on the figures in his paintings. The device could be applied mechanically and painted over or touched up as desired. Just how this was done is described by Dr. Stephen H. Goddard in an article about the painter.[24] He goes on to say this labor-saving device was in common use in northern Europe in the fifteenth and sixteenth centuries and that other mechanical devices for speeding up the making of art were used in Italy in the Middle Ages.

The reduction of the cost of producing something represents an increase in its supply. As a means of increasing the income of the producer, it is just the opposite of monopolistic practices or product differentiation because they try to reduce supply. In a competitive market, reduction of cost is the only way a producer can increase his income. If he raised his price he would lose sales to his competitors. Hence, cost-cutting can (but not necessarily does) indicate competition and also can indicate that what is produced has close substitutes. The product could be art. The annals of painting report how artists have tried to reduce cost, even artists who have not been in close competition with others. Some have used assistants, because they could not themselves do all of the pictures they could sell. An example from the present is the late Andy Warhol who did the initial copy of his multiples and had the others done for him. From the past, the examples are legion and include some of the greatest figures in the history of art: Giotto, Raphael, Veronese, Titian, Tintoretto, Tiepolo, El Greco, and Rubens, the last of whom was first among them in being a CEO.

There also have been lesser painters who tried to minimize cost. Reynolds was one, and he did so in order to meet the prices of his competitors.[25] In order to know if a painter who tried to reduce costs was a painter whose work was or was not distinguished [low or high cross elasticity of demand, respectively] we must know if the price he received for it was or was not similar to that received by his contemporaries for their work. If his prices were close to those of others, he was in competition with them, and his art, whatever may have been said of it after his death, was not thought to be much better (or worse) than theirs. Reynolds's prices were similar to those of others of his day, which suggests that as well-known as he was then, his work was not as distinguished as it became after his death.

Reynolds used assistants and priced his portraits according to the amount that he himself painted of each of them. Between 1753 and 1792 he painted more than 2,600 pictures which, if he worked five days a week, was about one every three days. At the start of his career he sensibly set his prices below those of his teacher, Hudson. As the demand for his work increased he set them equal to Hudson's, after which the prices of both increased equally (indicating that the art of Reynolds was not incomparable during his lifetime). Each painter at one time charged twelve guineas for a portrait of which he did the head only and forty-eight guineas for a portrait he did without any assistance. If Reynolds (or Hudson) utilized his assistants and studio facilities fully, either by doing only complete portraits or only partial portraits, the one must have taken four times as long to do as the other. If complete portraits took less time, he would have done only them; if more, he would have done only partial portraits. The fact that he did both indicates he could not keep busy by doing only one or the other which in turn indicates that by doing both he could make better use of his assistants or his studio. This deduction assumes that Reynolds kept a sharp eye on costs and returns, that he was, if you will, the economic man at the easel with the mind of an accountant behind the eye of the painter. He did, in fact, keep what his biographers call "pocket books" in which he recorded the names of his clients (painters like lawyers and astrologers do not have customers) and he also kept ledgers in which he entered the deposit he required from each client before beginning a portrait, the balance being payable when the picture was finished. His practice apparently was not to part with a picture until it was paid for; when he died there were a number of portraits in his studio.

Some of the work of Reynolds was gone over by his principal assistant, Giuseppe Marchi, whom he had brought from Italy and trained to imitate him with "the greatest fidelity." Reynolds also had portions of his pictures done by his pupils, by professional copyists, and by other painters, Hoppner and van Aken among them, the latter a drapery painter who clothed the figures.

There are other examples of specialization. Girolamo Mengozzi did architectural settings, ornamentation, and perspective well, and he collaborated for many years with Giambattista Tiepolo, the latter conceiving the picture and painting the figures while the former supplied their setting. Jan (Velvet) Brueghel collaborated with Rubens, in one work providing the floral setting for the figures. He also worked with de Momper and others. For some he would add flowers or animals, for others paint figures in their landscape or set a landscape against their figures. This is not specialization in the familiar sense (placing the head on the pin and nothing else, as Adam Smith illustrated it) but is specialization in the (James Mill) sense of doing that for which the painter had the greatest comparative advantage or least disadvantage. Rubens perhaps could do flowers better than Brueghel but could do faces even better, and Brueghel may not have painted animals as well as a floral setting or as well as the painters who engaged him could do themselves but could not do as well as they could paint other things. The interested reader will find the classic statement of this idea—the idea of comparative advantage—in the seventh chapter of Ricardo's *Principles of Political Economy and Taxation* (1821).

A collaboration of particular interest is that in which Canaletto participated with six or seven others in Venice in the 1720s. It was organized in entrepreneurial fashion by Owen McSwiney who was also a music impressario. He engaged them to do "tomb paintings" which were depictions of imaginary monuments to English notables of the day or of the recent past, a not unusual subject in England at the time. One was the *Allegorical Tomb in Honour of Lord Chancellor Somers* (who died in 1716), and it was the joint product of Canaletto and Cimaroli who did the perspective and landscape and of Piazzetta who did the figures. In two others the figures were done by Balestra, the landscape by Cimaroli, and the architecture by the Valerini brothers who were actually scene painters. An art historian of the day, G. P. Zanotti, said the artists had no idea of what the series was about. An art historian of this century, Tancred Borenius, said the "elements fused together with singular success."[26]

McSwiney had twenty-four paintings done and put them on the market. They did not sell quickly, and by 1730 he still had fourteen, whereupon he advertised them and also had them engraved. Mr. Borenius records that Boucher had a part in the engraving (thereby making the enterprise tri-national). A single buyer took the fourteen; the other ten had been sold earlier to one buyer. Was each of them so fascinated by imaginary tombs? Or did each expect to resell them at a profit?

The collaboration is interesting as an example of entrepreneurial activity in painting—interesting because of its scale, not because it was unusual, certainly not among the English. McSwiney had an idea for something that might be profitable; he brought together the resources to produce it; the artists divided their labor in a way that made their joint effort as efficient as possible; their product was put on a market where the demand was uncertain; and to inform the public, advertising was used which had the consequence of yielding additional income from the engravings that were a by-product of the advertisements.

So does the episode appear to an economist. Not so to all historians. While Mr. Borenius wrote favorably of it, F. J. B. Watson, writing later, did not. He described McSwiney as a speculator, adventurer, a bankrupt, mercenary of course, and (Pelion upon Ossa) an Irishman who drank too much. None of these qualities, if indeed that is what they were, troubled the artists who did their work and took their wages from McSwiney or at least did not trouble them enough to make them prefer other employment. Moreover, the character of the entrepreneur and his motives did not tarnish the quality of their work if we are to believe Mr. Borenius.

The McSwiney venture was not the only entrepreneurial activity in which Canaletto had a part or was it the most important or was it the only way he sold his services. J. G. Links is informative about Canaletto's business practices and relates that he dealt with collectors, their agents, and dealers as well as with entrepreneurs.[27] In Mr. Links' book and in just about everything that has been written about Canaletto, there appears the enterprising Joseph Smith, an English merchant in Venice who seems to have bought more paintings from Canaletto than anyone else did. Among them are a dozen or so he directed Canaletto to do of places along the Grand Canal, some looking east from the Rialto bridge toward the church of the Salute, and the others looking west from the church to the bridge, the group together constituting a tour of the central portion of the city which is what tourists were likely to remember. Smith had the paintings engraved and published in book form. All, or nearly all, were meant to be sold in England, where Smith later brought Canaletto himself and had him paint scenes. The Thames, Windsor Castle, and Greenwich never looked so sunny, so unlike England, and so much like Italy. There are said to be more paintings by Canaletto in England than there now are in Italy, certainly more paintings of Venice than in the museums of Venice itself. (For the consolation of the non-English, the city itself does not present the clutter and litter today which it has in many of his scenes, and there are fewer dogs though possibly more cats.)

Canaletto was given to cost-cutting and in being so was in no way unusual among painters (or pin makers or housekeepers or any who must rely on their own income to meet their expenses). He did variations on his paintings, some near to being copies; he made engravings of them or had them made by others; and some engravings (like those of the tomb paintings) were put together and published as books. His clients were familiar with his ways. One, according to Mr. Links, commissioned four paintings and stipulated they must be "original works." Canaletto complied to the letter but went on to make variations of three of them, two of which he did at least twelve times, then had them engraved and copied by others.

Another who copied himself quite obviously was El Greco. He did two views of Toledo and replicas of other works. Whether he did so to reduce his cost, I do not know, but that was the effect. A painter who was aware of the effect was W. P. Frith, the little-remembered Victorian who was so well-known in his day. "I found myself included amongst the popular men to such a degree, that scarcely one of my more important works escaped what Scheffer called being 'bred from'." An important work was his *Railway Station* (1882), of which an engraving was made and prints sold by subscription. Before the engraving was made, the painting was put on exhibition, and some 21,000 people paid to see it in a seven-week period. Frith said, "The critics contradicted one another as usual, without doing good or harm to me or the picture."[28] Like several other of his works, the painting was so popular that a rail was placed before it to keep visitors at a proper distance. Each time this was done, Frith recorded his gratification in his diary. If popular paintings were fenced off today, would the act be deplored by those who were offended by the velvet sash before the Metropolitan's Rembrandt? A nice question. The sash did not call attention to the popularity of the painting, and the rail did not call attention to the price of Frith's work. Yet popularity and price do vary in the same direction, and to call attention to the one is to call attention to the other.

Frith's wry observation about critics makes one ask how much they effect the demand for art. The people who review the theater for newspapers have been said to determine whether a play succeeds or fails. Yet a study of the American theater reported that reviews could account for only a third of the variation in the profits from producing plays.[29] In Frith's day the commanding figure among critics—and one who did not care for Frith at all—was Ruskin. He is said to have made the public understand why Turner was an important painter and was himself an important buyer of Turner's work. If Ruskin were living today and if Turner were General Motors, Ruskin would be suspected of insider trading. A personage of his day, Shirley Brooks, sent this jingle to Frith. "I ups and paints, hears no complaints/And sells before I'm dry/Till savage Ruskin sticks his tusk in/And all is up with I."[30] It could be a tribute to the influence of Ruskin or to his fatuity. Turner certainly is a major artist; but so too are Whistler who, Ruskin said, could not paint, and Canaletto whose work, he said, could be miserable and mechanical. Guardi did not think so and made paintings of his drawings. That—whether or not Canaletto received a share of the proceeds—was still another example of reducing costs by increasing production or of economies of scale in the making of art.

A tempting question is whether there are examples of economies of scale early in the Renaissance when the subject matter was a small number of religious themes. The painters did not have to range over the universe of reality or fancy or doctrine before they could decide what to put in their pictures. (To put nothing but paint on them was not done in that unenlightened age.) The limited subject matter reduced one of their costs—the time needed to choose a subject. On the other hand, they had to find a distinctive way to represent what had been represented many times before, the martyrdom of St. Sebastian, for example, and that must have been time consuming.

Painters use models and place them in a setting. Each comes at a cost. From the nineteenth century onward they have been able to use photographs for the setting instead of taking themselves and their paraphernalia to it (leaving that donkey's work to the photographers). Frith used a photograph of Epsom Downs when he painted *Derby Day* (National Gallery, London) which was as popular as his *Railway Station* (and was the kind of art favored by George V). In securing models, however, Frith did not skimp. Other painters have used their wives, children, friends, and servants. Or their imagination or photographs. What looks like a remarkable example is the *Virgin with Angels* of Cimabue (Louvre). There are seven figures. At first sight the Virgin and two of the angels seem to have been modeled on the same person and the other four angels on another person. On a second view all of the faces have so much in common that one may suppose the artist used just one model. Of less consequence but more unusual is an enterprise of Gerhardt Richter, a contemporary German who teaches in Düsseldorf (still a center of art though much less than it was in the nineteenth century). He painted portraits from portrait photographs, not the photorealism of Americans like Chuck Close but prosaic paintings of prosaic photographs. He then took photographs of the paintings. The process could, one imagines, be repeated indefinitely: a painting of a photograph of a painting of a photograph, *undsoweiter.* Mr. Richter came to a full stop at about thirty or forty faces, and they were hung together in the Wallraf-Richartz Museum in Cologne. They are, in addition to being an illustration of cost-cutting, an illustration of product differentiation.

The ways of Andrea del Sarto are noteworthy. He sometimes brought in models, sometimes "invented" them, and at times used his wife, a lovely but petulant lady according to Vasari. Browning in his verse about the painter went straight to the business heart of the matter. The painter coaxes his wife to sit with him by the window. "Both of one mind, as married people use,/Quietly, quietly, the evening through"—not just to exchange conjugal affection, not at all to idle the time away, but to refresh themselves for the morrow. "Don't count the time lost, neither; you must serve/For each of the five pictures we require—/It saves a model." Browning, never one to leave readers in doubt, goes on 200 lines later: "If you would sit by me every night/I should work better, do you comprehend?/I mean that I should earn more, give you more." Vasari is not that explicit but does imply enough to warrant what Browning made of the account. The incautious reader might think the prosaic Browning was infected by the manner of the merchants and mill owners of his day who looked sharp at the pence and shillings in each transaction. Actually, del Sarto and the other worthies Vasari writes about were of the same mind. After all, double-entry bookkeeping was invented in Italy (and accounting was first recognized as a profession in Great Britain).

PAINTING AS A FAMILY AFFAIR

An interesting question is how the income and employment of a painter was affected by his being a member of a family of painters. A noticeable number have been the son of a painter, or daughter, brother, cousin, nephew, niece, in-law, grandchild, husband, or wife. The della Robbia family was noticed early in this chapter, and the suggestion was made that Luca used the family to protect the monopoly he had acquired by using glazed terra cotta in sculpture. Giambattista Tiepolo taught his sons, Giandomenico and Lorenzo Baldiserra. They were not the equals of their father, but the former at times was so faithful to his father's manner that their work is difficult to distinguish, and he was entrusted to fresco the family villa, now reconstructed in the Ca' Rezzonico of Venice, where there also are frescoes by the brother-in-law of Giambattista who was Francesco Guardi who together with his brother, Gian-Antonio, was taught by his father, Giacomo. Jacobo Bellini was the head of a family of painters, one of whom, Giovanni, was the finest of them, although he by no means obscured his brother, Gentile. Their sister married the great Paduan painter Mantegna who contributed to the training of Giovanni.

Did learning to paint cost less if the teacher was the father of the painter? Was his lifetime income higher because his father had made the family name known? Or because he simply inherited a going concern when the family enterprise passed from his father to him? Were the costs of the father lower because he was assisted by his sons, or other relatives, instead of by workers outside of the family? A relative would have more desire to work hard than outsiders would have because the effort of the relative would increase family income and his or her share of it. The rotten kids would not want to be rotten painters or rotten anything. In these circumstances, being rotten is too expensive (compliments to Gary Becker).

The head of the family enterprise would feel more certain about the claim he had on the work done by his relatives than on that done by assistants. The claim was a legal right (and is echoed today in American law by which art students may not keep their work without the permission of the school, the stated reason being that what the student does has "a lot of teacher" in it).[31] The regulations of the guilds must have been less difficult to evade if the painter instead of using apprentices and assistants used his relatives.

There also is the matter of information: the inducement to acquire it, to share it, and the cost of exchanging it. In the family relation, one would expect there to be an inducement to acquire and share information about techniques, subject matter, materials, competitors, buyers, state of the market, and the like. One also would expect that the cost of exchanging the information would be lower than in a non-family enterprise. Still another advantage of a family enterprise is in its being a means of distributing risk and of bearing uncertainty at a lower cost.

Examples abound of families of artists, and they present questions. Did the van Eyck brothers simply succeed each other in the painting of the *Adoration of the Lamb* (St.-Bavon, Ghent), each doing every sort of thing, or did Hubert leave portions to be completed by Jan because they specialized (assuming Hubert had any part at all in the painting, assuming indeed there was a van Eyck named Hubert which at one time was denied)? Were the copies of the paintings of Pieter Bruegel more acceptable because they were made by his son Pieter? Were the original works of Pieter II more popular because he

copied his father so well? The same may be asked about Pieter III.
Then there was Jan, the second son of Pieter I, and his painter sons,
Jan II and Ambrosius, and their sons, who continued the floral paintings of Jan I who also influenced another grandson, Jan van Kessel.
Was Bellotto regarded as more than an imitator of Canaletto and as
a painter in his own right who carried on the tradition of view painting because he was the nephew of Canaletto (who was himself taught
by his father)?

Other families can be named. Luigi Vanvitelli was the architect
son of Gaspare Vanvitelli, born Caspar van Wittel in Holland from
which he emigrated to Rome to become one of the first to do scene
or view paintings, rendering the architecture in detail as Canaletto
and others were later to do of Venice. Next in popularity to them are
the genre paintings, and the most familiar were done by Pietro
Longhi, the son of a silversmith and father of Allesandro, who did
portraits. The largest painting in the city is the work of Jacobo Tintoretto and his son, Domenico (and others). It is 73 feet long and 22
feet high, covering the end wall of the Grand Council Chamber in the
Ducal Palace. (It may have been the longest painting in the world
until 1965 when James Rosenquist, the American pop artist, did *F-111*,
a collage 85 feet long. The collector who bought it said it was "the
most important statement made in art in the last 50 years." It was not,
however, as high as *Paradiso* and moreover was surpassed in 1976
by Bartlett's *Rhapsody*, which is 153 feet, 9 inches long, yet itself a
small matter when set against earth-art such as the project of Turrell
to smooth the crater of an extinct volcano in Arizona.)

The most interesting family (to one amateur) is the Lippis. Fra
Filippo, a Carmelite friar of Florence, was employed to do the high
altar of the Convent Church of St. Margherita. In the course of his
work, he saw Lucrezia Buti, a nun or ward, and was captivated. So
Vasari relates. He continues that Filippo made her the model of the
Virgin, and when the painting was finished they ran off and had a son,
Filippino, who became an eminent painter. Later historians have said
Vasari was spinning a yarn, and so he may have been. Nevertheless
they have not dispelled the magic entirely. One notices that the Virgin
in the paintings of the father and of the son are at times the same
person. It could be Lucrezia and very likely is since using someone
in the family as a model was a common practice. The child probably
was Filippino. When he became a painter, he painted his mother, and

she was as lovely as ever. Age had not diminished her beauty because Filippino reproduced the face of the Virgin in the paintings of his father.

There were other families. Among them were the Carracci of Bolognese origin: Agostino; his son, Antonio; his brother Annibale; and their cousin, Lodovico, from whom the brothers received their first lesson. Orazio Gentileschi, a Caravaggisto, and his daughter, Artemisia, were painters. Both spent time in England and were patronized by Charles I (that is, he bought pictures from them). Artemisia, who may have taken her name from Artemis and given it to the "women's only" galleries of the present, is a remembered figure in Italian art. Another is Elisabetta Sirani, whose father, Andrea, was a painter of the Emilian school. Still another is Marianna Carlevaris, the daughter of Luca Carlevaris who was one of the first Italians to do view paintings and did them of Venice. Marianna did portraits in pastel as did her contemporary and the most celebrated of the Italian women in painting, Rosalba Carriera, who was the sister-in-law of Giovanni Pellegrini, a Venetian who plied his craft also in northern Europe and England. Her pastels were celebrated and made her subjects look ever so handsome. But there is an exception, a self-portrait (Accademia, Venice) that depicts a plain, plump person who looks at us kindly with eyes that have seen all and would if they could forgive all. She takes such a modest view of herself that we can forgive the crown of laurel on her head. The outstanding figures of Venetian painting were "family painters" just as some of the lesser figures were. Tintoretto has been named. Tiziano Vecellio or Titian had a son, Orazio; a brother, Francesco; and a nephew, Marco—all painters. Three sons of Paolo Caliari or Veronese were painters and had a place in his large workshop as did his brother, Benedetto. Among the earlier painters of Venice, those of the Gothic school, were the Vivarini: Antonio; his brother, Bartolomeo; and brother-in-law, Giovanni d'Alemagna, all of whom collaborated on particular works. The son of Antonio, Alvise, was also a painter. But caution: Palma Giovane was not taught by Palma Vecchio, who was his great uncle and died sixteen years before the younger Palma was born. Yet he was taught by his father, hence was a family painter after all.

Art as a family affair was not confined to Italy. In the Low Countries, the van Eycks have been noticed and also the Brueghels, seven of them, who were outnumbered, however, by eight Halses. In Bruges where he settled and learned painting and became the son-in-law of his teacher, Blondeel, there was Pieter Pourbus, the first of three generations of portrait painters, the others being his son, Frans the Elder, and grandson, Frans the Younger. Jacob van Ruisdael, the eminent landscapist, probably was trained by his father, Isaac, and his uncle, Salomon, who spelled the family name Ruysdael. Rogier van der Weyden, the most important painter of Flanders in the fifteenth century, was trained by his father before entering the workshop of Robert Campin. Also in Flanders at that time, though of Dutch origin, was Dieric Bouts, whose style was carried on by his sons, Dieric the Younger and Aelbrecht. A remembered woman in Dutch painting is Judith Leyster. Her forte was genre and portraits, and she was married to Jan Molenaer, a painter and etcher of genre scenes.

In France, the outstanding family was the Le Nain brothers. Antoine, Louis, and Mathieu. A familiar name among women painters is Vigée-Lebrun, who was trained by her father. Even more familiar is Berthe Morisot, who was the sister-in-law of Manet. Chardin was assisted by his son, even to having his work copied by his son. Janet Clouet and his brother Pollet were trained by their father, Jean (or Michel?), who may also have trained another son, François. Henri Fantin-Latour was trained by his father, Jean-François. Gaspard Dughet was the brother-in-law of Nicolas Poussin, adopted his name, and painted in his style so well that his work has been mistaken for that of his relative. In this century one notices, *inter alia,* Utrillo and his mother, Suzanne Valadon; and Robert Delaunay and his wife, Sonia.

In Germany, there was Lucas Cranach the Elder, who was the son of the painter Hans, and father of Lucas the Younger. Hans and Ambrosius Holbein were the painter sons of Hans, the elder, whose brother, Sigmund, was also a painter. Elsewhere there was El Greco whose son was his pupil and assistant. The teacher of Velazquez became his father-in-law. Picasso, one learns with interest, was the son of a teacher of painting in Spain. How much he learned from his father is arguable. Somewhat more may have been learned by Piet Mondrian from his father and uncle.

In the United States, there were Charles Willson Peale and his sons Rubens, Rembrandt, Raphaelle, and Titian; and his brother, James—all painters or painters *manqué.* Of more consequence was John Singleton Copley whose stepfather was Peter Pelham, an English mezzotint engraver. One could go on, but let the list end with the Wyeths: Andrew; his son, James; his father, N. C.; and Carolyn, his sister who was a teacher of James.

How a family enterprise could raise the income of the artists in it was suggested a few pages back. Another question now occurs. Who in the family was likely to benefit most—the teacher or those he taught? One way the question might be answered is suggested by a review of the artists just named. The principal beneficiary was (one may assume) the member of the family who became the most important. An indicator of the importance of artists is the attention they receive in the *Encyclopedia of World Art* as measured by the length of the entry for each or the number of times each is mentioned, a measure (very) roughly analogous to a citation count. The teacher in the family (one assumes) was the oldest member: the father, uncle, older brother, or cousin.

Of the forty or so families named, a relation of elder/teacher to younger/pupil(s) can be noticed for thirty-seven. In twenty-three of them, the elder member receives more attention from the encyclopedia than the younger. The families in which the elder is more noted are the Brueghel, Canaletto, Tintoretto, Lippi, Carracci, Gentileschi, Sirani, Carlevaris, Titian, Veronese, Hals, Bouts, Chardin, Clouet, Fantin-Latour, Cranach, El Greco, Peale, Manet, Poussin, della Robbia, Tiepolo, and Holbein.

The younger is more noted among the Vanvitelli, Longhi, Vivarini, Ruisdael, van der Weyden, Vigée-Lebrun, Picasso, Mondrian, Copley, Wyeth, Utrillo, Guardi, Bellini, and Velazquez—fourteen in all. The difference (between fourteen and twenty-three) is enough to allow one to guess the enterprise was formed because the father (or other elder) believed it was to his interest more than to the interest of the younger members although they too benefited. They could not, of course, be expected to initiate the arrangement themselves, and one does not expect to find a son on record as having said, "Don't you think, Governor, that before I'm made an artist we should draw up articles of partnership?" Still, if the father meant only to increase the welfare of the family or of the artists in it and did not put his before theirs, one would expect the younger to be important as often as the older.

The families from whom this information was gleaned are not offered as a random sample. They are names I happened onto while looking into quite different matters. The first few were mere curiosities, but as the number grew it suggested something significant, namely, an example of one way the production of art has been organized, and the reasons for organizing it that way. That surely is an important part of the activity of art in its entirety. It is more important than who the principal beneficiary of the family enterprise was, although that is not uninteresting or uninformative. Historians who wish to inquire into it are welcome to the method I have used here. I advise a larger sample and await an answer. Did father not only know better but do better?

Is there anything singular about painting being a family enterprise, anything that sets it apart from other occupations? Nothing at all, really. Such enterprises are common among lawyers, physicians, and other workers at the highly skilled end of the labor market and also are common among relatively unskilled workers who operate small firms, usually in the retail market, such as a grocery or restaurant. Just why this is so can be explained by labor economists. The fact that it is so is what is to the point here. It is evidence that the activity of art is an economic activity and can be analyzed by economic theory. Completely understood? No, nothing can be completely understood by any one field of study, possibly not by all of them taken together. So the amateur who is a positivist would say. He would add that some are more helpful than others and some are not helpful at all.

TECHNOLOGICAL AND OTHER CHANGES

There are other circumstances that have affected the cost of painting. They are what economists call exogenous because they come from outside of the economy, that is, are not the product of a change in relative prices (although in fact they cannot always be separated from it). The invention of photography and how it reduced cost has been noted. An invention of even more consequence was the metal tube as a container for paint. The invention was English but seems to have had greater effect in France. Painting out-of-doors became easier and became still easier when the portable easel was invented. About the same time, the railroad appeared, and painters could take their tubes and easels farther afield. The Impressionists did this. The great change they brought about, which has been the subject of so much inquiry, may simply have been the effect of inventions that made outdoor painting easier which means cheaper. Art history records that one of their innovations was to render shadows in purple instead of black. Could that have been because purple was gotten more easily from tubes than by grinding and mixing it on the palette? We are also told that after 1850 artists used poppy oil and other substances that allowed them to apply paint directly onto the canvas (*alla prima*) which must have reduced the time required to complete a picture. The method changed the subject matter, or content, of pictures as well as the way they were made. We also read that artists began to apply paint to the canvas directly from the tube instead of brushing it on and that such a thing was unprecedented. It certainly could not have been done before the tube was invented, and if the French are to be admired for the use they made of the tube so are the English who invented it for them to use.

The changes that Impressionism made were slow in being accepted by collectors. That is what an economist would expect. The collectors of the day had invested in a quite different kind of taste, and the academic painters had invested in a kind of painting that was quite different from Impressionism or its predecessor, the Barbizon School. One would expect Impressionism to become accepted, if at all, only as investment in taste changed and as painters responded to it by investing in the skill a different kind of painting required. These changes take time and are made more cheaply by the young who begin with no taste or skill than by the old who prudently want to protect their human capital instead of allowing it to become obsolete.

Impressionism might have taken even longer to succeed if the established painters had allowed it to be shown in their salons. By excluding it, the prices of Impressionist paintings were reduced, and more may have been bought as a consequence. That is not certain because exclusion could also have reduced the demand. One can be certain that the demand was increased by the high incomes in America, by the price of Impressionist paintings being low relative to the price of Old Masters, and by the fact that Americans themselves had been painting for scarcely a hundred years when collecting in the United States first became substantial, which was after the Civil War. Whatever was the plight of the Impressionists, it would have been worse had the American rich not taken an interest in them—and also, one should add, had the French dealers not speculated on them eventually becoming popular. Thus can be laid to rest two of the cherished beliefs about the Impressionists. A third is that the academic painters did them in, concerning which one can say that while the Academicians made Impressionist work cheaper than it otherwise would have been, they also may have increased the amount of it that was sold.

There have been other exogenous changes which in the history of painting have had an effect on cost or on demand or both. Among them is the introduction of oil painting. Historians once sagely said it began in Flanders and now sagely say it did not. They still seem to believe it appeared there before it did in Italy and they no doubt always will agree that a painting done in oil has a different appearance from one that is not. We may deduce that oil painting changed the demand structure of the art market. How it changed the cost structure, I confess ignorance.

Political and social changes have affected the demand and supply of the market for art of all kinds. The fall of the Ming Dynasty in China, Professor Montias observed, brought about an increase in the production of faience ware in Delft by reducing the competition of Chinese porcelain.[32] He also describes how the faience makers artfully avoided the limit the guild meant to place on what each could produce. It limited the number of workers in each shop. But the shops then gave up making the tiles in their entirety, from the baking of them through to the final decorating. They turned to buying white tiles from makers outside of the guild and to finishing the tiles in the guild shops. The Reformation reduced the demand for religious paintings; the Counter-Reformation increased it and brought about a change in the style of painting. The change might have occurred even if there had been no Counter-Reformation since baroque painting was prefigured by the Mannerist art that began a little before the Counter-Reformation and was done in Protestant Holland as well as in Catholic Italy. But certainly the revival of Catholic power increased the demand for religious painting, increased the amount done, and the number of painters doing it. Architecture was also affected. As the Protestants stripped the ornaments from the churches that had been Catholic, the Catholics built new, more ornamental churches where larger congregations could be assembled and addressed by orders that were skilled at preaching.

Another notable change was the French Revolution. Among its consequences was the abolition of the Academy in 1791. The salons continued as periodic exhibitions for the purpose of marketing art; but there was no review by a jury, and every artist who wished to do so could exhibit. There was what economists call free entry (as today there is in some neighborhood art fairs in American cities). The number of paintings on exhibit doubled, and in the words of the historians, the "quality" fell. That could mean the worst paintings were worse than they would have been under the jury system while the best were as good as ever, or it could mean that both were worse. In either event, the average price of painting must have fallen, making due allowance for the inflation that was another consequence of the revolution. The painters, we are told, did not like the open market. That is not surprising. What would be surprising would be to learn that the people who bought art objected to its price being low. In 1798 the jury system was restored and returned with the approval of the artists, of the government, and of the body that replaced the Academy, all of which had a voice in choosing the juries. The artists, one reads with interest, voted for jurists with conservative tastes, namely, the tastes which had been propagated by the Academy and in which the established painters would have invested their skills. The consequence must have been to divide the supply of painting into that which was "officially" declared to be of high quality—the painting admitted to the salon—and that which had to make itself known on the open market. This was the same state of affairs the Academy brought about when it divided the market in the seventeenth century. In the nineteenth century the revolution in art returned to its starting point: the Academy was restored in 1816 as the *Academie des Beaux-Arts*. There was, however, a difference, and it may have had its origin in the first years of the revolution when economic policy looked toward the market. After 1816 the number of paintings admitted to the salon was greater. They were done of course by the Academicians whose output, however, was greater than that of their predecessors in the seventeenth century. This, as remarked above, is the predictable outcome of a cartel in which the number of producers is controlled but the amount each produces is not.

Another consequence of the revolution was the opening to view of the art which the French kings had placed in the Louvre. This was the origin of one of the great museums in the world, about which more is said in chapter five. The Louvre at first was open only to artists and was a source of valuable information to them. A museum is (or was) to a painter what a library is to a historian. Before there were museums, artists could draw on the past if they had access to private collections. Prior to the revolution, some worked in the Louvre and some lived there. Another source of information was the art in the churches. Painters in Holland were deprived of it after the Reformation when the Protestants removed art from the churches. The painters then had to travel to Catholic countries in order to learn what they wanted to know. To Italy, artists always had gone, and the artists of Italy for long had been invited to foreign countries where in addition to meeting the demand of collectors they influenced the work of native artists. What may be the greatest tribute France ever has paid to another country—a tribute which acknowledged that in art, if nothing else, France had a secondary position—was the Prix de Rome by which promising students were given a five-year fellowship to study art in Rome (at the French Academy there, to be sure).

In time museums came to be more than an artist's resource. They were open to the public and were influenced by what interested the public. That has always been the art of the past more than of the present. The artists then came to say museums interfered with the progress of art. That could mean, and probably does, that if people with an interest in art could not gratify it by visiting museums they might buy art, not that of the past (it is too expensive), but what living artists are creating. The same could be said of people with an interest in reading, that if they could not satisfy it by visiting a library they would buy books. In the nineteenth century the opposition of painters to museums was fairly mild in Europe and was unknown in America because it had few museums before the 1880s; in the twentieth century the opposition became intense in both places. In Russia soon after the Bolshevik Revolution, Proletkult, speaking for the avant-garde, declared, "In the name of tomorrow, we must burn Raphael."[33] The Politburo did nothing of the kind. It protected the Pushkin, Hermitage, and other collections and sold parts of them in the 1930s, when it needed dollars. (Proletkult, one learns with interest but not surprise, had a Department of Art Production.)

In the United States, the opposition of artists has taken a different form. They seem to believe museums are here to stay and want them to buy more contemporary art. The artists in expressing their wants deplore the conservative (or worse) taste of museum officialdom. Among their ready opinions about how public money should be used is that it should be given to museums to buy contemporary *American* art. They are like authors who believe the libraries should buy their books but they have not gone as far as the authors in Britain who have secured a law requiring libraries to pay the author a royalty each time his book is consulted. A British amateur, however, has said artists should be paid when their work is exhibited.[34] The analogue to library royalties for authors would be the museum paying the painter a portion of the museum admission fee each time a visitor pauses before a picture long enough to indicate he is looking at it. Once the practice began it could be extended to paying the painter in proportion to the time the visitor spends before his picture, which as chapter five reports is usually measured in seconds.

Exogenous changes, especially of a political kind, have affected the subject matter of painting as well as its cost and also have affected where it has been placed on sale as well as the structure of the market in such places. During the French Revolution the property of the upper classes was confiscated or pillaged. Later some reappeared in the shops of dealers where it was sold to other (or the same) Frenchmen and to foreigners. The English were among the buyers and were so again a few years later when Napoleon was in Italy and collectors there put their art on sale in the belief it otherwise would be seized by the French. Some of what went into English collections had been the property of Charles I whose collection of Italian, Dutch, and German art was most of it sold by the Cromwell government.

Earlier in the eighteenth century the Wars of the Austrian Succession reduced the number of visitors to Venice and the demand for the view paintings of Canaletto. He took himself to Padua and did *View of the Brenta*. He also did imaginary scenes (*capricci*) of Rome which some historians say are among his finest creations.

In the seventeenth century the Spanish power in South America brought about a market there for the painters of Seville, and they supplied it abundantly—over 1,500 pictures between 1647 and 1665. Among the exporters were Zurbarán and Murillo who seem to have priced their exports lower than their work for the domestic market (a practice that today is deplored by the General Agreement on Trade and Tariffs).[35] The trade was uncertain because Spain was at war with England, and England, when it could, confiscated Spanish cargoes. Whether they are still another source of English collections, I do not know.

SUMMARY: THE SUPPLY OF ART

Artists are like the rest of the world and try to do the best they can with what they have. Being so, what they do and how they do it invite the attention of economics.

One of its principles is opportunity cost which means the cost of painting a picture is the income the artist could earn if he were painting a different picture or not painting at all but working in marble or teaching art or doing something outside of art. If the income he could earn by doing something else is higher than the income he actually is earning, economic theory (drawing on the common sense of the ages) predicts he will turn to the more rewarding alternative. There is evidence that artists have been as familiar with the idea as anyone else.

The income of artists is not only money or the goods it will buy but in addition the satisfaction the activity itself provides, a nonmonetary return. There is such a return in other occupations also, and in all of them the sum of the monetary and nonmonetary returns tends toward equality if people can move from one occupation to another. In any of them a high money income indicates low nonmonetary returns and vice versa. In art, monetary returns are lower than in many other occupations. The nonmonetary returns presumably are higher because, if they were not, people would leave art.

The low income of painters cannot be explained entirely by their willingness to accept low prices for their pictures. Even at the low prices they ask, they cannot sell everything they paint. Some is bartered for the paintings of other artists, a practice that helps to explain why painters have been collectors. But not all is disposed of, and what is not must be explained as the by-product of a pleasurable pursuit just as the pictures of a Sunday painter are. No doubt he would be happy to sell his pictures and to be paid for doing what he is willing to do for nothing. If (as a great economist once said) it is better to play for nothing than to work for nothing, it must be still better to play for something than to play for nothing. To do anything for nothing (meaning a monetary return of zero) is to engage in consumption. The time artists give to painting pictures they know will not be sold is time given to consumption and is the equivalent of leisure activity.

However, nonmonetary returns buy no bread and feed no babies.

Hence one would expect that people who wanted money as well as pleasure from painting would take it up only if they came from rich families. The expectation is supported (though scarcely proved) by the fact that in the Delft guild the boys who were apprenticed to painters came from families with higher incomes than those who were apprenticed to the faience makers. Delft provides an example of another relation economic theory leads one to expect. It is that painters who do not come from rich families are more likely to be successful than those who do, because those from poor families can increase their monetary returns only by exceptional effort. The example is Vermeer, the only painter of Delft who received as much for his paintings as did Rubens, his contemporary in Flanders.

Not all painters have been poor. Those who have been successful have secured, along with a high income, the nonmonetary returns of renown, admiration, and the knowledge that their works might be among the few the world wants to keep. The high rewards of success help to explain why so many people wish to make a life for themselves in one of the arts. The probability of failure is high, but risking it is perfectly sensible if the reward is proportionately high. A fondness for risk is noticeable in the arts and is another reason why their money return is low.

One way to increase income is to restrict competition, and people in the arts no less than people outside them have succumbed to the temptation to try it. Both usually have been disappointed even when assisted by government. From medieval times onward, painters have come together in guilds and academies in order to restrict supply. The results appear (from the limited information available) to have been disappointing to the artists while nevertheless being a nuisance to the buyers of art. The restrictions have been incomplete, have been evaded, and at times have been simply flouted. That is what is predicted by the economic theory of cartels which is what the guilds and academies were. Some artists have eliminated competition by eliminating their competitors, literally.

Most, however, have simply tried to excel. When successful they have made their art more of a substitute for the art of others while making the art of others less of a substitute for their own. [They have reduced the cross elasticity of demand to their advantage.]

Another way to increase net income is to reduce costs, and the examples are legion of artists doing that. Some did it because the work of other artists was a close substitute for their own. Not being able to raise prices, they had to reduce their costs. Hence one may infer their work was undistinguished. However, distinguished artists also engaged in cost-cutting. An artist whose prices were similar to those of others was probably undistinguished in his own day—not necessarily later—as Reynolds seems to have been. Artists who received prices considerably higher than others probably were among the distinguished figures of their age, as Rubens was (and continues to be). Costs have been reduced by breeding one work of art from another: the artist making copies of his own work or of the work of others, by having his work copied or engraved, by his doing variations on a particular subject, by painting the drawings of others, by drawing the paintings of others, by selling the right to photograph his works, by staging an exhibition of them and charging admission (the equivalent of renting them).

The effort to reduce costs and increase returns could be a reason why a noticeable number of painters have been in a family relation to each other. One may guess that a boy could be taught at a lower cost by his father than by someone else, that his father could depend more on the assistance of his son than on that of a hired helper, that people will work harder to increase the income of their own family than that of another, and that members of a family who are in the same occupation can exchange information and help each other in other ways.

The income of painters and what they paint have been affected by external or exogenous changes, in particular changes in technology, religion, and politics. The tube, the easel, and the railroad made painting in the open air less difficult (less costly) and had a place in the development of Impressionism. The Reformation reduced the demand for religious subject matter and directed artists to genre painting. The Counter-Reformation brought about the baroque in sculpture and architecture, reinforced it in painting, and again made art an instrument for the propagation of the faith. Private collections, when they were opened in both Catholic and Protestant countries, furnished artists with information at a lower cost. The same occurred as museums came into being, and they affected the demand for painting also. In time artists came to resent museums because they are substitutes, to a limited extent, for private collections. The French Revolution changed both the demand and the supply of art, the immediate being more important than the lasting effects. The expropriation of the upper classes and confiscation of their art made it available to others in France and to foreign collectors. The first revolutionary government abolished the Academy in an act that in cultural policy was the analogue of the abolition of the guilds in economic policy. A free market in art and other goods ensued and was not to the liking of the artists any more than it was to the workers and businessmen who had been protected from competition. In time the practices of the Academy were restored as the government resumed its authority over economic activity.

The control of supply and price was never as effective as its proponents wanted it to be, in France or elsewhere, but they persisted in trying to make it so. No one likes the price the free market of things will produce, Dudley North, a seventeenth-century economist, said. That was not quite what he meant. No one wants competition in the markets where he sells but wants all there possibly can be in the markets where he buys. Artists are no exception. In this and other ways they show they are no better than they ought to be. As such, they invite the attention of economists.

4

The Art Market

Renoir, in recognizing the competence of the Hotel Drouot, is merely being shrewd and sensible. If he had left the verdict to contemporary critics and depended on what official mandarins and arbiters of taste had said at the time, he and his Impressionist friends would have come off very badly and lost their case. The sale room public thought otherwise.

—FRANÇOIS DURET-ROBERT
"The Verdict of the Sale Room"

THIS CHAPTER is about the uncertainties of art, attribution being the most important; about the misconceptions entertained outside of the market but within art circles of how it operates and the effects of regulating it; and about what the prudent buyer whether he is interested in art or money or both will take note of if he wishes to invest, to speculate, or to enjoy art.

The most common uncertainty about art is its authorship, and it also is the most important. We want to know who did what. As the Jamaican guard at the de Young Museum said to a visitor, "You want know who make that?—J. S. Copley!" So the museum must have believed if it identified the work (*Mrs. Daniel Sergant*) as being by Copley. Museums become more conscientious about attribution as time goes on, and the market does also. Both testify to the accumulation of knowledge, to the increase of interest in art, to the competition to satisfy that interest by the market, by scholars, and by museums, to the rewards for providing accurate information, and to the penalties for failing to do so. Yet even the purest conscience is fallible, and uncertainty can only be reduced, not eliminated. There is a cost to reducing it and another cost in bearing what remains.

Of course there is certainty about some works of art, or, more accurately, about some aspects of some works. No one doubts that Michelangelo did the ceiling of the Sistine Chapel and the altar wall. But there is disagreement over what the colors were now that the ceiling is being restored. It is not on the market, to be sure. Yet it is available for commercial use. A Japanese television company is paying for the restoration and must expect a return of some kind.

While there are no doubts about the work of Michelangelo, there are about that of other giants of painting and of painters of lesser standing. A celebrated instance is Leonardo. In the 1920s Joseph Duveen, the dealer, scoffed at the claim made by an American woman that she owned *La Belle Ferronière,* and she brought an action against him. Expert opinion, most of it, agreed with Duveen that the original was in the Louvre, and Berenson testified on his behalf. The lady persisted and in the end received an out-of-court settlement from Duveen.[1] There have been doubts about attributions to such leading figures as Dürer, Grünewald, Holbein, Cranach, Vermeer, Rembrandt, Rubens, and others. Some of the doubts were later shown to be well-founded.

ATTRIBUTION AND FRAUD

One consequence of uncertainty is that it invites fraud, which takes many forms, from simply lying about the authorship of a painting or changing or adding a signature, to making a copy and claiming it is the original, or making an original painting and attributing it to a valuable name. This does not mean fraud is more profitable in the market for art than elsewhere, because the rate of return from dishonesty should be the same everywhere after allowing for risk. What is meant is that art provides more opportunity for fraud than some other kinds of economic activity, hence there is more of it relative to the money value of transactions, hence there is a greater risk of loss per dollar exchanged. The buyers who make the market must be aware of the fact, because it is valuable information, and they will offer less for paintings than for goods that are not as risky. The amount by which their offer is less will vary directly with their estimate of the risk and with the aversion they have to bearing it. Some of the buyers are dealers who expect to resell to buyers as knowledgeable as themselves. They may all of them be mistaken about how risky particular attributions are, but there is no reason to think they all err in the same direction.

The risk is important enough to engage the interest of the police. At the 1983 World Art Market conference, the topic of one session was "Fakes, Forgeries, and Thefts," and the speaker was W. E. Martin, Detective, Los Angeles Police Department, Burglary Special Section, Art Theft Detail. Scotland Yard has an Art and Antiques Squad. The French police have long attended to crime in art, more so than the police of most countries since France has more laws affecting it. In the Foreign Ministry of Italy, there is the Delegation for the Retrieval of Works of Art, and the head of it has cabinet rank. It is more concerned with theft than with forgery. The reason may be that stealing art in Italy is easier than forging it.

In the United States, the extent of fraud seems to be exaggerated by outsiders who look in on the world of art, that is, by the people who read, talk, and look at it more than they buy and sell it. They have a keen interest in deception, and the market does what it can to satisfy them. So one concludes from noticing the books on the subject and their titles, for example, *Frauds, Fakes, and Reproductions* (Savage), *Forgers, Dealers, Experts* (Schuller), *The Art of the Faker* (Arnau), *The Art of the Forger* (Dutton), *Paintings: Genuine, Fraud, Fake* (Marijnissen), *The Fabulous Frauds* (Jeppson), or simply *Fake!* (Irving). The activity is amusing, except to those who lose by it, while honesty is less interesting if it is interesting at all. One looks hard and long for titles like *Honesty in Art, The Dealer of Square Deals, Authentic Auctioneering, Truth in Attribution, Successfully Scrupulous: or, It Pays to Come Clean.* One will also look to no avail because the titles are imaginary.

Is honesty less interesting than roguery because honesty is more familiar, and more familiar because it is more profitable? Who would be diverted by a letter of Rubens in which he promises to paint a picture in its entirety, and not just design, supervise, and put on the finishing touches (which he acknowledged he did with some works)? On the other hand, who would not be amused to read, "According to the enlarged edition of his *oeuvre* catalogue, Corot painted over 2,000 pictures. Of these, more than 5,000 are in the United States."[2] Who would not be diverted by the tale of the impudent forger who imitated Marc Chagall? He was brought to trial, and Chagall (to the consternation of the prosecution, no doubt) testified that one of the paintings on exhibit was not a forgery but had been done by himself. The accused (for whatever reason) said, No Maestro, you really didn't—I did.

Even more like the work of the master himself—in this instance, Vermeer—were the paintings of Han van Meegeren in Holland.[3] He sold one to an agent of Hermann Goering when the country was occupied by the Germans. After the war he was arrested for collaboration and for the export of a national treasure. The authorities were of the opinion that the painting had been done by Vermeer and was similar to other "Vermeers" which van Meegeren had painted and which had been acquired by Dutch museums in the belief they were authentic. He protested his innocence on both counts, asserting he had not collaborated with an agent of Goering but had swindled him and that he had not exported a national treasure but a forgery. He was not believed, however. A Dutch museum had made a chemical analysis of its Vermeer/van Meegeren and had concluded the paint was the kind used at the time of Vermeer and no longer used when van Meegeren said he had painted the picture. He offered to demonstrate he could paint like Vermeer and did so while imprisoned. The charges against him were changed to forgery, he was found guilty, and given the minimum sentence allowed by law. By then he was quite ill and did not live to serve the sentence.

The episode shows the limitations of expert knowledge and also shows, since some experts continued to believe the paintings were not forgeries, that expert opinion is not always unanimous at any one time let alone over a period of time. These limitations are a more important reason than forgery for the uncertainty of the art market. So one may infer from the fact that when attributions are changed, the stated reason seldom is forgery. Fraud occasionally is the reason, but the more common reason is new information about the painting or the painter, his contemporaries, or the history of the ownership of the work.

HOW UNCERTAINTY IS MANAGED

The market is aware of uncertainty. Buyers, sellers, dealers, and auction houses do as much as is worth their while to reduce it by collecting information and by making it known (a distinction that is not trivial). There are people who specialize in collecting it. Art historians do, and some are prepared to make a written declaration of authenticity. Alvar Gonzalez-Palacios, a historian of the present, states that Italian scholars have sold thousands of such declarations of which "a great deal [is] rubbish masquerading as the genuine article."[4] That is an implausible (and redundant) statement. It claims the buying side of the market is permanently ignorant, deceived not by just an occasional certificate but by "thousands," while the selling side is permanently informed. Since dealers buy as well as sell, just how do they account to themselves for themselves, that is, how does the inner man reconcile the innocent who is the buyer with the sharpster who is the seller, when both are the same person? Or are the certificates believed only by people who are not dealers? If so, why has no enterprising person offered to inform the buyers of what they ought to know and what they certainly would find worth paying for? Moreover, this profitable enterprise in selling information should elicit competition and in time would be no more profitable than any other use of labor and capital. Señor Gonzalez should know that ignorance is like innocence: once lost, it is never recovered.

Among the art historians who have provided the market with information, the most eminent was Bernard Berenson. For many years he advised Joseph Duveen, mainly about Italian painting, and received a commission from the sale of works about which he gave an opinion. The detractors of each have been numerous. Having disposed of Duveen some time ago, they turned on Berenson and they include people to whom he was hospitable, gave advice, instruction, and assistance in their careers. A recent detractor (not, as it happens, one of the ingrates) is Colin Simpson.[5] He learned that Berenson and Duveen had signed a contract and he cited the secrecy of it as evidence of intent to deceive. Actually, most of Berenson's attributions have been endorsed by later historians, and that is all the more remarkable in view of his having had less information than they. He made some mistakes, but there is no evidence they had an upward bias (which Simpson, to his credit, acknowledges). Some reduced the price of pictures and along with it the commission he received from their sale. He wanted to be accurate, he insisted, and said he would be most useful to Duveen when he was. He also wanted an honored place in art history and to be remembered. That his interest lay in being accurate should be obvious.

Duveen no doubt preferred to have a painting attributed to a more important artist than to one less important, and Berenson probably had the same preference. So did the museum people who consulted him. John Walker—who was a protégé of Berenson and always loyal—wrote in his autobiography of asking him to affirm the attribution he had made of an *Adoration of the Magi.* Berenson, at a time when other historians had attributed the work to Filippo Lippi, had said it was by Fra Angelico. Walker asked him to repeat the attribution because a donor had promised to buy the painting if it was by Fra Angelico and to give it to the National Gallery of which Walker was director. Berenson, much to Walker's surprise and dismay, said he had changed his mind and now believed as others had that the work was by Filippo Lippi. Walker pressed him to reconsider and himself adduced reasons for an attribution to Fra Angelico. At length, Berenson said, "Johnnie, I do think that just before he died Fra Angelico may have painted one or two of the figures."[6] The painting teems with figures, and the "one or two" that Fra Angelico "may" have done are a small part of the multitude unless they were two of the magi, which (one suspects) would have been mentioned by Walker if they were. The label on the painting now attributes it to Fra Angelico and Filippo Lippi. The account, *inter alia,* is a morality tale, namely, self-interest operates in the nonprofit sector as well as in others.

Information that bears on attribution is also available from private enterprises, the most familiar being the many periodicals about the visual arts. There also are firms that sell it, not clandestinely, but openly and advertise that they do. In *Art and Auction,* a monthly, there is an "International Directory for Collectors" that includes information for sellers, dealers, and museums. One section lists the services of consultants. Some specialize in identification. Others are advisers, appraisers, promoters, exhibition coordinators, or auction bidding agents with expertise in Chinese porcelain, Fabergé, Eskimo art, and so forth. The directory also lists the names of people and firms that provide financial services (installment loans to collectors, investment banking services, the financing of purchases); insure art;

pack, ship, and store it; see it through customs; and the many that frame it. Even more important is information about where buyers and sellers are. The directory includes a section on shows and fairs and another on the location of dealers and auction houses in the principal countries of the world.

Not all of this information has to do with authenticity, but all has to do with factors that affect the transactions costs of the art market. To a collector, they are the costs of buying a work which are in addition to its price. To a seller, they are among the costs that make his net return less than the price paid by the collector. In all markets there is an effort to reduce them. Information can do so, and there is a market for it, as well as for the art which it is about.

About the authenticity of paintings, the market reports information that is analogous to the grading of goods in other markets. Mention was made in chapter one, on value, that in both art history and the market there is a classification of works according to their authenticity and that the classifications resemble each other. The market classification was taken from *Art Prices Current.* An instructive example is also provided by Richard Hislop in his book on auction prices.[7] He states auction houses may indicate their judgment of the authenticity of a work by the way they state the name of the painter in the sale catalogue. Consider the work of Ommeganck, a Flemish landscape painter (1755–1826). When his name appears in its entirety, which is Balthasar Paul Ommeganck, the work may be considered authentic and the attribution as certain as it can be. If his name appears as Ommeganck, B. P., the attribution is not certain but one may have more confidence in it than if the name appears only as Ommeganck. If the name is followed by "circle" or "style" or "studio" or "after," the work is not believed to be by Ommeganck. Nevertheless, the information is important, obviously so to historians of art (although Ommeganck is not a good example since he has attracted little attention). The information also is important to buyers and sellers. A work from the studio of the painter is more valuable than one done by a member of his circle, and a work of the latter kind is more valuable than one done in his style. This supposes of course that other things are held constant (size, subject, period, condition, and provenance). It also assumes that attribution affects value.

DOES ATTRIBUTION MATTER?

Does it? The evidence shows it does. If it did not there would be no explanation of why the value of a painting changes when its attribution changes—"value" meaning, as it does through this book, its price on the market and its merit as an aesthetic object. Nor would there be an explanation of why when a painting is intentionally misrepresented the attribution is to a more rather than to a less important artist (except if the lying rogue means to create uncertainty about the work of the true artist because he has sold him short). Nor would there be an explanation of why museologists when they become scrupulous and reattribute works usually assign them to less and not to more important artists.

Should attribution affect value: Is it really important? The question is out-of-bounds to an economist who minds his own business and does not presume to tell people what is and is not important. It is not out-of-bounds to people who write about art, and a surprising number of them say too much is made of it. According to John Walker, "Attributions, of course, do not affect the beauty of works of art, but they do affect collectors and consequently values. They should be merely a convenient way of categorizing, but they often set up irrational standards of quality."[8] He seems to mean they are useful for making an inventory but not useful (or *as* useful?) for judging aesthetic merit. Gonzalez-Palacios states that when he studied art history, shortly after the Second World War, "One could say 'so and so is a good attributionist,' which would be found embarrassing today."[9] The contemporary philosopher Alfred Lessing seems to go further: "The plain fact is that aesthetically it makes no difference whether a work of art is authentic or a forgery."[10] Arthur Koestler once said that to dwell on attribution is "extraneous and snobbery."[11] These views are not shared by everyone in art, of course (certainly not by those who conduct the extensive enterprise in Amsterdam that is attributing, deattributing, and reattributing the works of Rembrandt). But the views are by no means eccentric or inconsequential.

They share the belief that the aesthetic quality of a work is independent of what is associated with it. That includes, in addition to the artist (no small association), the history of its ownership or the names of the people who had it in their collections, the museums where it was exhibited, the books and periodicals in which it was mentioned, the name of the subject if it is a portrait, possibly how it came to be commissioned and by whom, how much was paid for it, the title (whether or not it describes the subject matter), even infor- mation about the frame, especially if it is the original frame. Informa- tion of this kind is reported when the history of a work is recounted. From an aesthetic viewpoint, it is pointless, according to Alfred Lessing and such.

It is anything but pointless to other kinds of people, and they have more influence in determining value—economic and aesthetic— than do the aesthetes (if they may be called that). Why is attribution important? The question is different from whether or not it should be, because it asks for an explanation, not a judgment, of behavior. It lends itself to some observations and conjectures about how choices are made in the market for art. There, as elsewhere, the names of things are important. That would not have to be said were the impor- tance not denied or implied by those who claim attribution has no aesthetic significance. A collector usually does not buy an anony- mous painting, except as a gamble. He buys a painting identified as the work of a named artist, and it usually has a title. That in its entirety *is* the aesthetic object: painting, artist, title. The evidence for this can be supplied by a thought experiment. Imagine how a dealer would fare if he alone in the market did not provide information about the paintings he offered for sale: no name, no title, no prove- nance, no references to works of art history or criticism, no dates. Nothing but the price. On the other hand, imagine how he would fare if only he and none of his competitors provided this information. The world beats a path to the door where the mouse trap is known by its name and maker. A similar thought experiment is to imagine a mu- seum where none of the paintings was attributed and none had a title. Museums know this information is valued, and they supply it. At special exhibitions the works are sometimes identified only by num- bers, and if the visitor wants to know more about them he buys a catalogue where there are entries corresponding to the numbers. Does the practice increase the sale of catalogues? If one or more is sold, it must. When people of Professor Lessing's views disclaim any interest in attribution, they do so (they say) from the viewpoint of "aesthetics." Since it is about value in art (at least in ordinary lan- guage) they could mean they have no interest in anything that is not conveyed by looking at a work. If however they are more curious, they must believe there is more to art than aesthetics comprehends.

If they do they make "aesthetic" synonymous with "physical" and make an "aesthetic object" a piece of canvas on which paint has been placed. Yet even in this meaning attribution can be helpful. It can provide information about the merit of a work that enlarges the information the work itself provides. If on studying a painting we believe it was done either by Rembrandt or de Gelder but we do not know which, we are less confident of our judgment of its merit than if we do know who painted it. To say the information is extraneous is to reveal a limited understanding of how decisions are made and to say that wanting the information is snobbish is itself "extraneous." This function of attribution is complemented by another source of information. It is the history of the ownership of a work, its provenance.

There are other reasons why attribution is important, hence why it engages the interest of the market and of other precincts of the art world. The information is indispensable to art history as we know it. Conceivably it could be carried on if nothing was known about authorship and what the work was called. The history of the art of antiquity often must do without this information. But something has to be known about when things were made if they are not merely to be listed. If we also know who made them and what they were called we know a great deal more; and that is not always as much as we would like to know.

Apart from the information it provides—about the merit of a work and its historical significance—attribution also satisfies two other kinds of interest. One is simply our interest in names. We attend more to an object that has a name than to one that has not, and we are more interested in a named object that carries the name of the maker than in a named object that does not. This interest is independent of the information the names convey. If we had before us two paintings which as aesthetic objects were equally pleasing or displeasing and one carried the name of the painter and the painting while the other did not, we would be more interested in the former than in the latter. That I propose as an empirical proposition, and it is refutable, at least in theory. Behavioral scientists are invited to test it.

The other interest attribution satisfies is the interest we have in the associations of an object. The clearest example is things in a historical museum; a hat worn by Napoleon, Harriet Martineau's ear trumpet, a sprig of heather from the grave of John Stuart Mill, the skeleton identified as that of the scout who warned Custer not to enter the Valley of the Little Big Horn. A painting that was in the collection of Charles I would be interesting for that reason. Its having been a part of a distinguished collection would also be interesting. It would not have the latter but would have the former value if it once was owned by Abraham Lincoln, who is not remembered for a connoisseurship of art but is for other things. The value of a painting can be enhanced by quite lesser associations, for example, by being in the frame the artist himself put it in. If such associations are interesting, surely the title of the painting is also and more surely the name of the painter is. These considerations are meant to explain, not to justify. People to whom attribution is irrelevant have a place in the mansion of art. It has many rooms, and there is one for them. The others seem to be occupied by people of a different view.

RESTORATION: A LESSER UNCERTAINTY

The uncertainties related to attribution, while they are the most noticeable in the market for art, are not all that buyers and sellers take note of when they form their bids and offers. There is also the uncertainty about what physical changes were made in a picture after it was painted. Making the changes is itself a chancy enterprise, and the evidence is the continual arguments over how to conserve art and the continual and sharper arguments over how to restore it. Or whether to restore it at all. If *Hamlet* had come down to us with the soliloquy missing we would not want a publisher or library to commission a writer to create a pastiche of it. Apparently we feel differently about painting and the decorative arts (although not, for some reason, about sculpture any longer). So dealers and museums believe they must make objects as complete as possible, adding a leg to a Chippendale chair and a little finger to a Giovanni Bellini (but not arms to the Venus de Milo). The consequence is that in a gallery or a museum what appears before one—even if complete with attribution, provenance, and literature about which there can be no doubt—is a work that one cannot be certain is what it is represented to be. To state the point simply, we do not know what we are looking at. Is it a painting that providentially has been untouched by time or is it a painting that has been partially restored or more than partially done over, and has it been altered once or twice or three times or more?

This uncertainty is not as important as the uncertainties of attribution. They are of course related. One would be guilty of inconsequence if one were uneasy about attribution yet indifferent about whether the painting had been altered. Alterations can be detected and removed, then an attempt can be made to produce something, by the methods of restoration, that is more or less like the original, in a manner of speaking, if what the original was like is known, and there is an earnest desire to recover it. Satisfying that desire is expensive. Hence one would expect a dealer to be less earnest, because his clients are less so, than a museum is, the one having to support himself, and the other being able to call on the public for assistance. A common practice among dealers for long has been to give their acquisitions a coat of varnish before putting them on sale, often with a spotlight trained on them. That is why so many paintings known to the market (and at one time to the Customs Inspectors) as Old Masters were dark in color, so dark that darkness was believed to be a differentia of the class and that the painters of the Renaissance used a dark palette. In this century the museums have begun to take off the varnish, and the palettes of the past are now seen to have been lighter. The practice is not universal, however. The Hermitage in Leningrad, if it has heard of the practice, is not convinced. Its Flemish and Dutch paintings that toured the United States in 1988 were many of them heavily varnished. So, too, was Botticelli's *Primavera* when it was returned to its place in the Uffizi in Florence, the dark colors brought to a high gloss that was made still glossier by the lights trained on them.

Whether this is to be deplored, commended, or ignored depends on whose judgment is to rule. People who want to see a picture as nearly as it was when it was painted are more likely to be satisfied by one that has not been touched by restorers and has been conserved by conservators acting conservatively. But people who want to see more, who do not care for faded colors, visible seams, or patches of canvas showing through, will favor restoration—of just what kind they themselves must decide, understanding of course that in the end what they see may be different from what the artist meant them to see. This latter group seems to be in the majority, if one may infer from dealers' and museums' rarely showing works that have not been touched in one way or another by the restorer. If the inference is correct, it means the market does not discount substantially the value of a painting that has been restored. The reason is not that the probability of its having been restored is small (quite the opposite), but that the alteration has not substantially lessened the aesthetic interest of collectors and museum visitors. The minority that regrets restoration is left to its regrets and to the recourse of buying paintings in order to prevent them from being altered.

OBSOLESCENCE AND UNCERTAINTY

Obsolescence is another source of uncertainty. Before art deteriorates physically the interest in it usually diminishes. This was explained in chapter two. Of course not all art is subject to obsolescence. If it were, nothing would be conserved except those works in which the interest does not diminish as quickly as they deteriorate. They are few—very, very few—relative to all of the art that ever has been made. Some in fact has deteriorated and some has been destroyed or lost. Most has simply been discarded. If art did not become obsolete there would be a futures market in it, and there is not. That is not the only evidence of obsolescence. More obvious evidence is that what has survived is a minuscule portion of what has been created.

Since obsolescence is predictable, it is not itself an uncertainty. What is uncertain is what part of the art of, say, any one year of the last ten years of the twentieth century will survive indefinitely, and when will the remainder become worthless.

Among people who buy art and hope to resell it for a higher price, there are (a) those who wish to minimize uncertainty; (b) those who tolerate it if they are compensated enough; and (c) those who enjoy the experience of uncertainty. They are, in the language of economics, (a) risk averse, (b) risk neutral, and (c) risk loving. The a's will buy art of the distant past because less of it is likely to become obsolete (because more of it has already become so); the c's will buy art of the present because more of it is likely to become obsolete; and the b's will buy either depending on how much they expect the price of each to increase. If things work out as desired, the a's will make a profit in excess of what the same expenditure or investment of labor

and capital would yield in an undertaking that is certain, the excess
being their compensation for the disutility they experience from uncertainty. The *b*'s will make a profit equal to what their investment
would yield in a certain undertaking. The *c*'s will incur a net loss, and
it is what they pay for the utility they obtain from uncertainty. If this
is unduly abstract, it can be brought down the ladder by relating it
to gambling. Some people enjoy gambling and do not expect to break
even—the *c*'s. Some will gamble if the odds allow them to break
even—the *b*'s. Some do not like to gamble at all because they don't
like uncertainty, and to induce them to gamble the odds must be in
their favor—the *a*'s.

Then there are people who buy art for a different kind of return,
namely, the satisfaction it gives them or gives others whose opinion
they value. If they sell a work the reason is not to make a profit,
although that may be a consequence. They sell in order to buy something else that yields a greater return in the form of utility. The
obsolescence of art affects them but not in the way it affects a person
who speculates in art. They, or their heirs and assigns, may lose
interest in their art, hence they face the possibility of its becoming
worthless, indeed the probability. But this does not mean buying it
is wasteful. It means that what is bought yields a return for only a
time, the reason being that it becomes too familiar, not that it "wears
out" or is "used up." Art as an asset does not become depleted but
(if the expression is allowed) becomes repleted. We have all we want
of a particular kind and now we want something different. The event
is, or should be, altogether familiar, because it recurs throughout the
history of art. It is described as the pendulum of taste, occasionally
as the cycle of fancy, but neither is a good figure because each
suggests a change that is more regular, hence more predictable, than
can be observed. The origin of the movement is simple and was
explained in chapter two. Art is subject to diminishing marginal utility, or, in ordinary language, the more we have of one kind the less
do we want still more and the more we do want something else. As
a consequence, there will be artists who decline and fall and artists
who rise and glow by replacing them. Such change is inevitable
where people are free to choose and is all the greater the more
choices they have.

DEALERS AND THEIR POWER

However, that is not the explanation of change one hears from people in art, especially those having to do with contemporary painting. One is told that change is created, induced, or contrived; that it is the work of a few people of influence; that it is done for private gain of some kind; that it is to the detriment of art; and that it is all unjust. One hears of a collector who can make or break a painter by what he buys, sells, or holds; of a magazine that can make a style of painting fashionable and profitable by giving it undue attention; of a critic who buys the work of a painter, or wheedles it from him, praises it in print, then sells it at a profit; of a museum that has its favorites whose work is also in the private collection of the director; of another museum that has links to a dealer and favors painters under contract with him. One also hears that riches and fame come to artists who are able to promote themselves which not all have the ingenuity, energy, or crust to do. Then there are the favorites of fortune, those who happen to be noticed by a dealer, collector, critic, or journal. Why such things are believed, whether or not they should be, can be understood by reading the miscellany in the art periodicals, especially *ARTnews,* by noting the personal references in the *New York Times,* and by paging through books like *The Art Crowd* by Sophy Burnham (1973) which is a little out of date but is still diverting.

What these accounts have in common is that the market for contemporary art is not governed by aesthetic merit. That is another way of claiming economic and aesthetic value have no relation to each other. That they do and are consistent is the premise of this book and was explained at length in chapter one. How well or poorly it was done, the reader will decide, indeed should have decided by now, and he will not be troubled by additional explanation here. If he has been convinced, he will be no more than amused by the folk wisdom of art circles. He may also find it unsatisfactory, even if he does not accept my premise.

If success comes to the few artists who can promote themselves, why do not the others—the shy and retiring—hire someone to promote them? There are advertising agencies and such that do this sort of thing for a price. If the shy and retiring cannot afford the price, that only means the return from being promoted is less than the cost.

Dealers are reproached for being profit seekers. If that means they want to do as well at art as at something else, they surely are, just as everyone is if in the return from any activity we include, as we should, the nonmonetary rewards as well as the monetary. An art dealer must satisfy his buyers if he is to maximize his income. That, however, does not mean he provides them with all of the satisfaction he can afford, which would mean selling at a price that covers no more than the normal profit for the trade. His price may be above that. The reason is that he has some monopoly power, and it comes from each painting having unique qualities. A painting is the only one of its kind. This is true even of replicas, because they usually are not identical, and usually is true of graphics also. (Some multiples are identical, however, such as copies of a photograph.) The monopoly power of the dealer can be enhanced (that is, the price he obtains can be increased) by his having more information than the buyers have. He is unlikely to engage in gross deception, such as lying about attribution or provenance, because when it is discovered he will lose sales. But he may profit by withholding information the buyer does not expect him to have. He might keep from a prospective buyer of a work by X the information that other works of X are in an estate which in time will come to the market. Even that device cannot be used often if buyers keep themselves informed about the market whether they are actually making purchases or not. Moreover, even if the superior information of the seller enables him to sell at a higher price than he would receive if he knew no more than the buyer, the increment of price may be equal to the cost the seller incurs in acquiring the information. In that circumstance there would be no point in acquiring it. It would yield no gain and could antagonize the buyer. Information rarely is free, it may be incomplete, and it may be unreliable.

BUYERS AND THEIR POWER

Moreover, information may turn out to be common knowledge. Buyers have access to it as well as dealers and some know more than dealers. Museums are important buyers. They have learned people on their staff, far more than if the museums had to support themselves by their admission receipts alone. Being nonprofit organizations, they are less likely than the for-profit organizations which dealers conduct to pursue a line of inquiry only to the point at which the cost of the additional information is equal to its value. Or, simply stated, museums are likely to know more than dealers. So that if superior information confers power over price, the power is with the buyer.

There is another circumstance in which a buyer has an advantage. He may be one of only a few people who are interested in a work, perhaps the only one. The seller must deal with him or with no one. That would not eliminate the seller's monopoly but would reduce its power, meaning the price he could obtain. The price itself would be determined by bargaining and would be somewhere between the least the seller would accept and the most the buyer would pay. That is not an informative statement. It might be made informative by applying game theory to bilateral bargaining which, however, is an undertaking the writer prefers to shirk and the reader, if he were presented with it, might feel he could do without. Let the matter rest with the statement that if there is an exchange it will be at a price set by bargaining and will be within the obvious limits. Exchanges of this kind are not rare and do not call for making exceptions to economic theory.

REGULATING THE ART MARKET

Yet there is the feeling that such exchanges should be regulated. The feeling is that which Mrs. Ramsbottom expressed when she said, as she often did, "Soom-un must be soom-uned" (as her Lancashire sounds to an American). New York City has a Truth in Pricing Law which requires sellers to put price tags on their wares. Art galleries were once exempt but in 1988 were made subject to the law. It does not require them to sell art at the posted price but presumably they would not ask anything more. The stated reason for the law is the protection of the buyer. That he is gullible and deserving while the seller is strong and suspect is an article of faith as ancient perhaps as exchange itself. It is not of course held universally, certainly not by sellers in markets for goods. It is held by buyers except by those who can't get what they want because the law has reduced the amount offered for sale. The belief is reversed in labor markets where buyers are employers and sellers are workers and the moral is that prices (that is, wages) should be held up.

In the art market, requiring works to carry price tags seems innocuous. But what seems is not always what is. The requirement imposes a cost on the seller, the cost of putting price tags on things— small, to be sure, but noticeable and increasing if, as is likely, prices change from time to time (and from one prospective buyer to another). The seller will pass on to the buyer as much of the cost as he can. There is another and more significant cost—the cost of enforcing the law. In New York the law does not apply to everyone who sells art but is extensive enough to be costly. There are other objections. It could move sales from the markets where it applies to those where it does not, to the artist's studio for example. It could also move the market itself to places where there is no such law or to auctions.

These are more important objections. One is the presumption against interfering with voluntary exchange—of art or of anything else that affects only the buyer and the seller. A voluntary exchange is satisfactory because it is voluntary; otherwise it would not be made. The buyer would not make a purchase if he thought he was being overcharged, and the seller would not offer a good if he thought he would receive too little for it. Not every voluntary exchange is satisfactory at all times in all places to all people. But unsatisfactory exchanges will not be repeated if buyers and sellers know the difference between what satisfies them and what does not. That they do is a modest compliment to them. Among them there very likely are rogues and innocents, *in posse* or *in esse*, in the market for art and elsewhere. One cannot believe they dominate markets. To believe that, one would have to suppose most exchanges are unsatisfactory, whether because people do not know the difference between what does and does not add to their satisfaction (in which case the difference would not matter) or because they know but cannot or will not do anything about it. If the latter were so, the rogues would compete with each other in fleecing the innocents until the ill-gotten gains were eliminated along with roguery and the rogues. They would be unable to perpetuate their gain by conspiring not to compete because they are on both sides of the market.

Thus would a neo-classicist address the main point. It usually is not the point that is made. Dealers say they should not be treated like merchants who attract sales by making their prices known, as if there were something wrong about the practice and as if art dealers themselves did not do the same. Some willingly post prices and others disclose them. They could not do otherwise since a price is a necessary part of an exchange. Supporters of the law can counter that a dealer will not, for a given work, ask the same price of all buyers who inquire but will vary it according to the dealer's guess of how much the buyer is willing to pay. That is plausible but is not the point. The dealer who is required to post a price probably will set it as high as he expects anyone will pay (and still higher if the dealer is a risk averter). Buyers will learn this (as they have in the automobile market where such a law has been in effect for some time) and will believe the dealer will accept a lower price. The law, then, would "protect" the buyer by informing him that the actual price is probably below the price on the tag. The information is worth something. Whether it is worth the compliance cost in the form of a higher average price is uncertain. He would be indifferent to the enforcement cost since it is borne by everyone. It is not a matter of indifference to the rest of us.

If such laws are more than a nuisance and substantially reduce the transactions, the dealers and their clients will do business elsewhere, such as at auctions. To require such laws at auctions is something not even the most avid of regulators would propose unless he wanted to be certified. There is, however, a proposal to require auction houses to report the sales they make at a reserve price. It is the minimum price the seller will accept, and if no bidder offers as much the work is withdrawn or, in the language of auctions, it is bought-in. The practice interferes with an important function of the price system which is to provide information—information that is useful to collectors, dealers, museums, and other auction houses; to people who are thinking of making a gift of art and people who think it may be meant for them; to people who collect taxes and want to verify deductions; and to people who are interested in the activity of the market because they are interested in the activity of art in all of its aspects, a group that is numerous enough to warrant auction prices being reported in the newspapers. Buying-in should be especially objectionable to buyers.

These considerations seem to justify the law. But there is more to be said. It touches only one of the uncertainties of the art market and one that is much less important than the uncertainties about attribution, about provenance, and about how much conservation and restoration have altered a work. Moreover, while the law would remove one uncertainty about auction prices it would not remove another that is said to be present and, if it is, constitutes a greater deception. It is whether an actual sale at an actual price was made in order to inflate the value of a work. A owns one or more paintings by Z and at an auction bids for another that has been put up for sale by another owner or by A himself. A increases his bid as much as the rules of the auction permit. If his is the winning bid it establishes a new and higher value for the works of Z including those which A owns. If his is not the winning bid, the value of his collection rises even more. Thus is the chicanery described. Consistent with the account is the fact that auction houses frequently do not reveal the names of buyers and sellers. Also consistent is the theoretical consideration that the practice would be profitable if certain conditions are present, among them that in the course of the bidding actual buyers increase their estimate of what the work is worth (contract "auction fever") or that the spurious bidder has confederates who bid, that the increments by which the bids are permitted to increase are substantial, that the final bid inflates the price of a work by an amount more than the cost of the deception including the commission, usually 10 percent, the buyer and seller each must pay, and that the value of the works of Z which are not at auction is affected by those which are. All of these conditions are not likely to be present but they conceivably could be. Reformers and their legislative agents who are on the track of deception seem not to have picked up this scent. Or perhaps they are warming to it.

INTENDED AND UNINTENDED EFFECTS

About any form of deception there are two questions. One is how much it impairs the operation of the market as a means by which transfers of property are made, information disseminated, and mutual satisfaction produced. The other is whether regulation by law or other means can improve the market. If close observation of the market indicates that deception is not extensive, the second question need not be asked. If deception is extensive, that is good reason to consider regulation, and considering it means predicting its probable effects.

They can be different from what is intended. To require dealers to post prices, instead of adding substantially to the information of buyers, could in practice tell them no more than what is the highest price they need pay, and the information may not be worth its cost. To prohibit secret reserve prices could induce sellers to inflate prices by means that are more costly, more misleading, and more reprehensible, such as disguising an advertisement as the considered judgment of a disinterested critic and placing it in a periodical, a practice acknowledged in France.[12]

Laws that are meant to improve the market can bring about the very condition they are meant to prevent. This can be said of two other kinds of legislation affecting art, one now in force in some states and the other a proposal before the U.S. Senate that would apply to what now is nominally in effect in one state. The former is meant to protect what is said to be the right an artist retains in his work after he sells it. In California, by the Art Preservation Act, a museum is accountable to an artist for the damage it may do to his work by conservation, restoration, framing, and gross negligence. If the artist is dead, the museum is responsible to his heirs for fifty years. The reasoning could be that the income of an artist and the value of his unsold work are lessened if his work is altered or neglected. The artist (*pace* Iago) must believe that whoever takes his good name impoverishes him by shrinking his purse as well as by harming him in other ways. The principle also underlies the "artist's moral law" of France which authorizes the family of a deceased artist to order the destruction of works done in imitation of his.

The actual effect on the income of the artists is probably the opposite. The law, because it limits what a buyer may do with his art, must also reduce the price he is willing to pay for it. The price is also reduced by the risk of the owner incurring a cost to defend his right to do what he believes the purchase entitles him to do. Actually there is no need for a law to protect artists' rights. Those who want to retain control over their work after it is sold can contract with the buyers to do so. What the contract might be is indicated by a model commission agreement in *American Artist* (June 1983), a periodical as near to a trade journal as anything there is in the field of art. The agreement states, "The artist shall retain certain rights relating to the client's use and maintenance of the work." Among them are control over the way the work is displayed publicly, the right of the artist to be identified or not as he chooses, the right to prohibit photographic reproduction, to be consulted about conservation and restoration, to do those things himself if he chooses or to supervise their being done, and the assurance the owner will not alter the work and will protect it against damage. An arrangement of this kind reduces the price a buyer will pay, which working artists surely know, but the reduction should be no more than the value of the rights to the artist. If the reduction is greater than the value of the rights to the artist, he can sell his works unconditionally.

However, there is one right to what they make which artists do not forego—and cannot even if they would. Each work of art has a maker, and this is so whether he has been assisted by others in executing his conception or he has executed it himself. The maker is always a part of the object. Consider a person who, standing before the Mona Lisa, asks, "Whose painting is that?" He would think the answer odd if he were told the painting was Lo Giocondo's, the husband of the subject and the person who commissioned the portrait (and, by one report, never paid for it). The sensible answer to the question is, The painting is Leonardo's. The reason the answer is sensible is that he painted it. It is his in the sense that there is a right of ownership conferred on the maker of an object simply because he made it. Like all rights, it rests on a premise. The premise was used by Locke when he justified private property. A thing becomes our own when we have mixed our labor with it. That is so because to whatever we have imparted something of ourselves, that thing is a part of us, and we own it because we own ourselves. Each step in the argument is essential, and to question any is to question the conclusion. It is not the only justification that has been offered for private property. The Utilitarian justification is the more common (to allow people to keep what they produce gives them an inducement to produce more, and more is better than less). The view of Locke, however, is that on which the rights of an artist rest and which provides a reason for distinguishing them from the rights of the person who buys art. The idea can be read into what J. Paul Getty said to a Dutch art historian who had protested Getty's buying Rembrandt's *Maarten Looten* and sending it to America. Getty said it could not be lost to the Netherlands, "for it, like every Rembrandt, will be forever Dutch."[13]

The bearing of this on the law is that the right the artist has by reason of being the maker of the work cannot by its nature be taken from him. No law is needed to reserve it to him. Admittedly, the buyer of a painting can alter it (whether or not he should), and the result may be to misrepresent the artist to the world. The artist can reduce this risk by making a contract with the buyer about the way the painting will be conserved.

The other law (that put before the Senate) would do for the nation what a similar law is meant to do for California. Its salient provision requires that the artist be paid 7 percent of the profit made from the resale of a work of art if the resale price is more than 150 percent of the price received by the artist and if that price was not less than $1,000. The purpose is to prevent egregious acts of injustice (as well as those that are not egregious). "It is the fundamental inequity of the U.S. 'free' market system of art sales—which privileges the dealer's and the collector's financial interest over that of the artist—that S. 1619 seeks to redress," according to the *New Art Examiner* (March 1988), the voice of the anti-market in the Midwest. The law, then, if it did what it is meant to do, would protect the artist from the market. "I be protected and I be starving," an English farmer said about the Corn Laws of the nineteenth century that protected English agriculture from the world market.

The art law would not starve the artists, many of whom have a second occupation anyway because their sales are so small. But it would worsen their position. If it was enforced (as the California law is not), it probably would reduce the average price of art that was produced after the law became effective. (It would not apply to art that was resold before that time.) Buyers who believe that what an artist offers them may increase in value will offer less for it than they would if they could keep the profit. But the relative as well as the absolute price of such work would also fall. Original art that was purchased by dealers and collectors before the law became effective could be resold with the profit accruing entirely to the sellers. The artists who did the work would benefit indirectly if the value of what they currently do is affected by the value of what they already have done. They of course would receive less for their current work, because the law would reduce its price. But the reduction could be moderated by the increase in the value of the work they did before the law became effective, and the amount of this work would be greater the older they are. Younger artists, on the other hand, would have done less before the law was passed, and it would reduce the price of their current work relatively more. The law, then, in addition to making all artists worse off, could make younger artists worse off relative to older.

The price effect of the law would be different, probably less—possibly nill—if it required the artist to share losses as well as profits. It does not, hence has the effect of a capital gains tax without any adjustment for capital losses, the "tax" in this instance being paid to the original seller. The bill is represented as a royalty law, not as a device for sharing profits, and "royalties" cannot be negative. Its being represented in this way is consistent with its premise: that the buyers of art can look after themselves but the makers of it cannot. Indeed the law would compel the artist to come within its protection whether or not he wished to. He would not be permitted to make a contract with buyers that released them from profit sharing. If dealers thought he was a risky venture, they would not buy his work. He then would be excluded from the market, and his income from art would be zero. "He be protected and he be froze out."

Many of these effects were noted by Professor Ben W. Bolch in a *feuilleton* that is a model of analytic clarity and concision.[14] When they become known to artists, he dryly observes, they will think differently of the law.

Pertinent comments about it have also been made by Richard L. Feigen, the art dealer.[15] He reports the California law has been pointless because it has moved the art market out of the state. To reduce a federal law to ineffectuality is more difficult but is not impossible. The law could move the market for contemporary works to countries where it is free (a diminishing number) or could drive it underground as similar legislation has done in Europe where, Mr. Feigen states, collectors conceal their art in order to protect it and themselves (which must also reduce the price they are willing to pay for it). This restricts the work of scholars because they cannot see what they want to study and may not even know it exists. The work is also kept from museums that would like to exhibit it and is prevented from being reproduced in books and periodicals. There is still another consequence. People to whom art is worth more than it is worth to the owners are unable to buy it. That is a matter of some importance to those who believe (as Pareto did) that goods should be distributed in a way that provides more, not less, satisfaction.

Comments of a quite different sort, neither pertinent nor to their credit, have been made by the art dealers through their trade association. It has proposed that, in place of the profit-sharing law, Congress enact a law that would give the owner who sells a painting a tax credit if he uses the proceeds to buy another painting. The effect would be the same as that of a federal subsidy to buyers of art and would give a fillip to the dealers who sell it.

Artists, in seeking satisfaction for themselves, now can contract with buyers to share the profit from the resale of work. No law is needed, as the *New Art Examiner* itself acknowledges. It reports that Hans Haacke in 1975 sold *On Social Grease* with a contract that called for his receiving 15 percent of the difference between the resale price of the work and the price at which he sold it; it was resold in 1987 for $90,000, and Haacke received $11,000. Or painters can hold their work until its price rises as high as expected. But if they do not want to divide their time between painting and speculating, they can sell their work at the best price they can get and let the buyer bear the uncertainty. There are thousands who are willing to bear it and have done so for centuries. They are dealers, and selling to them and to collectors is what most painters have preferred to do.

Actually, there is only a small probability that the value of a painting will increase, and there is a high probability that it will fall to zero. Between the very large number of painters who are not remembered at all and the very small number who are remembered there are those who were eminent at one time in their lives, later became less so, and now are names in the book of time. An example is William Frith. He was renowned in Victorian England, then became a painter whose public diminished, and now is an artist recalled only by name. When an artist dies, the interest in him usually declines and with it declines the price of his work. Examples from the present century are Mark Tobey and Ivan Albright. The exceptions are so unusual that when they occur they are noted with interest, as they were by Daniel Grant in *American Artist.*[16] He stated the work of Gauguin, van Gogh, Jackson Pollock, Milton Avery, and Philip Guston increased in value after their death. They are not the only painters of whom this can be said but when they are all of them brought together they are far fewer than the artists whose work once had a considerable value and later lost it.

Price changes of this kind have a different origin from changes in the price of the work of painters in whom there is a continuing but irregular interest. The latter are to be explained by the value of novelty (which in turn is explicable by diminishing marginal utility),

by changes of real income, of investment in taste, and of changes in
the relation of income to human capital. These things were set forth
in chapter two. The Pre-Raphaelites were popular in their own time,
became less so after their deaths, came near to being laughed at
(which indicates they were not forgotten), then regained the interest
of the public after the Second World War. William Adolph Bouguereau, the quintessential Academician of the nineteenth century in
France, enormously popular when the Impressionists were begging
for attention, fell from his high place when they finally became popular, was scorned for years, and now has re-engaged the interest of
collectors and, in a different way, of museum people (as a period
piece more than as a master). The Impressionists meanwhile continue to reign in glory. One result (which economic theory would have
predicted) is that as the price of their paintings has soared, there has
been an increase in the demand and price of work done in their
manner by artists in other countries; and now the market distin-
guishes French Impressionism from American, Scandinavian, and
others. There is moreover a market, perfectly legal and open, for
acknowledged copies. They are commissioned by collectors who
cannot afford an original or have one and do not want to risk hanging
it. The prices range from $5,000 to $17,000, very little relative to those
of originals ($54 million for van Gogh's *Irises,* which has been cop-
ied). At next remove are expensive mechanical reproductions, with
"simulated brush strokes, cracks, and fissures, $499.75 including
frame," beyond which are less expensive reproductions, for which
the frame usually costs more than the picture, and on and on to
postcards.

The market for substitutes, while at present not the object of
regulators, has not escaped their notice. There are grumbles about
painting coming from the Third World and sold for less than American artists and dealers expect for what they do. The work is said to
misrepresent itself, hence to debase the market with shoddy. Something of the same was said in the seventeenth century when the Dutch
guilds wanted to prohibit the painting of non-guild members from
being sold.

The stated purpose of regulatory laws is to protect something
or other the public wants protected, such as the buyers of art, the
nation's artists, the national heritage, and so forth. The most important of the laws are described in this chapter except those which
are related to the export and import of art, and they are described

in chapter six. About the actual effect of the laws, one cannot readily generalize. While they usually make the market for art smaller than it otherwise would be, that is, reduce the number of exchanges, not all do that or are they meant to. Subsidies to museums and to painters make the market larger than it otherwise would be and should be, although probably not as much as the subsidies to the performing arts enlarge their market. The price effect varies. Some laws (and government action) related to the visual arts are meant to increase price and do; others are meant to increase it and do not; and vice versa. In the language of economics, the laws more often reduce than increase the quantity exchanged; they may either increase or decrease price and the money value of exchanges; rarely is either of the latter unaffected.

EXPLAINING REGULATION

Why are there such laws? The question at one time would have been nudged out of economics into political science, sociology, psychology, or limbo. If pressed for an answer, a neo-classical economist in the past would have shrugged his shoulders and recalled Burke's remark about "the prolific imbecilities of reform." Today, however, he might relish the question, and answer it in either or both of two ways. One is that the market doesn't do everything which even market economists believe should be done, which is to direct labor and capital to their most efficient uses and to distribute their output in a way that, given the division of income, brings about the greatest satisfaction. In certain circumstances, the market is said not to do this. Just why is explained in chapter seven, which has to do with whether the government should assist the arts.

The other answer employs the new political economy, the premise of chapter six, which is about why governments assist the arts, whether or not they should. Briefly stated, the theory attributes the same motive to political conduct that it attributes to economic conduct, which is the desire to maximize returns of some kind. The government intervenes in the economy because certain people outside of the government and many inside it obtain higher incomes as a result and obtain them at the expense of those for whom the government does not intervene or intervenes less. Intervention, unlike a caucus race, is not a game in which everyone can win. To say this is to say what has been said for generations: the government intervenes on behalf of favored interests. Yet there is reason to say it again, and it is said in the sixth chapter which is about rent-seeking in the arts.

Neither of these explanations will satisfy people who do not care for the market, and they are many. The idea of market failure does not come near to capturing their moral outrage while the idea of rent-seeking ignores it. Their feelings run deep and lead them to countenance things they must know are mistaken. Works of art have been exchanged for thousands of years in both domestic and international markets. The editor of the *Oxford Companion to Art* knows this. Yet the entry on French art (unsigned) claims that in the nineteenth century "the artist had to find his own market and his own public" because of "the loss of official patronage," the consequence being "the first stirring of that sense of spiritual isolation—the so-called divorce of art from life—which has harassed the creative artist until the present time." The writer, in addition to being wrong in implying there was no market before the nineteenth century, is also wrong in imputing the feelings he does to the artists. How could the feelings be known—the inner thoughts of the thousands of artists of the century and of the thousands who followed them? We do happen to know what two leading painters thought. While what they thought may tell us nothing of what others thought, it does make us want evidence that the views of the others were just the opposite. Monet deplored the practice of "courting this or that Maecenas" and of soliciting commissions from a patron. He told Renoir that painters would prosper by selling their work to large dealers. "While our dealers are busy attracting customers, we will be able to do our painting far away . . . where we find subjects that inspire and please us." Renoir told this to his son, Jean, who does not record that his father disagreed with Monet.[17] One would not expect him to have disagreed, believing as he did that the market was the best register of aesthetic value.

Then there is Hugh Trevor-Roper, the Oxford historian of renown. In *The Plunder of the Arts in the Seventeenth Century* (1970), he gives an account of the dispersal of three collections: that of Charles I of England, of the Gonzagas of Mantua, and of Emperor Rudolph II of Bohemia. The dispersal of each is described as "aesthetic cannibalism, looting, plundering, and infamous robbery." The author acknowledges there were works in each that were not commissioned from the artists but obtained from other collectors, hence each collection was the outcome of earlier collections. His point, then, cannot be that every collection should be kept intact. If it should not be, one then would conclude, although he does not, that the exchange of art is not in itself objectionable. His point might have been that these particular collections were of such importance that they should not have been dispersed. But if that was his point he did not justify it and perhaps could not have since art history is not his forte. What he does claim is that each dispersal was an act of violence. But, as he himself reports, two of the collections were simply sold. They were not stolen, plundered, looted, or cannibalized. The Gonzanga art, owned by the dukes of Mantua, was put on the market because they needed money. The art collected by Charles I became the property of the Cromwell government after the monarchy was overthrown and was sold or taken by men high in government. Whether the collection of Rudolph II was sold or seized is not made clear in the account. Actually, some of the collection had been sold earlier, some later, some in fact was pillaged during the Thirty Years War; and, marvelously, a part of the collection survived to be discovered in the 1960s, according to R. J. W. Evans (*Rudolf II and His World,* 1973). That this information should be missing from Professor Trevor-Roper's account is perhaps to be expected. Including it (if he was aware of it) would have hobbled the moral indignation he wished to convey. So would the fact that there were pieces in Rudolf's collection for which the seller was never paid. That is not surprising because the author does not distinguish between voluntary and involuntary exchange, the way of the market and the way of the thief. Does he wish us to believe there is no difference? Or that there is not always a difference? Or that there is no difference in the matter of art? Or that there was no difference in the particular instance of these collections? The questions are pointless, actually. One should not ask for a demonstration of the undemonstrable or what is the proper price of the unpriceable.

ART AS INVESTMENT, AS SPECULATION, AND AS ART

While there are people who deplore the attention that is given the money value of art, there also are people who are pleased the attention is given and study the information with relish. The first comprise the anti-market party, and the second the party of art-as-investment. Some people are in both, their day being long enough to lament the way of the world after working hours and to make the best of it during them.

The art-as-investment people believe it can be bought at one price, sold later at a higher, and meanwhile can be enjoyed. They believe the same of houses (live in them while the price goes up), jewelry (wear it while it gains value), land (farm it while it appreciates), and oriental rugs (stand on them while they rise). The belief is not necessarily mistaken. A real asset, which these things are, can increase in value while it is being used, not a common occurrence when the price level is stable but possible. The mistake is to believe such assets are superior to financial assets, such as a bond, and yield a higher return than they do. Actually, financial assets can also increase in value while they yield an income. In an economy where the value of each real and financial asset was constant, the only income from them would be the utility of the real asset and the money income of the financial asset. We do not live in a stationary economy (which is what that is) and, so far as we know, we never have. But thinking about it is useful because it helps us to understand the economy we do live in. It is one in which the price of assets of both kinds changes. A moment's thought tells us that if the changes were predictable they would be small. If I expected the price of stock Z to increase in the next twelve months at a rate higher than the interest rate on loans, I would want to borrow and buy the stock now. So would I if Z was a painting instead of common stock. Other people would want to do the same, and we would bid against each other until the price of the asset was equal to the expected future price minus the interest expense of borrowing the money to buy the asset. Conversely, if the price of the asset was expected to rise by less than the interest rate, the owners would want to sell it and lend the proceeds. That would reduce the present price until it differed from the expected future price by an amount equal to the interest rate times the present price.

We know from observation that the value of some assets does

rise at a rate greater than the interest rate. We know from our thought of a moment ago that the increases could not have been expected because if they had been they would not have occurred. Further thought brings us to the conclusion that a work of art can be bought and held for a period and enjoyed, then sold at a profit (that is, for a gain greater than the interest rate). But the same thought tells us we don't know what that work of art is. So that if we are going to buy art in order to resell it we must be prepared to take risks. The best preparation is more than a willingness to take them. It is the capacity to enjoy them in the way a speculator enjoys speculation for its own sake and a gambler enjoys gambling. Risk lovers have the capacity, and if they are also art lovers, the art market is their oyster. It is not for them, however, if they have no interest in art as art. That is because compared to roulette or options it offers fewer thrills and calls for more patience.

Another consideration is relevant to investing or speculating. Art is an asset that yields its own return to people who value it for its own sake, the return being the aesthetic satisfaction, pleasure, utility, enjoyment, or (in economic prose) its viewing services. The aesthetic yield is one of two components of the total yield, or return, the other being the changes in its price over time. The total return to art, if the market for it is informed, should equal the total return to equally risky assets, such as financial assets like stock or bonds or real assets like buildings and land. People who buy art only to resell it at a higher price and for no other reason, that is, speculators, have a lower yield from it than people who enjoy it. To speculators, the aesthetic yield is zero. If they are to resell art at a profit, its price must rise by an amount at least equal to the price increase of other assets plus the yield (dividends, interest, rent, and so on) of the assets. For example, if the total return to common stock is 15 percent, of which 5 is dividends and 10 price increase, a speculator in stock could make a "profit" of 15 percent in one year from buying and selling it. If he is to do that well with art, its price alone, which is just one component of its total yield, must rise 15 percent. That would mean the total return to art for people who enjoy it would be more than 15 percent. Such a relation is conceivable for particular works at particular times. But it cannot be common, and it cannot obtain for long. If the total return to art was expected to be higher than that to equally risky securities, the demand for art and its price would rise until its total yield fell to that of the securities.

What does this signify to people who do not speculate in art but "invest" in it, in other words, those who buy it in the hope its price will increase and meanwhile enjoy it? The significance is that investors are more likely than speculators to make a "profit." A given increase in the price of art produces a larger total return to investors than to speculators. If investors value the aesthetic yield at 5 percent and the price increases 10 percent, they have done as well as they could have done by buying common stock yielding 15 percent in total. Speculators on the other hand would do worse because their yield is only 10 percent. Of course investors must realize that their allegiance is divided between the enjoyment of art and the enjoyment of money (meaning the enjoyment of things other than art). The more important is the latter, the less will they enjoy the art they hope to resell.

There is a third group that has good reason to wonder about the future value of their art. It consists of people who buy art only because they enjoy it, yet cannot sensibly ignore how much it costs them to hold it. If the value of their collection increases after they have acquired it, the cost of holding it also increases. That is because they could sell it and buy other assets. Suppose a collector for a song bought a painting after the Amsterdam project said it was not a Rembrandt as it once was said to be, then suppose it was found to be a Rembrandt after all. Suppose its price increased to half a million dollars and the rate of return on a security of equal risk was 7 percent. The annual income from the security would be $35,000. That is the cost to the collector of keeping his painting, about $100 a day, including the days he is away from home or doesn't look at it. Of course the aesthetic yield of the painting is not taxable and the money yield of the security is. Yet again, in an economy with well-ordered markets, that could only mean a higher nominal yield for securities and a lower yield for art.

We pass from people who enjoy taking risks to those who are either averse or indifferent to them. For neither is art suitable as an investment and even less so as a speculation. The reason is that there is not enough information about its return to enable them to make decisions about it. What the empirical studies described below report is that the total return to art is less than that to securities. The explanation could be that there is less information about art than about securities (which, however, could also make its return higher). Or securities on the whole may be more risky than art. Or the studies could be mistaken and more inquiry is called for. They do not all report the same return to art which makes for still more uncertainty. These matters should tell with an investor even if he is indifferent to risk. He is not indifferent to yield and does not want to hold an asset about the past yield of which he has no clear information. Uncertainty about the future, while it may be regretted, cannot be avoided. Uncertainty about the past can be.

What applies to the risk neutral applies even more to the risk averse. The former cannot find the art market inviting. The latter find it dismaying. If either buy art they do so because they like it and not to make a profit from it. The reason is not of course that making money from art degrades it but that profit-seeking is a mistake for collectors. Art for art's sake has a firm grounding in neo-classical economics whatever it may have in aesthetics or in the socio-politico-historical view of it which is entertained at present by younger art historians.

THE VALUED AND THE VALUELESS

A noteworthy feature of the art market is the large variation among the rates at which individual prices change. They range from positive values exceeding 100 percent in one year to a negative 100 percent (and nothing lower is possible). The high values are necessarily unexpected. The very lowest are those for art that cannot find a buyer, may not even be offered for sale, and is about to be discarded because it no longer interests anyone. Negative rates of price change are not of course unique to art or are very large price decreases. Other assets may have the same fate. But rarely do they decline in value as much as 100 percent, that is to say, become worthless, because they usually have a scrap value. Paintings, alas, do not; sculpture may have. What is unique about the price of art as an asset (though not as a consumer good) is the frequency with which price falls to zero. As most of the art that has been created has not survived—and its disappearance cannot be accounted for by depreciation or destruction—most of it must have become worthless, and its price must have fallen 100 percent. If we were to construct a frequency distribution of rates of price change at any one time, we would see a very small number of very high rates, a very large number of very low rates, and an average equal (when aesthetic yield is added) to the total rate of return on equally risky assets.

Most works of art lose their value entirely because in addition to being assets they are also durable consumer goods which are subject to obsolescence (as explained earlier in this chapter). A work yields aesthetic pleasure for a time, then no longer does. The owner would like to sell it when he tires of it, would like even more to sell it at a profit but knows he probably cannot. When people look for art to buy, they know they probably will not want to keep it indefinitely, and the price they are willing to pay is what they think the enjoyment of the art will be worth for the time it interests them.

The probability of art becoming worthless is greater for that which is very new: the very-very-contemporary or as Mr. Jingle would say—latest thing—novel novelty—top hole—bottom line—cutting edge—far out—just in—right off easel—still wet. The greater the age of a work, the less is the probability of its losing all of its value. For art that is very old and important, say of the Flemish or Italian renaissance, the probability is lowest. However, art that survives does fluctuate in value. The explanation in art history is that tastes change. Economics can add they change because old art, like all other, is subject to diminishing marginal utility. The more we see of it, the less do we want to see still more—just now. But we know the interest in it, unlike that in very new art, probably will not fall to zero or if it does will not remain there. The reason we believe it will survive is because it has.

The value of art that has survived (taking it in the aggregate and over the long period) is likely to increase at a modest rate. It has been exposed to the judgment of buyers and sellers and those they rely on. Its having survived indicates they believe it is worth conserving. In an economic sense this is what is meant by a work of art having met the test of time. Another economic description is that while its marginal utility may diminish it will not fall to zero permanently. This in itself only means the price of older art will not fall to zero. There is, however, reason to believe it will increase. That is because the demand for it increases over time as the income of buyers increases. Art, as explained in chapter two, is a "superior" good, one for which the demand is income elastic. Its income elasticity, taken together with the small changes in supply, causes its price to rise over time.

Its supply can also increase even though the artists are dead, because paintings get reattributed and unknown work is discovered (and there may be successful fraud). But the increase is likely to be small. Moreover, reattribution decreases the supply of the work of some painters (hence increases its price) while simultaneously increasing the supply of others' work. The price of older paintings then, if it changes, usually increases. In an informed market the increase cannot be more than the interest rate. If the market is not informed, the increase can be greater. Or less.

THE PRICE OF ART: THE STATISTICS

Among the empirical studies of the price of art, there are five of which I know that are either important or interesting, and some are both. They are "The Appreciation of Paintings" (1973), a doctoral dissertation at the University of Chicago by John Picard Stein; "Unnatural Value: Or, Art Investment as a Floating Crap Game" (1986), a journal article by William J. Baumol; "Paintings as an Investment" (1974), a journal article by Robert Anderson; *Money and Art* (1971), a book by Geraldine Keen; and "Is Art Such a Good Investment?" (1988) by Bruno S. Frey and Werner W. Pommerehne, a report to the general reader and to economists as well.[18] A summary of their findings is a fitting end to this chapter.

Before describing them, something must be said about a different kind of price information. It is of no particular significance to an economist and should be of none to the art lover, the investor, or speculator but nevertheless is interesting to them. The prices are the big numbers that get onto the front page after a spectacular sale, usually of Impressionist or Postimpressionist work and occasionally of the work of living artists. A million or so for a work by a member of the New York School is newsworthy; even more is $30 million for one of the six paintings of sunflowers by van Gogh and still more is $54 million for his irises. The public would like an explanation. To say it is supply and demand does not satisfy and leads to another question: Why would anyone pay that much for a picture? The answer is that it is worth that much to the buyer (and more than that if there is consumer surplus, an economist would add). That merely repeats the original answer, but there is nothing more an economist can say. Not so the world outside of economics from which comes a volley of expletives: "excessive—unreasonable—senseless—outlandish—scandalous—obscene." And of course, "incredible." Just such words were used about the van Gogh sales. They come within the category of what linguistic analysis once called "oo-oo" and "ah-ah" statements—lower on the scale of meaning than statements of preference ("I like vanilla, or sunflowers, better than chocolate, or irises") that do convey information however inconsequential it is.

Admittedly, prices of this order are unusual, hence are not representative of the value of most art, not even of those works that retain enough value to come to market. Not only do the prices tell us nothing about the average price of art at present. They tell us nothing about the course of prices over time. They are of course large numbers, but so are other prices, like that of the Stealth Bomber, ten times as much as the *Irises*. They would be informative if they were related to a relevant magnitude and compared to a high price of a standard commodity like wheat. How many bushels of wheat does a Jasper Johns command today, and what was the wheat value of the Correggio (*The Sleeping Venus*) that Walpole reports was sold in 1650 for £1,000? In the Middle Ages the ruler of a petty domain offered to pay the public debt of another such domain if its ruler would give him a certain painting in his collection. Today is there anyone in the world (a Japanese insurance magnate perhaps) who would pay the national debt of France in return for the Mona Lisa? Are the highest of the high prices today higher than the highest of the high of the past? Or is it conceivable that the van Gogh prices presage a downward trend? That would be something to gasp about.

We leave the land of oo-oo and ah-ah and turn to the empirical studies. Dr. Stein computed the (geometric) average of the prices of all paintings auctioned in the United States and, separately, of all of those auctioned in the United Kingdom between 1946 and 1968 (the paintings being by artists of all countries and of all periods). In the United States, the number auctioned each year varied between 190 (1964–65) and 837 (1947–49); in the United Kingdom, the variation was between 1,097 (1954–55) and 2,297 (1947–49). The lowest average price at American auctions was $375 (1949–50), and the highest was $4,904 (1965–66). In Britain the lowest price was $276 (1949–50) and the highest was $2,923 (1967–68).

From the auction prices, Dr. Stein computed the annual percentage changes and did so on the assumption that these changes indicate the changes in the value of the entire stock of paintings, whether or not they come to auction so long as they are "auctionable" (that is, if they have any value). He did not, as the next study to be described does, compute the change in the value of the same paintings at two or more sales.

He found the "average annually compounded rate of price appreciation" (what I have called the price yield) to be 10.47 at American auctions, 10.38 at British auctions when the prices are stated in dollars, and 13.12 when stated in pounds, a distinction that need not detain the hurried amateur. One that should is between values which are and those which are not adjusted for changes in the purchasing power of money. For the period Dr. Stein studied, the annual average increase in all consumer prices was 2.5 percent which should be subtracted from his annual rate of price change (10.47 percent in the United States) to get the rate adjusted for inflation (about 8 percent).

These rates are substantially above the rate of interest on the highest grade (AAA) corporate American bonds; they averaged 4 percent for the period. That indicates the paintings either entail more risk than bonds or that the art market is not as well informed as the bond market or both. Another relevant comparison is between the price yield of painting in the United States, 10.47, and the total rate of return to common stock (price appreciation plus dividends) which was 14.3 percent annually. The comparison is relevant to the merit of painting as a speculation and shows at that time painting was inferior to common stock. Finally, a comparison is in order between the total rate of return to stock, 14.3, and the total return to painting, which Dr. Stein places at 12.1 percent annually, the difference between that and the price yield of 10.47 being the "service return" or aesthetic yield of 1.63 percent. The comparison shows that painting was not then a superior investment, was not something to be bought, enjoyed, then sold at a profit with a total return in excess of what could be obtained from stocks or bonds.

About painting as an investment or speculation, Dr. Stein has this to say:

> To the investor primarily interested in financial gain and valuing the return from viewing pleasure at only about 1.6 percent per year, paintings are not more or less attractive than other assets. They yield the going rate for their systematic risk. Contrary to a

misbelief that lures some collectors, investment in paintings is not particularly lucrative. The expected appreciation from such investment is only 73 percent of the return, including capital gains, in the equities market. And contrary to another misbelief, the value of paintings contains a substantial element of non-systematic risk, a factor that should persuade collectors to keep most of their wealth in other forms. Any superior performance derivable from paintings can be attributed entirely to the viewing pleasure they provide, not capturable by speculators.

The study by Professor Baumol is of particular interest because he is a pioneer in analyzing the economics of the performing arts. His study of the visual arts measures the rate of price change over a 300-year period of the paintings listed in Gerald Reitlinger's *The Economics of Taste* (1961), a highly personal account of painting, collectors, auctions, prices, artists, and economics as spoken by Uncle Gerald, as one reviewer called him. Example: "Of the paintings of other schools, for which names had been supplied by Richter, I cannot help thinking that the man who bought a roundel Holy Family for 13 guineas, whether or not it was by Raffealino del Garbo, was exceedingly lucky." Professor Baumol in his search for prices in Mr. Reitlinger's book was exceedingly lucky he did not have to get them from Part I, where this sentence appears, although Part II, where the prices were obtained, is not simplicity itself; for example, in the list of paintings by Poussin is the entry "1794/Joshua Reynolds. C. Adoration/£546."

Professor Baumol computed the average annual rate of price change, adjusted it for changes in the value of money, and found it to be .55, about one-half of 1 percent with a median of .85. That is surprisingly low, and not what economic theory predicts except in a market where values are consistently and mysteriously understated. The finding of course is consistent with the observation that art is not a profitable speculation, that it is not a superior investment, and that its value increases by no more than the interest rate. If its price yield was in fact only .55 it would be an inferior investment, so inferior as to be nearly no investment at all. That rate does not of course include the aesthetic yield of the paintings.

The study by Professor Anderson also uses the prices in Mr. Reitlinger's book and in addition those in *International Auction Records* by E. Meyer. Professor Anderson's purpose was to explain (by regression analysis) what determines the price of painting but in the course of doing so he also measured the rate of change of prices and did so in two ways, one by a regression equation in which time is a variable and the other by averaging the change of the price of paintings that were sold more than once. For the former he had no fewer than 13,000 prices for the period 1780 to 1970 and for the latter 1,730 pairs of prices between 1653 and 1970. The annual rate of price change by the former method was 3.3 percent and by the latter 4.9 percent. Both are less than the rate of return to securities for the comparable period, which Professor Anderson estimated to be 6.5 percent. Its being higher indicates that art would not have been as profitable a speculation as securities but does not necessarily indicate it was inferior as an investment, because in addition to its price yield it yielded an aesthetic return.

The study by Geraldine Keen describes a large number of separate indexes (fifty-seven of them). Each measures the rate of change of prices paid for the work of particular painters (for example, Renoir), of particular schools (late Renaissance), accepted categories (Old Masters), subject matter (English sporting), and others. The prices usually are not those at which the same work was sold at different times but the prices of works that are comparable, and the comparison is made by the Sotheby staff. For Old Masters, the average yearly price increase was 11 percent from 1950 to 1960 (remarkably close to Dr. Stein's estimate of 10.5 percent for painting sold at American auctions). The rate was 24 percent for the works of Chagall and 8 percent for late Renaissance paintings. The Times–Sotheby index is computed from many fewer prices than those used by the other studies. It does not shirk the problem of comparability and addresses it in a straightforward way. But the comparisons are made by a small number of people, experts to be sure, and their judgment may not reflect that which the market would make. Moreover, the number of prices in each index is uncomfortably small. If the investor/speculator is not disquieted by these doubts about the indexes, he can find evidence in them that painting can be an investment superior to financial assets and can be a profitable speculation. On the other hand, the prudent amateur who is not fond of risk taking will buy art for art's sake and invest and/or speculate in other assets.

Professors Frey and Pommerehne used the prices of paintings that between 1635 and 1987 were sold more than once. The prices were taken from Reitlinger and also from auctions in London and elsewhere that were held after his book was published, and all prices were adjusted for commission charges. There were 1,200 sales, or (in their terminology) "turnovers," and they disclose an annual real increase of 1.5 percent. That is about three times the rate reported by Professor Baumol (.55) who used much the same information but did not use it as finely. The other three studies did not adjust the change in art prices for changes in the value of money. But all except that of Ms. Keen give the same answer to the question, Is buying art simply to resell at a higher price likely to be profitable? The answer is no.

SUMMARY: THE MARKET SURVEYED, THE AMATEUR ADVISED

Works of art have been bought and sold for millennia. Trade in art between countries is itself at least 4,000 years old and trade within them must be older since domestic markets usually antedate foreign. In the exhibit from Israeli museums, Treasures of the Holy Land, which toured North America in 1988, there were alabaster ornaments made in Egypt in the second millennium before Christ and unearthed in Canaan. Silver work of Mesopotamian design has been found in Etruscan tombs of the seventh or eighth century B.C. Concerning domestic trade, there is information in the letters of Cicero, Horace, and Caesar about dealers in the city of Rome.

The longevity of the art market is evidence it is useful and that it is an indispensable element in the activity of art if the activity originates in the discrete decisions of the many who create art and the many who want to own it. The two need to be brought together: producers and consumers, sellers and buyers, people who have more art and less money than they want and people who have more money and less art than they want. Bringing them together is the function of the market in all things. The more specialized is the making of art, the more specialized is the selling of it and the buying also. Dealers rarely paint. Painters are known to deal in art, that of others as well as their own, but the principal activity of the principal painters has been painting, and so much the better for them, Monet told Renoir. Collectors who can afford to be serious about their collecting do not rely on their judgment alone; they call on that of others and pay for it, indirectly in the form of dealers' commissions and directly by engaging experts.

Simply stated, there must be the exchange of art if there are to be artists. It is the necessary consequence of the division of labor, as Adam Smith said and went on the say that the more extensive is the market, the greater will be the division of labor and the more productive will it be. More does not always mean better but it cannot mean worse. So that while one may not say the extension of the market has improved the quality of art (by any of the dozen or score of standards of excellence), one may say the quality has not lessened. If it had, there would be less bought, collected, seen, read about, and (of course) produced. By all indications (though not by the Census of Manufactures, which is silent on the matter) there has been an increase in the making and using of art. That means it provides an increasing amount of enjoyment to the population, or in the language of economics, greater total utility. There may also be an increase in the utility per person, since the interest in art is influenced by education and the population is becoming better educated (at least in the sense of spending more time in school).

As the art market becomes more extensive, so do the differences become greater among the works that are traded on it: differences in subject matter, how it is treated and with what skill, the originality that is shown, the power to engage the viewer's interest, the quality of the visual experience—in a word, aesthetic merit. This explains (if an explanation were necessary) why the prices of art vary from a few dollars to $50 million. In this, the extensive view of the art market, it is more than the market for "fine" or "serious" art or what is desired by important collectors who buy from the great dealers of the world and the principal auction houses. The market, as seen here, includes small galleries, neighborhood art stores, paintings sold by painters from their studio or at art fairs or local exhibitions, and the art galleries of department stores and the wares of interior decorators (which have been known to include the work of artists like Buffet, who are also represented in museums). Then there are the mountebank auctioneers who on a Sunday afternoon knock down a Giovanni Bellini for a few hundred dollars.

Just what the limits of the market are is a pretty question and also a solemn question because it asks, What is art? That is not a question for this book. All that need be said here is that the market for art includes goods which are substitutes in some degree. The prices of the goods are therefore related but are not competitive because the substitutability is not perfect, in many instances is slight. Each work of art is unique in one way or other, and that gives the seller of it some power over price. The power obviously is greater if there are many rather than few buyers who want it. But buyers usually specialize, which limits the demand for any one work, hence limits the price power of the seller. The relation between seller and buyer is then a bargaining relation. All that can be said is that the price will be no less than what the seller will accept and no more than what the buyer will pay. That is not particularly informative except that it indicates sellers do not have their own way as is so often said. One who said it was Maurice Rheims, a prominent figure in the cultural affairs of France and the author of a noted book about the market: "Dealers and the trade in general impose their will upon amateur buyers."[19] If that were true, dealing in art would yield a higher rate of return than other uses of labor and capital, and the number of dealers would increase continuously, which does not appear to be happening. One reason is that amateurs are knowledgeable, and if they are not, they learn to be.

There are other misconceptions about the market. They invite the attention of people who are predisposed to regulation. New York City has a law that requires dealers to post prices. A proposed regulation would require auction houses to disclose which of their sales are at reserve prices, hence represent the withdrawing of a work from the market. California has a law that prohibits museums from altering works in their collection without the consent of the artist or his heirs. The state also has a law that requires the owner of a work who resells it to share the profit (but not the loss) with the artist. A similar law has been put before the U.S. Senate. Regulation is difficult to enforce, usually is expensive, and frequently brings about the opposite of what is desired or brings about nothing at all. To require the owner to share the profit from the resale of art would in all likelihood lower the price the artist receives and also make some art too risky to buy, reducing its price to zero. Regulation on the Continent is extensive, of long standing, and has been concurrent with decline in the market for art there. Another result is illegal trading and the concealing of art in order to safeguard it and the owners.

A salient but not unique feature of the art market is its uncertainties. We cannot always know when we look at a painting just whose work it is, and even if we can be certain of its attribution we cannot always be certain about how much the work has been altered by conservation and restoration or the want of them. Of the two, the uncertainty about attribution appears to be the more important and to have the greater effect on price. There of course is uncertainty (that is, disagreement) about the aesthetic quality. The uncertainty is greater, the greater is the uncertainty about attribution and the less is the information about provenance.

The art world is not of a single opinion about the importance of attribution, and if a vote were taken the majority might be found on the side that says attribution is not important. This seems to place expert opinion at odds with the market. But the difference could be trivial, the result of hair-splitting. It is that when a museologist says the attribution of a painting is not related to its aesthetic qualities and at the same time he is quite careful about it when he recommends an acquisition. If he is to be taken literally, he must be saying that a work of art is not only (not merely?) an aesthetic object but an aesthetic object plus objects of a different nature which in their entirety constitute what is called art and is placed in what is called an art collection. A more useful approach is to wonder why the market makes attribution important, and several reasons suggest themselves. One is that objects which have an identity are more interesting than those which do not. Another is that the names of the makers convey information about the merit of what they make. Another is that things are valued for the associations they have as well as for being what they are. Then there is the considerable convenience names have for art history, those who read it as well as write it.

An uncertainty of another kind is about price, and here too the art market is unusual but again is not unique. About most of the art that is produced at any time, there is no uncertainty over what its price will be in the future because the art will cease to interest anyone and will be discarded. About the art that survives, there is some but not much uncertainty about its future price. The demand for such art rises as real income rises, and its price rises also. The better informed is the art market, the more nearly will the price increase be limited by the rate of interest on assets that are equally risky. What is uncertain is which of the works of art created at any time will survive to have a price in the future. Experience shows that the longer a work of art has survived, the more likely is it to survive still longer and the more likely is its price to be higher in the future than at present. Conversely, the greatest uncertainty is about the most recently created art because a large part of it is likely to lose all of its value. Latest thing dicey—careful! Mr. Jingle would say.

Of five empirical studies of the price of art, three report the long-term trend is upward with no account taken of changes in the value of money. One makes it 3.3 percent annually, another 10.5, and the third 11 (for Old Masters). A fourth study reports the increase to be only .55 percent annually after adjustment for changes in the value of money. The fifth reports the annual rate to be 1.5 after adjustment. The difference among these estimates is a warning to people who would invest or speculate in art unless they happen to enjoy taking chances. If they love art as well as risk, the art market can be their playground. It is not for people who are risk averse or risk neutral. Even if they were certain of the price history of art (which they cannot be), they would not find the market attractive. By the most detailed study, the total rate of return to art (aesthetic yield plus price appreciation) was about 12 percent from 1946 to 1968 when the total return to common stock (dividends plus price appreciation) was about 14 percent. As a speculation, the only return to art is its price appreciation, at that time 10.5 percent which was still lower than the 14 percent total return to common stock.

The prudent amateur—the art lover who is not a risk lover—buys art for the pleasure of owning it. He invests or speculates in other things. Art for art's sake has a good grounding in neo-classical economics.

5

Art Museums

> It is the intention of the Trustees that
> the rentals shall pay the interest on
> the debt and the care of the building;
> that the tuition fees shall pay the ex-
> penses of the school; and that the
> membership dues and door fees shall
> pay the gallery expenses.
>
> —*Annual Report*
> Art Institute of Chicago
> 1888

ART MUSEUMS are an aspect of the supply of art in the sense that they make it available to the public. They are related to the visual arts in the way a repertory company is related to the literature of the stage. This chapter then continues the subject begun in chapter three, but an economist's view of an art museum is quite different from his view of a painter and his studio. The reason is that museums are not conducted for the purpose of increasing the money income of the people who own them. They are, with a few exceptions, nonprofit organizations. This does not mean they are conducted for the benefit of the public at large (which, if it means anything, means for no one in particular), or that the benefit they provide has no money value. What it does mean is that the benefit is not received by the people who own the museum except the satisfaction they receive from doing what they believe should be done.

Most of the museums outside of the United States are owned by government. So that in principle they are the property of everyone, even and particularly in Communist states where what is public is virtuous and what is private is usually more efficient. Something that in theory is the business of everyone is in practice the business of no one until it becomes the responsibility of someone in government, and then it no longer is everyone's business. In Western Europe, the museums are the responsibility of the national government, usually the ministry of culture if it has one, or a local government. The Louvre is a museum of the national government, and the Musée d'Art Moderne of the government of the city of Paris. In the United States the ownership of most of the large museums is divided between a local government that owns the land and buildings and a board of trustees that in a formal, legal sense owns the collection as a private (that is, nongovernmental) body but may not use it for the benefit of the members. The Metropolitan Museum in New York is an example. There also are museums that are owned entirely by the government— building, land, and collection—as the National Gallery in Washington is. Then there are privately owned museums, the property of an organization or individual, such as the Fogg Museum at Harvard and the Terra Museum of American Art in Chicago. What all of them have in common is that they are not operated for a profit in the way Disneyland is and the museum of Charles Willson Peale was.

THEIR SEVERAL PURPOSES

A nonprofit and a for-profit organization are alike in one way. They both try to maximize something or other by doing the best they can with what they have. A for-profit organization tries to maximize the rate of profit on its capital. Because long-run profit is more important than immediate gain, the organization must respect the standards of business conduct as they are revealed by the buyers and sellers with whom it deals. A nonprofit organization maximizes something other than the rate of return on capital. What it maximizes depends, in the best of circumstances, on how the people who conduct it interpret its stated purposes. In other circumstances, it maximizes the private returns of the people who direct and operate it. That can be their money income, the security of their jobs, the perquisites of office, their professional standing, or anything else that adds to their utility.

How well a for-profit organization does what it is supposed to do is quickly determined—by looking at how much profit it returns on its capital. Admittedly, measurement is not always accurate, especially of the value of capital, and the amount of profit may be over- or understated by the external effects, negative or positive, that are engendered by what the organization produces. But the problems are manageable and those related to the measurement of capital are managed daily (actually, moment by moment) on the stock market. How well a nonprofit organization does what it is supposed to do is difficult to determine. That is not because what it is supposed to do and what it actually does are impossible to measure. They can be measured and usually in money. The cause of the difficulty is elsewhere. It is that the purposes are unclear and that the cost incurred in pursuing them is usually not reported accurately. This is notably true of art museums.

In the United States they have several purposes about which the community of museum professionals is in agreement. But there also are purposes about which there is disagreement. Moreover, in each of these categories there are purposes which were not among those which the people who began and paid for the museums had in mind. Finally, some of those they did have in mind are no longer held. That is a fourfold classification, and an example of each is in order.

1. All museologists agree that museums should conserve art. They may and do differ about what should be conserved, how it should be, and about what conservation means in relation, for example, to restoration. But everyone agrees that art museums should conserve art. They also agree that museums should do more than conserve it, in other words, they should be more than warehouses, although they are that in part. A common and recommended practice in the United States is to allot as much space for storage as for exhibition, according to G. Ellis Burcaw (*Introduction to Museum Work*, 1975). This must mean—since more space is given to an object on exhibit than in storage—that more than half of a museum's collection is in storage at any time. In Europe, the proportion in storage, one would guess, is even higher.

2. Museologists disagree over the kind of art that should be exhibited. Should it be that which attracts the largest number of visi-

tors, or that which is more interesting from a historical point of view, or that which trains the eye of the visitor by giving him the opportunity to compare and discriminate, or that which pleases the visitors who come with the discerning eye, the connoisseurs, or that which is the fancy of the moment in the world of art?

3. Today the major museums as well as some that are minor are engaged in research as well as in exhibiting and conserving art. Among the purposes stated by those who began the American museums one would have to look very hard to find research of the kind museums today undertake to do. This is not to say they should not do it but is to say they should explain why they do.

4. When they were begun an often-stated purpose was to improve the taste of the common man and to provide him with an innocent diversion. Today museums certainly do not turn the common man away, yet what they show him may not engage his interest as much as other art would do (and which they may have in storage), and the hours at which it is on view are not as convenient as others would be (surely Monday evening is more convenient than Monday morning).

That the purposes of art museums have changed is not in itself to be regretted or is there anything alarming about there being disagreement among professionals over what they should be doing. But change and disagreement do make difficult a judgment about how well they are doing their work. The difficulty is increased by there being in addition to the stated purposes of museums others that are only implied or quietly sought. They and all other purposes may be perfectly legitimate or they may not. They are if they add more to the return of the museum than to its cost and are not if they add more to cost than to return. Just which they are would be clear if a museum were a private enterprise operated for a profit. Whatever increased its rate of profit would be desirable and whatever did not would be mistaken. The museologists of the world do not for a moment accept this, the market, test of their conduct. They can draw some comfort (how much is debatable) from the economic theory of externalities and public goods which acknowledges the market is unable to make some judgments. The museum people ought either to use this theory or to explain just how they do make their judgments. That requires a clear statement of the purposes a given museum is seeking, whether or not they command the agreement of all museologists, and requires also a clear statement of how the museum knows if it is or is not fulfilling its stated purposes. To say this is impossible comes near to saying, "I don't know for sure what I'm supposed to be doing and if I did I would have no way of being sure I was doing it—but I would like to go on doing what I'm doing, whatever that is, and I ask you to give me the money I need to do it."

THE UNDERSTATEMENT OF CAPITAL COSTS

Museums, apart from not being clear about what they believe they should do, are also not clear about how much they should spend to do it. Specifically, they do not make a full acknowledgment of their costs. That is because they do not consider their capital to have a cost. It of course does, and its cost is the income that would be received if the capital was invested in another form. Museums, unlike painters, are either not aware of opportunity cost or are opposed to the idea in principle. The cost of capital would be obvious to a museum if it borrowed money in order to buy a painting. The annual cost of the painting would be the interest paid to borrow the money. That cost is distinct from the price of the painting. The price would appear on the balance sheet as an asset and the loan as a liability. The interest cost would appear on the income statement as an expense. The idea can also be illustrated by supposing a museum had a sum of money which could be used either to buy a painting or to buy a security which would yield an amount of interest that would pay the salary of a curator. Certainly the salary would be considered an expense, and just as certainly the implicit interest cost of the painting should be. By the conventions of accounting, the implicit interest cost of a private enterprise does not appear as an expense as the explicit interest costs do. But in the theory of accounting as in economic theory the former is an expense as much as the latter is.

The people who now keep the accounts of the Art Institute of Chicago, or the people who decide how the accounts should be kept, would find the annual reports of 1883 and 1888 instructive. The former records the receipt of $60,000 from the sale of 5 percent bonds and the disbursement of $66,865 for "real estate and buildings." A part of the property so acquired was used for exhibition and another portion was rented for more than enough to pay the annual interest on the bonds which would have been $3,000. Five years later the annual report stated, "It is the intention of the Trustees that the rentals shall pay the interest on the debt and care of the building." That is not all an economist would like to see, but it is a beginning. It acknowledges that the capital the museum has in the form of a building has an interest cost. It does not say the art inside has an interest cost also. The omission conceivably could be explained by saying the trustees of that age of innocence were ignorant of opportunity cost. That, while conceivable, is improbable. They were no-nonsense men of business. What is likely is that they believed there was not enough art in the Institute to incur a cost worth noticing. "We have a few pictures but no collection worthy of the name," the report of 1888 stated.

The omission of the cost of its capital has an effect on the way a museum is conducted, and the effect is compounded by its being a nonprofit organization. The collection of a museum is one component of the real capital it uses, that is, its building, equipment, and other material goods as distinct from its financial capital, such as the securities it owns. If the museum does not own its building, as many museums do not, its collection is by far the most important component of its own capital. The actual cost of that capital—irrespective of the recorded cost, which is zero—is a large part of the actual total cost of operating the museum. That total, in addition to the implicit interest cost of the collection, includes operating costs such as salaries, heat, and light. The extent of the activity of an organization, whether the activity is measured by the number of shoes a factory produces or the number of visitors a museum has, is governed in the long period by the cost and income the organization chooses to recognize. If it does not choose to recognize all of its costs, then what appears to be an excess of income over cost will, in fact, be less than it seems; or if income is less than cost, the actual loss will be greater than it seems. The effect of either—of an overstated gain or an understated loss—is to induce the organization to do more than it efficiently can do: to produce too many shoes or to become too large a museum. The inefficiency of the shoe factory will come to an end because it is a for-profit organization and must give its owners a satisfactory return on their capital or go out of business. The museum, on the other hand, can endure because it is immune to the discipline of the market. It cannot of course be flagrantly wasteful of capital or of anything else. Its board or a government agency would put a stop to that. But it can hold an excessive amount of capital indefinitely if it manages to meet its other costs.

Even failing to meet them does not necessarily harm it. "It is suggested that the apparent continuing financial difficulties of the performing arts may well be in part a strategy designed to induce maximum assistance from potential patrons." So it was politely said by C. D. Throsby and G. A. Withers in *The Economics of the Performing Arts.*[1] They go on to say (following an idea of Geoffrey Brennan) that a feature of the strategy is to deliver an ultimatum to prospective donors. If they fail to give they will not have less art but no art, not less opera next season but no season. Such a warning was issued at one time by an official of the British Arts Council who said: "If half a million pounds of public money now invested annually by the Arts Council and Local Authorities in opera, ballet, music and drama in this country were withdrawn, nearly all the national institutions of music and drama in this country would have to close down."[2] Whether the strategy is effective is arguable. It is if frequency of use indicates effectiveness. Many years ago Benjamin Ives Gilman in his book on museums (1918) said, "To conduct a gainful enterprise with an annual deficit is to invite ruin. To conduct a charitable enterprise with an annual deficit is to invite re-endowment."[3] If this is true, museums would elicit more donations if they recognized their capital costs and reported them.

WHY MUSEUMS GROW

The consequence of not recognizing capital costs is that museums are larger than they should be. This would be denied in the world of art which, like the world of morality, believes there can never be too much of the good thing which is its responsibility. Ian Finlay, the British museologist who was mentioned in chapter one as representative of the anti-market mentality and who of course is much opposed to the acquisitiveness of a commercial society, is of the opinion that a museum must "grow" or perish.[4] That is almost certainly wrong. There are museums that were small when they began and have remained small; they also have remained distinguished, such as the

Wallace Collection in London, the Frick Collection in New York, and the Cognac-Jay Museum in Paris. Nevertheless, Mr. Finlay correctly expresses the opinion of the large museums and of some of the small as well. Kenneth Clark said that when he was made director of the National Gallery in London, "My only thought was to buy some good pictures for the gallery and to re-hang certain rooms."[5] One must add he did try to reduce the stock of things in storage by offering to lend them to museums outside of London which, however, declined them when they saw what he offered. On the other hand, there is evidence that a museum would not care to dispose of any part of its collection even in return for something to replace it if by so doing the growth of the museum would be retarded. And it would be still more averse to disposing of anything if the result would be a decrease in the size of the collection.

The size of museums figures in an important way in a unique study of how visitors conduct themselves. It was made some sixty years ago by E. S. Robinson, a psychologist, and two associates.[6] It is unique because of what it investigated and for the way the investigation was made. A visitor was not asked his age, income, occupation, education, what he had come to see, whether he had seen it, and whether he could remember the name of the artist (all of which figure in other audience studies). The investigators asked scarcely any questions, but, equipped with a notebook and a stopwatch, picked out a visitor and followed him as he made his way through the museum, noting how many paintings he looked at, measuring the time he paused before each, counting the number of rooms he entered, and measuring the elapsed time between the start and the end of his visit. The behavior of eighty-seven visitors was observed in four museums of different sizes, none identified.

The visitors were observed to spend more time in the small than in the large museums, to spend more time before each of the paintings in the former than latter, and to have seen a larger proportion of the total collection of small than of large museums. But neither engaged the attention of visitors for long. The average time of the entire visit was less than half an hour. The average time spent before a painting—at which the visitor spent any time at all—was nine seconds.

The investigators used a novel measure of "museum fatigue." They noted how the time a visitor spent before a painting changed as his visit progressed. What they found is consistent with diminishing marginal utility—but not completely consistent. As the visit progressed, the visitor spent less and less time before the paintings at which he spent any time at all, the diminution being taken as a sign of increasing fatigue, until he was about midway between entrance and exit whereupon the time began to increase and continued to do so until he departed, the last picture engaging his attention for longer than any he saw at mid-passage but for fewer seconds than those he looked at when he began his visit. The variation in his attention span may possibly be accounted for by his taking a break during his visit and recuperating. If this is so, it makes the time he spent looking at art still briefer—and is consistent with diminishing marginal utility. However that may be, the data on museum fatigue do establish one principle and in doing so dispose of another. They dispose of the belief that museum fatigue is the product of tender feet on hard floors and establish the belief it is in the eyes of the beholder. The measured value of fatigue was highest in rooms where visitors walked least over hard floors but had the most pictures to look at. A few years later, Professor Robinson made another such study and then did ask a question or two. Most visitors said that in their opinion there was too much to see in museums.[7]

Museologists, their patrons, and their partisans, if given this information would no doubt smile. *Sans pertinence mais drôle.* In neither their actions nor their words is there any indication that museum people are aware of it. The trustees of the Art Institute (men of the market during business hours) said in their annual report for 1978–79, "Because the Art Institute is a comprehensive museum the acquisition of works of art is a never ending, necessary, and vital part of its program." To be accurate, one must add that museums at times do dispose of works in their collections, but there is no evidence they dispose of more than they acquire or would like to acquire. The director of the Toledo (Ohio) Museum of Art, one of the small, distinguished museums of the Midwest, said, "I could not work in an environment where there is not great art and the opportunity to acquire more."[8] The desire of museums to grow, while it has several causes, is the predictable outcome of their acting as if the most important part of their capital were free. It is so regarded whether the works in the collections have been given them or have been purchased. To act as if a thing were free when it has a cost, as art has, is to increase unduly the amount of it demanded or to make an inefficient use of it or both.

Or to make no use of it at all. As stated above, the museums of the United States taken altogether probably have more than half their art in storage. Some exhibit all they have, as the Cleveland Art museum once did and may still do. Others exhibit much less than half of what they have. So for the entire country, a visitor who goes off to a museum to see a particular work will see it there less than half the time. If he wants to see a popular work, like Calder's *Circus* in the Whitney, or a work of which the museum is rightfully proud, like the *Victorious Athlete* at the Getty, he is not likely to be disappointed, and he certainly will not be if he goes to the Art Institute to see the *Sunday Afternoon on the Island of La Grande Jatte.* But if his interest runs to the unfamiliar, like the Italian paintings in the Walters Gallery in Baltimore, he probably will be disappointed. He may be told, as one visitor was, to submit a written request that in due course would be answered by mail to the visitor's home, a thousand miles away.

A few museums have made the paintings in storage accessible without undue waiting. At the Metropolitan at one time, visitors were admitted to a part of the storage area after a word with a guard and his telephoning the proper office. The Brera in Milan has glass-enclosed storage areas where paintings are hung closely together on sliding panels, but alas the doors to these inviting places usually are locked, and the guard when found shakes his head in sympathy. The Kunsthistoriches Museum of Vienna for some twenty years has had a "secondary gallery" where less popular paintings are hung. However, not even the primary galleries are always open during the posted hours. The reason is not given. It could be that on some days not enough guards appear for work, as has happened at the Louvre where on a given day upwards of half of the galleries may be closed. The reason is different at the Rijksmuseum of Amsterdam where the administration in 1988 said it had not received enough money from the government. The conduct of this distinguished organization is what economic theory predicts will be done by a nonprofit establishment that understates its capital costs and attends only to its variable, or out-of-pocket, costs. When its income falls, it curtails its activity, that is, does less, which is just the opposite of what a for-profit organization may do when its income is reduced. It may reduce its price and produce more and will do so as long as the additional income covers the additional variable costs.

When the Centre Pompidou in Paris opened, there were paintings on panels that descended from the ceiling like theater scenery. The paintings were listed in a catalogue and each was given a particular number or letter for which there was a corresponding button on a control panel. The visitor leafed through the catalogue for what he wanted to see, pushed the proper button, and the painting appeared. Later the buttons were pushed by an attendant. Still later, the facility was removed—panels, paintings, buttons, and attendant—and their place was taken by disappointed amateurs.

Museums will explain why everything in their collections is not on exhibit. Some of it is fragile and could be damaged by exposure in a gallery. Exhibition, while universally acknowledged to be a function of a museum, is not all it is expected to do and is subordinate to conservation if a choice must be made. A museologist, if he is candid, will go on to say that some of what is in storage is not worth exhibiting but nevertheless is being saved. Just why is a question that is considered later in this chapter. The museologist then will certainly offer what his profession claims is the most important reason for storage. There is not enough exhibition space to show everything that can safely be exhibited and is worth exhibiting.

Yet this reason, offered as the most important, is the least convincing. It would do if the shortage of space was a temporary condition, brought on, say, by an unexpected bequest of Maecenian (or Gulbenkian) proportions. This seems to have happened in France during the wars of the Revolution and the Empire. The French acquired art in the territories they conquered and brought some to Paris where a new museum was created for it. That which was left where it was acquired was placed in academies created by the French. After 1815 what was in France was returned, whether to the original owners or to the governments of the territories is unclear. The academies remained under other names, and one would not be surprised to learn that some of the works in them stayed there even though they had been appropriated from churches, monasteries, and private collections.

In Paris, there must then have been a surplus of exhibition space, a condition most unusual in the history of museums. In a survey of the 1970s, 80 percent of the museums in America said they needed more exhibition space, and (what is truly startling) 74 percent said they needed more storage space.[9] Why, one may ask, do they allow their collections to grow or, rather, why do they avidly seek to add to what they have? They do, to be sure, campaign for larger buildings. Yet the new buildings allocate a smaller proportion of space to exhibition—about one-third is common—than was allocated in the buildings they replace. This does not necessarily mean total exhibition space is less because the new buildings are larger than those they replace (and some are additions to them). It does mean the administration of museums, and the resources it uses, have become more important relative to exhibition. Germain Bazin, a distinguished figure in the French museum world, wrote, "It is a contest between collection and services. . . . Little by little, administrative offices have encroached upon exhibition space."[10]

The art a museum has no space to exhibit or does not choose to exhibit is put to unusual uses. Some of the collection of the National Gallery of Washington is in American embassies in various countries. Art as an instrument of foreign policy, perhaps, or aesthetic diplomacy? The Uffizi of Florence at one time had some 7,000 objects on loan to embassies and government offices where they did not receive the care they would in a properly conducted museum ("paintings . . . hung to cook over radiators" in the Quirinal Palace; "tapestries, like those in the Palazzo Pubblico in Siena . . . reduced to faded rags").[11] Hence one should not be surprised to see a Renoir over the desk of a museum administrator where it adds to her total income, in a nonmonetary form of course. If it has a market value of $500,000, and the interest rate is 5 percent, the cost of that nonmonetary satisfaction is $25,000 a year. Would the museum consider borrowing $500,000 at 5 percent in order to buy a painting to hang in the office of an administrator? Would she prefer to receive an additional $25,000 in money instead of its equivalent in aesthetic satisfaction?

WHY THEY GROW TOO LARGE

Yet what a museum does is understandable when account is taken of the economic circumstances in which it operates. They do not alter the judgment an economist makes of the use of museum capital. To understand is not to forgive (*pace* Mme. de Stael) but it is informative. The circumstances are related to museums being nonprofit organizations and (what is logically distinct) to their reliance on gifts and subsidies.

A nonprofit organization is deprived—by choice, of course—of the clearest and simplest, although not the only, measure of efficiency. That is, profit determined by transactions on the market. An enterprise so engaged knows when it is efficient and when it is not. The profit it returns on its capital tells it. A nonprofit organization could in theory determine the rate of return on the capital it uses. How that might be done is described a few pages farther on.

Why do they not do so? The answer that immediately occurs is that they are enfeebled by the anti-market virus and cannot bring themselves to believe the market can furnish any guidance whatever. As important as that is, there may be another.

When the National Bureau of Economic Research in the early 1960s tried to get information from museums about the value of their collections, it was told that such a thing was impossible. One of the reasons (as noted in chapter one where the episode was first described) was that the collections consisted of irreplaceables whose value could not be stated in money. That is a droll notion. Sometimes it is expressed by saying art is priceless. Since some works are obviously valued above others (those on exhibit above those in storage) one must conclude that while all of them are priceless some are more priceless than others. And if none of them were replaceable, none would be insured. Yet they are. The museums did say that insurance values are less than the actual value of the works insured, which implies the actual values are known. They said that the value of any one painting depended on the other paintings in the collection of which it is a part, citing as an example a Fragonard for which the National Gallery had paid $875,000 but would have been worth less to a museum that already had a Fragonard of "the same size." This curious statement may mean that because a good is worth more to one buyer than to another its value is indeterminate or, what comes to the same thing, it cannot be valued. If that is what it does mean it implies the price of a good has nothing to do with what it is worth, except if it is worth the same to everybody. The idea did not appear in economic theory before that time and has not found a place there since. One which has been there for some time is the quite different idea that the value of a good is the price it brings on the market, and that, surprisingly, was also expressed by the museum representatives. They advised the National Bureau that an indication of the value of museum collections could be gotten from auction prices because "bidders are knowledgeable" (as in chapter two it was said they are).

In time, the economists of the National Bureau persuaded the museum people that their collections should not be omitted "entirely" from an inventory of the national wealth whereupon the museums did provide some information. In return the National Bureau concurred with the declaration that the "need for public support of the cultural and educational activities of museums must not be de-emphasized by the publication of the value of museum collections."[12] The declaration suggests what is probably the main reason why museums treat capital as they do: they expect it to be given to them. Would it not be used differently if it had to be paid for? Would it not be thought to have a monetary value, to have an annual cost, and to be acquired only in those amounts that could be exhibited, not necessarily at all times, but for such time as to use it properly? Would museums not refuse to allow their works to be put to extraneous uses, such as ornamenting government offices or the offices of their administrators? Would they not maintain a complete record of what was in their collections and would they not think it cavalier to be ignorant of what works were in it and where they were?

THE CARE OF "COSTLESS" CAPITAL

Museums now are said not to keep proper records of their collections. In a report made for the International Commission on Museums (ICOM) concerning the protection of collections from theft, fire, damage, and other loss, Robert Tillotson said that a necessary condition for security is a complete record of everything a museum has. "It is admitted within museum circles, however, that this is often badly neglected," he also said.[13] The result is that a museum may not know when something is missing. One may wonder how many museums keep a satisfactory record of their holdings even as they themselves define "satisfactory." Some do not have photographs of even the principal works in their collections. The Getty Museum has a photo archive program by which it is assembling photographs of "the important works of art in the Western European tradition."[14] It places an order for prints of each work with the museums it surveys, and the order is large enough to pay for the photography. The museum retains the negatives and the copyright.

Some of the recipients of this bounty will thereby acquire a photographic record of their principal holdings. It will not be complete, since the Getty does not want photographs of everything, so it will not fully meet the minimum requirement which the ICOM report lays down for security. That requirement of course would have also to be met if the museums were to report the value of their collections. As matters now appear, they are not only withholding that value from the public but from themselves. Hence if they are to be reproved for one they are to be condoled for the other.

They have a friend in the security division of the ICOM. "To discourage speculation, illegal trafficking, and blackmail, museums should not publicize the monetary value of their objects nor tolerate exorbitant insurance valuations," the report states.[15] The statement does not expressly advise concealing the total value of the collection but it can be read to mean that. The museum people in their discussion with the National Bureau said that if the public knew how valuable the collections were it might stop giving. And start stealing, Gilbert Ghez said, as much in truth as in jest.

Museums do not keep all of the components of their capital off the balance sheet. The value of buildings and equipment usually is included. Once upon a time, there was a major museum that did report the value of its collection. The collection was not as valuable as it now is or was the museum as major as at present, but both were of some consequence for their time and place. In 1919 there was published *The Art Institute of Chicago: The Collections Illustrated. With a Historical Sketch and Description of the Museum*—the sketch by the director, William M. R. French—and it stated: "The value of the permanent collection is estimated at about a million and a quarter dollars." *Mirabile dictu.* At present a few museums of a different relative position (for example, Denver and North Carolina) report the value of their collections.

The American Association of Museums estimates the value of collections in the United States but does not identify them. Museums themselves may do that about specific works. When they make an important acquisition, they often announce the price paid for it, as the National Gallery did about its Fragonard and the Metropolitan about its expensive Rembrandt. Whether doing so increases the risk of their being stolen, hence increases the cost of protecting them, is arguable. Art thieves can be skillful and know not only how but what to steal. But some are amateurs (both as Redon used the word and as it is used by the American Association of Amateur Athletics) and have to be directed to what is valuable. The information is available outside of the museums as well as in them. Thomas Hoving, with the enterprise for which he is known, made a list of the thirty works of art in America that he considered to be the most important and estimated the value of each. Their total value of $176 million in 1984 was, he said with characteristic verve, slightly less than the gross national product of Gambia and only twice the annual income of the Getty Museum.[16]

Whether or not thieves have to be told what is worth stealing, museums appear to have to be reminded there are thieves. When several Impressionist paintings were stolen from the Art Institute in 1978, the Chicago Police Department said they really should not have been stored in a broom closet. They were recovered, and the thief turned out to be an employee who had access to broom closets.

Negligence of a different kind was found in the Gallery of Modern Art of Milan in February 1975, when thieves stole twenty-eight paintings, including works by Renoir, Gauguin, van Gogh, and Cézanne; the total loss was $5 million at the prices of the time. The museum was equipped with burglar alarms but the guards, wanting to sleep, had turned them off. In Urbino the same month, a Raphael and two paintings by Piero della Francesca were stolen from the Ducal Palace. The thieves demanded a ransom of $4.6 million. The minister for the Italian Cultural Patrimony said to pay it would be to invite more theft. He also must have known that art thieves, unlike a kidnapper, have no inducement to destroy what they have seized. If they cannot ransom it, they can sell it, if for less than the ransom, still for something.

The issue of valuation is addressed by W. H. Daugherty, Jr., and M. J. Gross, Jr., in their manual of museum accounting. It states a museum is not obliged to report the value of its collection on its balance sheet and advises against its doing so. "When a museum elects to value the currently held collection, it has elected to undertake a tedious and time consuming task," they state.[17] That is not altogether consistent with the accepted accounting procedures for nonprofit organizations of all kinds. They are advised to report the value of their capital just as for-profit enterprises are expected to do by their accounting procedures. The reason is that both have a fiduciary responsibility to the providers of capital. The handbook does not say the value of the collection should be omitted from the balance sheet. It says reporting is optional and continues that if it is done the value of each work should be entered at its original cost or its market value, whichever is lower. A museum that chose to report the value of its collection by that rule could seem to be more in need of gifts than it actually is (on the supposition that the deserts of the deserving vary inversely with their net worth). A museum that chose not to report the value of its collection could appear to be still more deserving.

THE GIFT RELATION

A dependence on gifts (and subsidies) is not a necessary consequence of a museum being a nonprofit organization. It could, from the services it renders, earn an income sufficient to cover its costs. There are university research departments that do this (if one can accept their accounting practices—a large "if"). Moreover, an organization that does not derive much income from what it does—and most nonprofit organizations don't—need not be an organization that loses money. Nonprofitable does not necessarily entail unprofitable, as Professors Throsby and Withers properly say.[18] A museum conceivably could meet all of its costs with the income from an endowment, or that together with admission and other income, and some do. However, nonprofit organizations usually do rely on gifts and subsidies and declare what is a robust non sequitur—that losing money is simply their nature. "The very nature of performing [arts] groups along with their need for artistic freedom and goals make it both impossible and undesirable for them to limit their spending to what they can earn." This is the considered judgment of a 1974 Ford Foundation study and is so much like the judgment of the performing arts groups themselves that one may be excused for wondering if it was supplied by them.[19] It no doubt would be endorsed by art museums also, possibly more fully than by performing groups were that possible. Information about the finances of the two—information that is admittedly fragmentary—indicates the performing arts groups received about 55 percent of their total income from admission fees, while the art museums received between 5 and 6 percent, the former in the years between 1965 and 1971 and the latter in the fiscal year 1971–72. The remainder of the income of performing groups came from the yield on endowments, from government subsidies (at that time mainly local and state), and from gifts. Art museums also drew income from these sources and in addition received a substantial portion—19 percent, or three times the income from admission fees—from their restaurants, shops, and parking facilities.[20]

The gift relation between museums and the public does not induce them to accept anything and everything that is offered. There are no perfectly free gifts any more than there are free lunches (a first but not invariable principle of economics). Gifts in kind increase the cost of storage whether the works they replace go there or they themselves do. They add to conservation, insurance, and possibly restoration costs. They may even have to be photographed at an expense not borne by the Getty. Another factor that gives pause is the conditions that go with the gift. A donor may want it to be on exhibit at all times or may insist it not be in storage most of the time, may never want it to be loaned or may want it always to be kept within a larger collection he offers and want it to be exhibited in a particular way. Mark Rothko offered the Museum of Modern Art a gift of fifty of his paintings on the condition that they be on exhibit at all times, and his offer was declined. Some donors want to be assured that what they give will never be disposed of by sale or any other way. Then there is the effect of the gift on the quality of the collection and the standing of the museum among people whose opinion it values. They probably are not the people who comprise the majority of their visitors. This last consideration would apply to gifts of money as well as gifts in kind. One guesses the Art Institute would decline money which had to be used to distribute to the public at large a colored reproduction of what was once the most popular painting in its collection, *The Song of the Lark* by Jules Breton which before the remodeling of the 1980s was seen if at all high on the wall of a rapidly traversed corridor and now has a place in a gallery of nineteenth-century curios.

Another consideration is how the acceptance of a gift will affect the relations between the museum and the donor in the future. Will he call on it for information or services which it is not meant to furnish the public, such as verifying an attribution, advising about the care of his collection, or directing him to acquisitions? Will declining a gift of what the museum does not want turn the donor away from it when later he has something to give that the museum does want?

There is another consequence of the nonprofit status of a museum. The administrative officers have more power and the board of directors less power than each would have in a for-profit organization. This is observed in empirical studies and is attested by museum people. It is also what economic theory predicts, because the directors of a museum have less incentive to monitor its operation than they have to monitor that of a corporation in which they have a material interest. The administrators and professionals of a museum have an inducement but it is not to use resources in a way to secure the best economic return from them. Their purpose, if they were asked to state it, is to satisfy the standards of museology as those standards are enunciated by their colleagues in the field. That calls for building a distinguished collection, for staging exhibitions of what professionals believe is of particular importance at a particular time, for mounting the exhibition in the most advanced way that can be afforded, for conducting scholarship and research, and for employing advanced methods of conservation and restoration. In brief, the purpose is to excel. How well it is realized is another issue and is irrelevant here. The relevant point is that there is a difference between conducting a museum according to the canons of museology and conducting it according to the canons of economic efficiency even when the latter take account of the value of all of those things museum professionals believe they should be doing. A museologist believes money should be used to satisfy as many as possible of the criteria his profession says should be satisfied. An economist asks if those criteria are as comprehensive as they should be and if they take into account, for example, the interests of museum visitors, not by mounting expensive exhibitions but by inexpensive measures like being open at hours convenient to the public as well as to the employees, and by taking some art out of storage and putting it in the galleries which, admittedly, would make them less attractive to an interior decorator but more attractive to those whose interest is in the fine and not the decorative arts.

To be noticed also is that the status of the professional employees is related to the size of the museum: the larger it is, the more important they are in their field and the higher their salaries are likely to be. This obvious statement yields the obvious inference that the employees have a reason to increase the size of their museum. Not as obvious is that an increase in size may serve their interest even if the average quality of the collection slips (just as a university administrator may find his interest lies in lowering admission requirements a little in order to increase enrollment).

Still less obvious is that professionals have reason to resist measures by which a museum could support itself in lieu of being supported by the government. The museums of Britain acknowledged the reason in 1987 when they opposed two measures that were meant to provide them with income or capital. The proposal came from the Conservative side of politics, but would not have altered the position of the museums as government-owned organizations. The proposals seem to an impartial spectator to be of benefit to museums or at least of no harm to them. That is not what the museums believed. Or would an economist.

One proposal was to permit them to sell works they did not care to exhibit. The National Portrait Gallery of London, for example, has more pictures of some notables than it has space to exhibit or would care to exhibit if it had the space. Among its holdings are ten likenesses of Nelson, thirteen of Charles I, twenty of Wellington, and twenty-one of Queen Victoria. When the arts minister made the proposal he said the proceeds of the sales could be used only for the acquisition of other art. The museum people at first opposed the measure. Their stated reason was that if they obtained money in this way (which is obtaining it from the market) they might receive less from the government, not penny for penny perhaps, but net. One guesses they also opposed it because it would limit their authority to use their funds as they saw fit. Later, when the arts minister said he would consider allowing them to use the sale proceeds for other purposes, which would include administration, the museums modified their view, and some came to support the proposal.[21] The other proposal was to replace the annual grant the government makes to each museum with a capital sum and to direct the museum to use the income from the capital to meet all of its costs. This is equivalent to telling the museum it will get no more from the government than the income from its capital. This would not necessarily arrest its growth, since it could and probably would ask for more capital, but would make further growth more difficult, hence would limit the progress of the professional staff.

This is not what the editor of *The Burlington Magazine* (July 1987) said. She opposed the idea of a capital grant and did so disdainfully and forcefully, then deplored the idea that the arts organizations of Britain should solicit voluntary contributions as those of the United States do. "Private benevolence is too whimsical, too geographically selective, to be relied on," she said. Warming to the task, she deplored the idea that museums should be subject to the "insidious vocabulary of cost-effectiveness and consumerism," and they must not, she declared, give way to "the primacy of marketing." Oddly, a few months earlier (March 1987) the magazine reported it had itself received financial assistance from individuals and foundations, some of them American.

While the museums were looking after their interest, there were two other groups in Britain that faced a similar challenge and tried to turn it back in the same way. The BBC was confronted with the proposal that it sell advertising, and the British Council that it sell more of its services (and give away fewer). Each said the proposals jeopardized the essential contribution it made to British culture.

There is a droll side to the unremitting effort of museums to grow. It seems at times to make them overlook the distinction between a gross and a net increase in their stock of capital, or in plain language, to make them attend more to increasing their collection than to knowing what is in it. The Victoria and Albert Museum in London has such a large collection of so many things it does not always know the difference between what it has and what it is supposed to have. By one report, it does not even know what it is supposed to have because it never has had a "comprehensive stock-taking." It believes it has 7 million objects, more or less, and knows it has 7 miles of galleries, which comes out to a million per mile or 190 per linear foot if they were all exhibited which they are not. That is understandable but not always to the good, because in 1987 the basement of the V. and A. was flooded and objects in storage were damaged. The administration of the museum placed the responsibility with the Conservative government which had proposed to reduce spending on the arts, although the reduction had not gone into effect. At one time a painting by Teniers (an object of some consequence) was stolen, and the museum did not know it was missing until the police recovered it. Another time it did notice in the course of a "routine stock search" that sixty-eight objects were missing, valued at £68,000. The press officer of the museum stated, "The items could have been stolen, it could be an inside job, or the objects could have been misplaced within the museum."[22] In Chicago, at the end of the year when the Impressionist paintings were stolen, the chairman of the board reported: "In the midst of the turmoil the acquisitions and exhibitions of the museum continued unabated" and that the "collections were enriched by a record 1,624 objects."[23] In a history of the Baltimore Museum of Art is a chapter entitled "How to Govern Growth"—which arrested the attention of one economist. But it was not, as he expected, about limiting growth or holding the size of the collection constant, but about "how to fill the gaps in the existing collection and [how to] balance our collection so that all fields of art are well represented."[24]

The acquisitiveness also has what appears to be an irrational side. In North America the second largest collection of Italian painting done before the nineteenth century is in the Walters Art Gallery, also of Baltimore, and many are never exhibited, according to a census of holdings in North America.[25] Such behavior is irrational if museums are assumed to want to maximize the utility of their benefactors and visitors. But there is no reason to make that assumption. The people who conduct them want to maximize their own utility and do so as long as the effort which additional acquisitions entail is no greater than what they add to their utility.

Conceivably a museum could estimate the value of what it does and relate the value to its cost, that is, could try to make a benefit–cost analysis. In reality, an effort of that kind is one of the last, if not the very last, things one would expect of people who believe the values they advance are not among those within the scope of economics. The belief is not warranted, as I have tried to explain; nevertheless it is a fact to be reckoned with. The belief serves their private interest of course, but is not to be laid to that alone. All passes, even art, but the last to go are illusions about it. To conduct a museum in the way one would manage one's personal finances would be (by this illusion) to debase it. In the introduction to *All the Paintings of the Rijksmuseum in Amsterdam* (1976), the editor saw fit to commemorate the liberation of the museum from such a notion, which, he said, was put to rest a century earlier by a writer, Victor de Stuer, in an article "Holland at Its Smallest," who said among other things, "A smile will appear on the lips of many when they hear that art and the colonies—Rembrandt's *Nightwatch* and Java coffee—are lumped together in our index of interests."

People who are given to the anti-market mentality are also given to the foodstuff analogy in order to clinch their argument, as if nothing could better show the absurdity of placing an economic value on art than by comparing it with something to eat. The dealer in Paris who was mentioned in chapter one acknowledged he was engaged in buying and selling, but he did want it known that his buying and selling were quite different from the merchandizing of frozen vegetables. Where, one may wonder, would he place the dealers of the edible (though not frozen) art of the 1970s, if any of it found buyers (or eaters)? The paintings, a subclass of Food Art, were confected of sugar, gingerbread, and other comestibles. Let it not be passed by as another frantic attempt to be novel, even though that is probably what it was. Vasari in his life of Giovan Francesco Rustico (or Rustici) relates that at a banquet Andrea del Sarto presented the host with a model church. "The pavement was formed of jelly, resembling a variously coloured mosaic; the columns, which looked like porphyry, were large sausages; the bases and capitals parmesan cheese; etc., etc."

One may also wonder if the learned curators of the Rijksmuseum were troubled by the reference to the *Nightwatch* which after cleaning was discovered not to be a "night watch" but a group portrait (*The Militia Company of Captain Frans Banning Cocq*) done on commission in the brisk art market of Amsterdam where Rembrandt was a dealer as well as painter.

The aversion of museum people to the market shows itself in various ways. There are others. Several are related to the question of how important the number of visitors is. The question has a bearing on what admission fees should be, on museum hours, on its educational activities, on the kind of special exhibits it suggests, and on what is called its outreach activity.

ATTENDANCE VERSUS———

Art museums have never, to my knowledge, expressly made maximizing the number of visitors their primary objective or have they been inclined to compare their attendance with that of other museums. Of museums of all kinds, the most popular are those having to do with history and historical sites, except when zoos are classified (as they sometimes are) as science museums.[26] Art museums do report their attendance and use it when soliciting private and public money. The Metropolitan reported that one million people visited it in the four weeks of 1963 when the Mona Lisa was exhibited. The attendance the following year was considerably less because the World's Fair of 1964 "attracted many thousands of New Yorkers who might otherwise have visited the museum"—a remarkable acknowledgment of what can substitute for art. The Uffizi of Florence said it had 1.5 million visitors in 1980, and the Centre Pompidou in Paris claims to be the most popular "building" in the world.[27]

Moreover, attendance figures can be put to use in museum controversy. In a philippic against the new administration of the Victoria and Albert (and the Thatcher government responsible for the reorganization), John Pope-Hennessy said, "In any national museum, attendance figures are important because they form the acid test of whether or not the museum is doing a decent job." (His colleagues might think that a bit of an overstatement.) By this test, Pope-Hennessy said, the evidence is clearly against the V. and A. because its attendance fell some 50 percent between the early 1970s and 1989 (*The New York Review of Books,* April 27, 1989).

The reported number of visitors is not necessarily the actual number. John Walker said that when he became director of the National Gallery in Washington he found the actual number of visitors was about half of what was claimed, and he ordered the inflation to cease. He regretted his scruples on learning that the number influenced the amount of money the government gave to the Gallery.[28]

There are special exhibitions that increase the number of visitors substantially—the blockbusters—and there is disagreement about them in the museum world. The popular exhibits of the 1960s were dismissed as "jazzed-up dumb shows" by Sherman Lee, a commanding figure among museum directors. An opposite view of attendance was expressed by another commanding figure, Henry Francis Taylor, who said museums must abandon their ivory towers and "become truly popular."[29] He was the director of the Metropolitan Museum, one of the founders of which, Joseph H. Choate, said in 1880 that it was meant to serve "the vital and practical interest of the working millions."[30] He did not only mean the museum should welcome the masses. It should also enlighten and improve them, the former rather more, as education was to be more important than changing behavior. Improvement was the more important to the first secretary of the Smithsonian, Joseph Henry, who in 1874 said museums and religion could alter the kind of behavior that comes with the growth of cities, behavior that is inimical to "the progress of society."[31]

A later director of the Metropolitan, Thomas Hoving, is credited with or blamed for being responsible for originating blockbusters. His name reverberates through a solemn collection of articles about them that *Art in America* published in June 1986. Only Albert Elsen, the art historian, defended them. He did so on grounds that would be considered relevant by readers of the periodical, that such exhibitions were a unique opportunity for art professionals to obtain information, but he also defended them on grounds that many would not find relevant, that popular exhibitions are a means of thanking "the public that pays for our enterprise." Brian Wallis objected to them for the very reason that they are attractive. Being so they turn people away from what they ought to notice—the nature of capitalism—to an aesthetic experience they value. So Mr. Wallis seems to have said in what he wrote about the sponsorship of art exhibitions by corporations: "The contradictions of this moral program are nowhere more apparent than in the conflicts of its humanitarian pretenses with the neo-imperialist expansion of multinational capitalism. . . . The sponsorship of art exhibitions helps to conceal these contradictions by providing both the museum and the corporation with a tool for enriching individual lives while suppressing real cultural differences, for promoting art 'treasures' while masking private corporate interests." Mr. Wallis takes us beyond the species, anti-market mentality, to the genus, anticapitalism, and prepares us for the heady stuff of Marxism, such as the discovery, made by Eva Cockcroft, that the New York School of the 1950s was an instrument of American foreign policy and a part of the military-industrial-*cum*-abstract art complex.[32]

Before the age of the blockbuster, the very idea was deplored by Daniel Catton Rich, at one time director of the Art Institute. He objected to "the mass approach in our culture."[33] Concurring with Mr. Rich is Alan Shestack, who said, "One of the realities of big, popular shows . . . is that they are not necessarily helpful to the museum, since they cause such wear and tear on the physical plant and on the psychic well-being of the staff."[34] A museum in Kentucky reported how it was taxed by the exhibit of the collection of Armand Hammer which in a few weeks attracted 100,000 visitors to a museum that until then had an attendance of 30,000 each year. Of special interest to an economist is that illegal parking was not a problem because there were substantial fines and towing charges. Had the same principle been applied to the other arrangements, the exhibit would have been less taxing and more rewarding. And the museum would have shown it knew as much about economics as the police department did.

APPLYING THE PRINCIPLE OF PRICING

The principle could be applied to all of the functions of a museum: exhibition, conservation, restoration, education, scholarship, and what others there may be. Each could be valued at the price it would command or—what comes to the same thing—the (marginal) value it has to the recipient, and from these values could be obtained the value of what the museum does in its entirety.

The value of the exhibition function could be estimated from the admission fee the visitors would be willing to pay, specifically, by what the least interested visitor would pay, which (economists will recognize) is the marginal value of what the museum exhibits. Many museums already have some idea of what that value is because they now charge admission. The value multiplied by the number of visitors is the total value of exhibition.

Yet, is that what the pictures are worth—wholly, entirely, really and truly? No, it is not. They are worth more than the marginal value to all of the visitors except the marginal visitor himself. They would be willing to pay a higher price than he. A museum could capture this total value if it charged each visitor the highest price he would pay. It is not advised to do so, not only for the offense it would give to the sensibilities of art lovers and not because it probably would be more trouble than it is worth. It is a mistake. As a measure of value it causes the rate of return to be overstated when it is compared to the rate in the for-profit sector and makes the museum look ever so much more profitable, hence to be using capital ever so much more efficiently, than, say, a dairy farm. If each mother had to pay the highest price she was willing to pay in order to get milk for her children, curators would be out and cowherds in.

There also are ways to estimate the value of other functions of a museum. Conservation is worth what private enterprises charge to do it. The value of research could be estimated by the cost of having the research done. Then there is the income from private gifts, the income being the entire gift if it is used entirely in the accounting period or, if the gift is a capital sum, the income from the capital. Since gifts are voluntary, they must represent the value the donors place on what the museum is doing and for which they expect no return other than the satisfaction of contributing to a worthwhile endeavor. (Receipts from the sale of memberships are not of this kind or are gifts that entitle the giver to privileges.) All gifts are a part of the total value of what a museum does. What it receives from the government may or may not be a part. As explained in the next chapter, it probably is not. At any rate, it cannot be said to be a voluntary transfer from the public to the museum as a private gift is.

From the total value of all of the functions, the cost of performing them would be subtracted, the remainder constituting "net value." That in turn would be divided by the net capital of the museum, and the resulting ratio would be the average rate of return. Just as was said a few pages ago.

That is a big order, admittedly, but it is feasible. A start could be made by the museum world's overcoming its aversion to the principle of pricing and applying it to particular functions. An obvious candidate is exhibition. The capital cost of the collection is incurred twenty-four hours each day and every day of the year, irrespective of when visitors are admitted to see it. The more hours they are admitted, the less is the capital cost for each hour the museum is open. For a given amount of capital, that cost is now less in the United States than in Europe because American museums are open more hours each day and more days each year. The Art Institute, to its credit, is closed only one day of the year. Like all museums in this country and others, it conceivably could reduce its total cost per hour by being open longer hours. That would increase some expenses (on guards, light, heat) but not necessarily total expenses for each hour it is open. The decline in capital costs for each hour it is open could be greater than the increase in other costs. In order to know just what total costs are, the cost of capital would have to be recognized. As it now is not, when a museum estimates how its costs would change if it changed its hours it considers only operating or variable costs, and the estimate is incorrect.

An even more obvious application of the principle would be to the admission price. It is either nothing at all, or is a fixed amount, except for special exhibitions for which an additional charge often is made, or is a "compulsory contribution." Whatever it is, it does not vary according to the hour of the day or day of the week which it should do in order to make the best use of the museum's space. If the price was higher on Sunday afternoon there would be less crowding then and if it was lower on Monday morning there would be fewer empty galleries at that time. Just what the price ought to be at any particular time depends on how much attendance is affected by price and time. If the museum hours are taken as given, the proper price is that which produces the largest total admission receipts. A price above that would reduce receipts and a price that was lower would reduce them. The same principle applies to determining what hours the museum should be open if the price of admission is given. When both are to be determined, the proper combination is that which allows the museum to receive as large a return over its total cost as it can or to keep its losses as low as possible. This requires estimating, on the one hand, the relation between the price visitors are willing to pay and the number of visits they will make and, on the other hand, how the cost of exhibition varies when the museum is open more or fewer hours. This is an application of marginal cost pricing and means an organization—in order to do the best it can with what it has, that is, in order to operate efficiently—should engage in an amount of activity such that if it did more the additional cost would be greater than the additional activity was worth. This never can be done literally, but an organization can compare the cost and the income from different amounts of activity and choose that amount which yields the highest return.*

By choosing the most suitable hours to be open and the proper admission fee (there probably will be more than one), a museum can perform its exhibition function in an efficient way. But that is not its only function. It should attend also to the cost and return from the others, a more difficult thing to do. But until it is prepared to undertake them, it nevertheless may improve its efficiency by doing what is least difficult. One must say "may" rather than "can," because an improvement in the performance of one function can have an adverse effect on another. Whether that will occur depends on the circum-

*I am assuming that (a) a museum can change the position of the demand curve of visitors by changing the hours it is open; (b) given these hours, it can change the number of visitors by changing the admission fees; and (c) the museum does not operate under long-run decreasing costs.

stances of the museum: on the prices it pays for what it uses to perform its functions, on the way it performs them, and on the prices it receives for performing them. Beyond this, no general statement is possible.

If admission fees were fixed for the purpose of increasing net income (or reducing losses), they could be lower or higher than they now are. They certainly would be lower for the hours of the week that are least convenient and higher for those that are most. Whether on average the fees would be more or less than they now are depends on how much attendance is affected by changing them, hence on how the change affects the dollar amount visitors spend on visits. In the language of economics, all depends on the elasticity of demand. For the performing arts, elasticity is such that an increase in price would reduce attendance by a smaller proportion, hence would increase the amount spent on tickets. The same is probably true of art museums since the people who visit them are the same people—or very much like the people—who attend the performing arts. This does not mean they set the same value on each of the arts, does not mean they would pay as much for an hour in a museum as an hour at the opera, the dance, or the theater. It only means they probably would pay more than they now do if they had to. One piece of evidence is that they now do when they buy tickets from a scalper. But the additional payment can also be made in other ways: in the form of time spent in obtaining tickets or in standing in a queue to use a ticket already purchased as Americans did to see the Gauguin exhibition of 1988. Then there is the fact that for some arts preformances there are not enough tickets for all who want to buy them. Hence, an efficient schedule of admission fees would probably be higher than the present fees.

This is not to the liking of many or any museums. Even though their income from visitors would increase, their income from gifts and subsidies might decrease by a larger amount—so the museums may believe. If they do, they cannot claim they need gifts and subsidies because their income from admission is insufficient or at least they cannot claim they need as many gifts and subsidies.

Another objection to higher admission fees is that they would expose the museums to the charge of depriving the poor of art and of becoming even more "the preserve of the rich" than they now are. In fact, they are not. They are the preserve of the comfortably situated, well-educated middle class. While fearing such an accusation, the museums nevertheless deny that maximizing attendance is their principal objective. "There is no question, even for those in charge of museums, of considering attendance an end in itself," it has been said by Jean Chatelain, the director of the national museums of France,[35] two of which claim to be the most visited museums in the world, the Louvre and (as already noted) the Centre Pompidou.

WHO VALUES MUSEUMS?

Perhaps what the museum people mean is that whatever is the desirable number of visitors, among them should be the poor whom they take (mistakenly) to include all students, all of the young, the entire working class, and the unemployed. The museums propose to help the poor by giving them more art. That is interesting but is not surprising or is it unusual. Teachers believe a poor person should have more education, social workers that he should have more counseling, dairy farmers that he should drink more milk, and tobacco companies would not object to his smoking more cigarettes. What each group has in common with the others is that each believes the poor should have more of what the group itself provides (that is obvious), that the way to increase what is provided is to sell it at a price below cost or give it away (not as obvious), and that the money for the undertaking should be furnished by the government which is to say by people other than the providers (which is artful). What none has proposed is to provide it at its own cost. Nor has any proposed to help the poor by giving them money—not theater tickets, schools, milk, family counseling, medicine, or housing, but simply money—to spend as the poor wish to spend it. If they wanted any or all of these good things they then could buy them. If they did not buy any, that would mean none was as good as its advocates claimed.

What museums now do in the interest of the poor is to provide free admission at certain times. Visitors do not actually have to show their need before being admitted, and the result is that those who are not poor benefit as well as those who are. The Boston Museum of Fine Arts in 1973 had free evenings. Attendance was noticeably higher than when there was an admission charge, and the checkrooms, according to the attendants, were quite stuffed with mink coats. When the free evenings were abolished, there was a substantial decline in the number of visitors and presumably fur coats also. In the Hague, the Gemeentemuseum made Saturday a free day in order to attract workers and new visitors. The number of visitors did increase but they were professional people, or people who frequently visited museums, or people who lived in the neighborhood of the Gemeentemuseum. In Mexico, a study reported that 60 percent of the visitors who were not from foreign countries were from the neighborhoods near the museums.[36] (The fact that people who live near a museum are visitors is not trivial because it indicates a part of the cost of making a visit is the time needed to get to and from the museum.) In the 1980s, when unemployment increased substantially in Britain, the museums of all kinds expected the number of visitors to increase. Actually the number decreased 5 percent when the unemployment rate increased 100 percent. "Other" uses of time increased 93 percent, "other" being time spent at "picnic areas, leisure parks and pleasure beaches." Gardening and "wildlife" experienced the same fate as museums.[37] Museums wondered why. Why they wondered is to be wondered. Yet they did and after investigating the matter concluded, "the demographic characteristics of the non-visitors . . . suggest that they are likely to be the manual workers who attended a non-selective school, left at the minimum school-leaving age and did not attend a college of further education. . . . This overall pattern of results is well-supported by evidence from other surveys."[38] They learned, in brief, that working people do not visit museums.

The income of a person has something to do with whether he is interested in the arts. Working people with low incomes (which is not all of them) do not show much interest. But among people with higher incomes, the interest while greater is by no means extensive. So money does not govern the division between those who are fond of art and those who are not, the amateurs and the non-amateurs. Moreover, the amateurs have distinctly conservative tastes, "conservative" meaning nineteenth century and earlier. Linda Nochlin, the prominent art historian, has said that "the dimension of art works which sophisticated art historians, critics, avant garde artists or enlightened museum workers consider 'aesthetic' has generally been irrelevant, incomprehensible or antipathetic to the people as a whole." She noted a UNESCO study of the 1960s reported that museum visitors disliked a work by Léger done in 1917.[39] A French study reported Renoir was the painter most frequently recalled by visitors when they were interviewed as they were leaving.[40] The International Commission on Museums reported in 1969 the findings of a study of the "preferences and judgments" of the public about modern art. One part of the inquiry consisted of showing postcard reproductions to 500 people in Toronto. There were four decks of ten postcards, each deck containing paintings of a different kind. In each group, "the choice went unerringly in favour of the least radical, the most nearly conservative paintings available." The work of Mondrian (who by then had been dead twenty-five years) was widely disliked, and the fact was noteworthy because shortly before the study was made there had been a major exhibit of his work in Toronto (suggesting the amateurs of Toronto either had seen too much or not enough of his work to like it).

The *rapporteur* of the study was the art historian Theodore Allen Heinrich, who said the findings brought him to the melancholy reflection that "those who are buyers for the 'art galleries' of department stores do know what they are doing." He was not despondent, however, and said the taste of the public could be improved "with a little effort on our part."[41] Professor Heinrich's opinion is itself conservative if the word may be used to describe an idea of ancient standing. The opinion was held by the authorities of Athens who gave the poor money to attend the theater.

The museologists who conducted the inquiry were put to unnecessary trouble because what they discovered was already known—and known by themselves as the reference to other surveys suggests. A number of years earlier, the British Arts Council issued vouchers that entitled the holders to buy tickets at reduced prices, and the Council did so in order to cultivate an interest in the performing arts on the part of "an apprentice or working person who left school at 15."[42] Some 5,000 people asked for vouchers each month but alas most of them were not the deserving poor. From 93 to 98 percent were full-time students. Another British study reported that about 5 percent of theater audiences consisted of working people.[43] A study of American theaters reported there were still fewer "uneducated workers" in the audiences of the 1960s—between 2 and 3 percent.[44] This need not mean American workers were less cultivated than British workers. It could mean, and probably does, that they were less subsidized. In the United States in the early 1970s, about 40 percent of the tickets to the performing arts were given away or sold at reduced prices. The number of working people in the audiences did not increase appreciably. There probably would have been more had the subsidy been large enough to take account of the time of Americans being more valuable than that of the British. Time is one component of the total cost or price of attending a performance or visiting a museum.

The presence of students at arts performances and in museums is consistent with the absence of working people. The students are more likely to be enrolled in the leading universities and colleges than in those of low academic standing, hence are likely to be of families with relatively high incomes, certainly above the median and probably the average also. Moreover, some will be students of subjects that create an interest in the arts (as explained in chapter two).

One may guess that the students who have an interest in the arts are not representative of the entire student population. It includes those who are enrolled in undistinguished as well as distinguished universities, who are studying subjects like engineering and accounting as well as literature and music history, and who come from families that are poor as well as from those that are not. This is not inconsistent with studies that show the proportion of people in the arts audiences who have attended college is higher than the proportion in the entire population. What is shown does not mean that everyone who has attended college is interested in the arts, does not even mean most of them are, but only that those who have are more interested than those who have not. The gross national product of Bulgaria is a larger proportion of the world's product than is that of Albania while it nevertheless is an inconsiderable proportion.

Hence to make special provision for students, such as offering them tickets at reduced prices, cannot be justified on the ground that without art the students would be deprived of what so many of them want, or (in the language of the art world) would be denied the opportunity of satisfying "a felt-need." The special provision can be explained however. A student majoring in English if he attends the theater at a reduced price is more likely to pay the full price later than is an English major who has not gotten a cheap ticket. Or, simply, cheap tickets are an investment in future audiences.

How advisable an investment of this kind is depends on how effective it is. It is most effective when spent on students and less so when directed to all of the young or to workers or to the unemployed. How justifiable the investment is—a question altogether different from its advisability—depends on how it is paid for. The *Wall Street Journal* offers students a subscription at a reduced rate, and if the rate is less than the cost the difference is borne by the enterprise (private and operated for a profit of course) for reasons it no doubt considers sufficient. Milk is provided schoolchildren at less than its cost, and the difference is borne by the government for reasons the dairy farmers no doubt consider sufficient. Art is said to be different from newspapers. It is not said to be like milk, yet such losses as are incurred in providing it are said to be a proper cost of government. Two questions ensue: Why has government for so long assisted the arts, and should it do so? They are considered in that order in the remaining two chapters.

SUMMARY: THE MUSEUM AS AN ENTERPRISE

Art museums are an aspect of the supply of art and one of the two places where the process of supplying it comes to an end. The other is private collections. The process begins in the training of the artist (in which museums may have a part), continues in his studio, goes on to dealers or auctions, and there the art passes to the final owners to be seen, to be known, to be stored, held for bequest, or to be put up for sale again. If the best use of art was that which made it visible to the largest number of people, it would be better in a museum than in a private collection. But that is not the criterion of best use. If it were, the busiest street corners and the most traveled expressways would be lined with the greatest art of the world if it would not thereby be damaged. It would be, but that is not why it is exhibited in a different way.

From the point of view of economics or from any viewpoint, the best use of art is the use that provides the greatest satisfaction. What separates economics from the others is that it takes market prices as indicators of satisfaction. That is not all. It asserts the individual is the best judge of what satisfies him and, what is a quite different idea, that he should be the best judge of what satisfies him so long as it does not affect others without their consent. The satisfaction he gets from the visual arts may be no more than a fleeting stimulus to the optic nerve or it may be nothing less than spiritual communion. Whatever he wants from them, he alone decides and he is not obliged to justify his choice. This is what the amateur probably means when he says, often defiantly, I don't know anything about art but I know what I like. The remark has called forth untold mirth and unmeasured pain to people in art. There is no cause for either. He is only confessing to what they are known to accuse each other of being. So divergent are their opinions that if the amateur wanted to know all about art he would not know to whom to listen.

They differ over the most fundamental ideas, such as the meaning of aesthetic value, of its relevance to judging the importance of a painting, and about the place of aesthetics in the history of art if any. They differ over what an aesthetic object is, about what constitutes the aesthetic dimension of the object, and about what the non-aesthetic aspect is or should be or could be or was. They differ about what art is. If it is Tinguely's *Homage to New York: A Self-Constructing and Self-Destroying Work of Art,* by what definition is it also *The Ecstasy of St. Theresa* by Bernini? That is not a rhetorical question but a request for information from outside of economics. Inside, the answer is clear. Art is what people say it is and will pay for.

About museums there is disagreement over what their purposes should be and there is difficulty in discovering just what they are. There is disagreement over how important the different functions are, over how they should be performed, disagreement even about what a museum is. An argument of the present is about how (or, why or what or where) an art museum differs from Disneyland. In one exhange, the clearest statement and the statement most favorable to museums was made by the man from Disney.

The disagreement is more consequential in museums than in the market for art. While people with a high place in art discourse and debate over the relevance of aesthetics and such questions, people in a lesser place, that of buying and selling, go about their business. Buyers want what they want which is what they like. Sellers profit if they supply it and lose if they do not. For museums there is no such single, simple guide. As nonprofit organizations, they are directed by other purposes, goals, ends, motives, desires, aspirations, and the like—which taken together or separately offer no clear guide to how they should conduct themselves or how well they have done so. Of course a museum knows it should exhibit pictures, but how does it decide what those pictures should be? Whose interest does it mean to engage by its exhibition, and how large is that audience? Does its size matter? How much of the work of living painters should it acquire? Of works of the past, should it collect extensively or intensively: a few works each of many periods, countries, and styles, or many works of just a few? Are five different landscapes by Monet (which most visitors would find interesting) a better choice than five of his haystacks (which scholars might find more interesting)? The Art Institute chose the latter. Not even special exhibitions are simple. In "The Arcimboldo Effect," an exhibition in Venice in 1987, there were several versions of a single painting done by the artist (which made a bibliophile look like books or the other way around), and they were borrowed from a Swedish museum. And they were all copies. Were they included for their interest to scholars or to allow a rather minor museum to participate in what professed to be a major exhibition? And why did the museum itself ever collect copies, exhibit or store them at some expense, and send them travelling at an additional expense? How much of any museum's space should be used for exhibition and how much for storage? How should it allocate its resources among conservation, restoration, research, education, exhibition, administration, and possible outreach and uplift? In a word, how should it spend its money?

Not to make a profit, surely, because that is expressly not one of its purposes. They do not expressly include incurring a loss, yet doing so can be the consequence of omitting from its expenses the cost of the capital represented by its collection; that cost is simply normal profit. The omission is common in the accounting practice of museums. It makes them act as if capital were free (except when it is borrowed) and to make their collections larger than they should be. That they are too large is indicated in two ways. One is that museums usually have a deficit, even though their costs are understated. The other, not a certain indicator but highly suggestive, is the large portion of the collections that is in storage, more than half in the U.S. and probably more in Europe.

Whether the other things a museum does, in addition to collecting and storing, are carried too far or not far enough is, with one exception, impossible to answer because there is no information about how the other functions are valued and what they cost, that is, information that allows the functions to be compared. The exception is such peripheral activity as the restaurant, gift shop, and parking facility, the rental gallery perhaps, and events for which there is a charge. The value and cost of these things are measured by the market. Measuring the value and cost of the major functions is also possible by estimating what they are worth to those who benefit by them and by what they cost.

What would a museum be like that made such estimates and was guided by them, that is, allocated its spending among the various things it did in such a way that what was spent on each of them was no more than their estimated value? Or, what comes to the same thing, what would a museum be like if it was a private enterprise operated to make a profit? The question seems to be an invitation to think about the unthinkable. Actually, it is not. Most art museums in America are private organizations. While they receive some assistance from government, including tax expenditure, their principal support is the voluntary payments made by visitors, including what they spend in the gift shops, and by benefactors. A museum must decide how to spend its money and in doing so it implicitly values its different functions, asks if they are worth their cost, asks if more should be spent on one and less on another, and how much should be spent to raise money in order that more can be spent on all of them. Of all of the questions, the last—how much should be spent to raise money—is answered, one must suppose, in strict accordance with the marginal principle in economics. One would scarcely expect a museum to spend more than a dollar to raise a dollar. If it was an enterprise operated for a profit, it would apply the same principle to everything it does.

Admittedly, this is the lore of the nicely calculated less and more. Is an attention to cost and income befitting an institution of such high purpose as an art museum? Its original purpose was "to fortify the cultural reserves of the mind" (Bazin) and today is said to be one of the "objective, disinterested foci for the on-going cultural life of society" (Fry), a center which is responsible for interpreting the visual arts "in terms of philosophical principles" (Russoli).[45] Pinching pennies on the cost side and wringing a few more out of the public by raising admission fees—is that not the way of the corner grocery rather than a cultural institution? Actually both of them dwell in a world of scarcity and must make the best of it or not dwell at all. The difference lies in who says what is best for whom.

If museums so conducted themselves, what would be the outcome? Would they be smaller, have smaller permanent collections, fewer works in storage, more on exhibit that was borrowed from among themselves and from collectors and dealers, possibly for a rental fee? Would exhibition become relatively more important, research less important, and would administrative costs decrease? Would admission fees vary according to the hour, day, and what was on exhibit? Would there be more special exhibitions, and would they be simpler, and would installation costs be less? Would attendance be larger? Would amateurs be happier and professionals unhappier? The answer to all of these questions seems to me to be yes. Just why, I have tried to explain in this chapter.

6

Why Does Government Assist the Arts?

Not art for art's sake, but not art for the people's sake either. Art for my sake.

—D. H. LAWRENCE

WHY HAVE the arts received government assistance in one form or another, and why do they continue to seek it? The question is not whether they are entitled to it—that is considered in the next chapter—but why in fact they have received it for literally ages. The ancient Greek theater was assisted by the *theoric* fund out of which people were paid to attend performances. Adam Smith objected to the practice, not because he objected in principle to subsidies, but because men were paid more to attend the theater than to serve in the army. Cultivating the martial spirit was more important to Smith than cultivating a taste for the arts. He did not advocate subsidizing them but probably would have if he had thought the market would not support them. He said they served the useful purpose of diverting people from religious enthusiasm. Like all utilitarians, he believed government should have a part in improving the manners and morals, the tastes and the temper of the lower orders. Just such a thing is said today by people who advocate government assistance to the arts, some for no other reason, and although they do not allude to the religion of the lower orders they do shake their heads over the moral majority.

RENT-SEEKING AS AN EXPLANATION

There are economists of the present who have studied the issue of government assistance to the arts, and most have declared themselves in favor of it in principle. They have not looked closely into the question of why the arts have, in fact, received assistance, possibly because the economists believe the arguments they have made for it explain why assistance has been provided. I shall separate the questions because they are logically distinct and also because I am not convinced by the arguments in favor of assistance, hence must find another explanation for it. That which I find plausible is rent-seeking. The economic structure of the arts lends itself to rent-seeking; the arts not only receive assistance but solicit it; and the assistance is clearly to the benefit of those who solicit it while others benefit less if at all. Such are the leading features of my argument, and it is made here in a way that will be understandable to the general reader. It has been made for economists in a precise way in a journal article, "Rent-Seeking in Arts Policy."[1]

I do not claim rent-seeking is the only reason why government assists art; I do believe it is important and would claim (if a claim had to be made) that it probably is the most important. Rent-seeking, as explained earlier, is the use of government to improve one's economic position, specifically, using it in order to sell at a higher or to buy at a lower price than one gets or pays on the market. Rent-seeking is more common among sellers, including those who sell their labor, than among buyers who, however, are also known to engage in it and in the visual arts do so more than do sellers who create those arts. People who visit museums, who look at art, and who operate the museums get more assistance from government than the painters who create the art in them.

Individually and in groups, people importune the government to tax, spend, and regulate in their favor, and the importuning if it is effective brings about a redistribution of income and wealth in favor of those who importune at the cost of those who do not or of those whose importuning is ineffective. The "rent" of the successful is the difference between what their actual income or capital is and what the market would provide them. The consequence is not only redistribution but equally if not more important a smaller total income and wealth for the nation. The rent-seeking itself uses labor and capital that otherwise would be engaged in productive activity and in addition causes the remaining labor and capital to be used less productively than the market would use them, which is another cost.

The register of rent-seekers is long in the United States and elsewhere, and the people in art are far down the list. What they receive, while the total is not altogether certain, is far less than the beneficiaries at the head of the list, like farmers and homeowners. If a campaign were mounted to cleanse the economy of rents, it would not get to the arts for a long time. The head of the National Endowment for the Arts truly said on one occasion, in order to reassure his beneficiaries, that they need not worry about the effort to reduce federal spending because even if it succeeded (which it did not) the NEA would not be touched. It spends so little compared to other offices of the government. *Lanthano*—I am not noticed: In obscurity lies safety. In economic analysis, however, nothing should go unnoticed (except what is not worth the cost of noticing).

The term *government assistance* to the arts makes one think of cash subsidies but they are not the only form in which it can and has been given. A government can itself create or produce art just as it carries the mail, operates passenger trains, conducts diplomacy, and educates the young. The Hermitage and the Bolshoi Ballet are organizations within the government of the Soviet Union. The National Gallery of Art in Washington and the other museums on the Mall are a part of the federal government of this country. It does not have a dance company but does employ more musicians in the military than there are in all of the major symphony orchestras of the United States and buys more musical instruments than any other organization west of the Bug.

In addition to being what might be called a supplier of first resort (i.e., engaged in the production and exhibition of art), the government commissions art from the private producers and puts it in public places. A certain percentage of the cost of constructing federal buildings must be spent on works of art for them. The federal government also offers information, advice, technical assistance, and other services to arts organizations in the private sector. This assistance is a subsidy in kind as distinct from money. An example is the Arts and Artifacts Indemnity Program that assumes responsibility for the safety of traveling exhibitions and in effect insures them at no cost to the exhibitors but will not reimburse losses in excess of $50 million. When the exhibition of works from the Vatican museums toured the country in 1983 an additional amount was provided by private contributions. The fact will interest anyone who wondered about the economic cost of the exhibit. The interest cost alone was at least 12 percent of more than $50 million for the time the art was away from the Vatican where the economic cost would have been higher, in a nominal sense, because the prime rate in Italy was higher than the 12 percent it then was in the United States.

There are so many ways government in the United States (state and local as well as federal) assists the arts that the number of them is not known with certainty, not even those of the federal government. Linda Coe has compiled the *Cultural Directory: Guide to Federal Funds and Services for Cultural Activities.* It was first published (by a private enterprise) in 1971 and revised in 1976 to include 100 programs that had come into being in the interim or had not been noticed in 1971. She now lists 252 programs and in addition 47 groups within the federal government that render cultural advice and she states there may be others of each kind that have escaped her notice. Those which are listed range from the very prominent, like the National Endowment for the Arts, to those known only to a few, like the Joint Committee on Printing.

HOW IT IS DONE

When President Reagan took office in 1981 he wanted to reduce spending on such activity and he appointed a Task Force on the Arts and Humanities. It consisted of a university president, an actor, and a collector (Hanna Gray, Charlton Heston, and Daniel Terra, respectively). In his charge to the group he said, "Our cultural institutions are an essential natural resource; they must be kept strong." He also stated his belief that the institutions were more the responsibility of the private sector than of the government and he directed the group to consider how the government's activity could be reduced. The task force in its report concluded "the strength of America's arts and humanities is essential to the well being of the nation" (which seems to be a paraphrase of what it was told by the president) and recommended there be no change in the spending on the National Endowment for the Arts or the Humanities (which was not a paraphrase of anything he said). Other advisers to the president had recommended a 50 percent reduction. Thereupon the world of the arts mustered its forces. What they did and to what effect are reported by Fraser Baron in the *Journal of Cultural Economics.*[2] It is an instructive description of rent-seeking although that was not the intention of Mr. Baron (then an employee of the NEA) who meant to describe a staying action.

The National Coalition for the Arts was formed by the American Arts Alliance, the National Assembly of State Arts agencies, and the American Association of Museums. The last includes museums of all kinds, and the first is comprised of the American Symphony Orchestra League, Theater Communications Group, Opera America, Dance/USA, and the Association of Art Museum Directors, each of which has to do with an activity of the arts that is eligible for assistance of some kind, subsidy or other, from the NEA. An "avalanche" of letters, telegrams, and phone calls "descended" on the White House, the Office of Management and Budget, and the Congress. So Mr. Baron reports. Celebrities appeared before a congressional committee, one of whom, Leontyne Price, broke into song, "Save the Performing Arts" to the music of "God Bless America." (How the visual arts felt about that, Mr. Baron does not say.) The support of business groups was enlisted, and a conference call was arranged between several oil company executives and President Reagan. Oil companies are prominent among the corporations that advertise by making grants to arts groups, and the audience of the advertising is greater (or the cost is less) if the groups also get money from the government.

The National Coalition was probably the source of what Mr. Baron calls an "outpouring of popular support" which however is not the only reason he gives for the effect the campaign had. There was also, he states, "quiet but highly effective lobbying by conservative supporters" of the president. In Congress there was an Arts Caucus that regularly had advocated federal assistance. Its leader is Representative Sidney Yates, of Chicago, who in his biennial campaigns for re-election has been assisted by members of arts organizations. Finally there was the Presidential Task Force, two members of which, the university president and the museum owner, represented organizations that receive assistance from the federal endowments for the arts and the humanities.

The result of the campaign was that the appropriation for the NEA in fiscal year 1982 was 29 percent less in money and 39 percent less in purchasing power than in 1980, the last Carter year. That is less than the threatened 50 percent (money) reduction and was good enough for Mr. Baron to say that NEA had "survived." It continued to do so through the Reagan administration and indeed inches forward. By 1988 its purchasing power was a trifle larger (about half a million). Compared to its initial appropriation in 1966 ($2.6 million), its purchasing power had advanced by leagues (1,650 percent more in 1988 than in 1966). Yet when its partisans, i.e., its beneficiaries, went before Congress in 1989, they said the arts were endangered.[3] Just what did they want? "More," as Walter Reuther, president of the United Automobile Workers, said when he was asked what his union wanted.

Rent-seeking is more likely to be effective if the number of seekers is small relative to the number of people who must bear the cost in the form of higher prices, higher taxes, or lower incomes. There are only a few people who are engaged in creating art or performing it, and while the number of people who are interested in what they are doing is greater they are few relative to the population. On the other hand, there are tens of millions who have no interest in providing art or enjoying it. The few can more easily come together than the many to make their demands on government prevail, and that is all the more true if what the many lose as a result is a trifling amount for each person. An indication of that amount can be gotten from *Patrons Despite Themselves: Taxpayers and Arts Policy* by Alan L. Feld and his associates. They estimated the direct and indirect subsidies made to the arts by the federal, state, and local governments. In 1973, the total was about $700 million or $3 per person and $12 per family.[4]

The millions of families who paid this much more in taxes (or fewer public services) could have come together in a common effort to save, each of them, $12. But had they done so, they probably would have had, each of them, to spend more than $12 to save that much. Had the amount been great enough, making the effort would have been worthwhile. Such efforts in fact are made, as the movements to reduce property taxes demonstrate. On the other side of the $12 transfer—the side of the recipients—the matter was different. Each of those who benefited from the spending of $700 million did so to the extent of many times more than $12 per family because there were fewer of them.

Another example of rent-seeking is provided by an action of the Art Institute of Chicago (to which I am indebted for numerous illustrations, of a non-graphic kind, of the application of economics to the visual arts). In 1977 it learned the construction costs of new facilities for its school would be $14.5 million more than expected and it did not want to draw on its endowment fund for the money. The board learned of a state law that made bonds issued for educational purposes tax-exempt but required the issuer to secure the bonds by a mortgage on the land or building. The Art Institute could not provide such a mortgage because the land and building are the property of the Chicago Park District. The board thereupon persuaded the State Assembly to change the law, and bonds were issued at 5.75 percent instead of 9 percent. The saving was $487,500 each year, "a nice piece of change," in the words of the banker who managed the affair.[5] What the Institute saved, the rest of the population in Illinois and elsewhere paid in the form of higher taxes or fewer public services. That comes to a fraction of a cent per person per year, not enough to pick up from the sidewalk, let alone being a nice piece of change. Over the life of the bonds, it is something more—at a guess, say two dollars per family if the cost were borne entirely by people in Illinois (which in fact it would not be since federal tax revenue is affected).

Did the public object? It probably didn't know about the affair, and finding out would have cost each family more than the cost it could have avoided. Yet would it have at least objected had it known? The answer is suggested by a thought experiment. Suppose the Assembly instead of changing the law respecting tax-exempt bonds had made a small change in the state income tax, by which change each family if it wished, but only if it wished, would pay an additional two dollars, the amount to go to the endowment fund of the Art Institute. How willing the public was to subsidize the Art Institute would have been clear. This leaves aside what economists call the free-rider problem—that each family would refrain from making its contribution in the belief that every other would. Whether people in fact do behave that way can be disputed and especially can be when the amount is small.

How the nation at large feels about subsidizing the arts can be answered by the same kind of thought experiment: Ask the taxpaying families if they want to add twelve dollars to their tax liability in order to provide the subsidies estimated by Alan Feld. That is not the way their opinion usually is discovered. It is taken from polls; and to an economist, polls reveal less than observed choices. But even the polls (as noted in chapter two) do not show substantial support for subsidies. Thirty-eight percent of those asked favored subsidies for cultural organizations of all kinds, 34 percent did not, 14 percent were not sure, and another 14 percent said "it all depends." For art museums, 41 percent favored subsidies, the proportion being higher for young people and for people with incomes above the median. It was highest of all for "frequent attenders," and if it had been anything else the poll would have been odd indeed because it would have shown that people prefer high to low prices.[6]

The rent-seeking of the audiences for the arts comes at a low price because most of the effort is made for them by the arts organizations, like museums and performing companies which of course capture some of the rent themselves. People who like art differ in this respect from people who like the out-of-doors and want to regulate the environment. The latter come together in organizations like the Sierra Club which seems to rely more on its members than a museum relies on its members and which encounters stronger opposition, for example, from business and other interests that do not want their property made into a wilderness area. In contrast, the opposition to the rent-seeking of arts organizations is diffuse and more likely to take the form of grumbles by taxpayers (and a few economists) than to show itself in lobbying. By all accounts, the strongest opposition an arts organization faces is the rent-seeking of other arts organizations, because each believes, as Humpty-Dumpty did, that the more there is of yours, the less there is of mine.

THE RIGHTEOUSNESS OF THE RENT-SEEKERS

A feature of the rent-seekers of the arts is their righteousness. What they are doing—which is transferring income from other people to themselves, voluntarily by gifts and involuntarily by subsidies—appears to them to be something no one could object to except a philistine. In an article on the national heritage of Britain, the authors wrote: ". . . few would wish to be so ruthless and, perhaps, philistine, as to maintain, as in a letter published in the *New York Times* in 1961, that 'It has never been a principle of our society that the people as a whole should be forced to pay for the benefit of a few.'"⁷ What the statement implies, intentionally or not, is that a non-philistine or anti-philistine (an exquisite?) is a person who wants his art paid for by people who do not value it. Of course the advocate could say people who do not care for art nevertheless benefit from being made to finance it for others because the others are a cultural asset from which everyone benefits. The English economist A. C. Pigou divided people into those who produce welfare by making something for others, like their shoes, and those who provide it simply by being what they are, by "emanating" welfare (my word, not his). What the idea does not explain is why the lower-many have never understood the benefit they receive from the upper-few and must be compelled to support them (not entirely, of course, because the arts are not completely subsidized).

The disinterest of the public should give pause to people in the arts, but does not. Instead it directs them to still greater effort to make the public know how much it can benefit from what art provides and why the public should help to pay for it. The American Association of Museums has a Legislative Program that engages in lobbying. It was, by its own account, pleased to have had a part in the campaign of 1981 described above. In 1982 it organized the successful campaign to restore the $1 million museum subsidy by which the Art Institute, the Chicago Historical Society, and the Field Museum benefited. It announced it "was once again successful in defeating the Reagan administration's efforts to rescind the Institute of Museum Services' budget, thereby enabling the IMS to award grants to more than 430 museums in fiscal 1982." The Association's president in a statement to the members said, "I am pleased to report that fiscal 1982 has been a very successful year for the American Association of Museums, one in which we have been gratified to see the fruit of our labors realized to an extraordinary degree."⁸

There are other groups that engage in rent-seeking but they seem not to go at it as righteously. The farmers, the auto industry, textiles, shoes, steel, and others do of course claim that what they are doing is defensible. Rent-seekers of any kind are not known to say that what they are doing is indefensible. They may say that what they are doing is of value to others as well as to themselves. A sugar beet farmer may say that protecting him from foreign competition is perpetuating a way of life that should be perpetuated but he will not inform the public that protecting him has at times made the domestic price of sugar four times as high as the world price. Workers and stockholders in the American automobile industry are quick to say that limiting Japanese imports is beneficial but are slow to inform the public what the cost of the benefit is (which they probably don't know themselves). In 1984 it was a $14 billion welfare loss to Americans who did not work in the industry or own its securities.[9]

People in the arts not only are convinced they are entitled to assistance. They proudly speak their conviction. They are also convinced that the way the assistance is to be used is to be decided by themselves and not by those who provide it. That seems to be what freedom of art means to them. For the government or a private donor to tell a painter what to paint or a museum what to exhibit would be a violation of that freedom.

As stated in chapter two, most of what has been written on behalf of artistic freedom has been written on behalf of those who provide art: the painters, playwrights, and producers; the museums, theaters, and publishers. Yet the people—collectors, dealers, audiences, et al.—who provide the resources artists need have in fact had an influence on the content of art when it has supported itself on the market. There has, in other words, been freedom on both sides—on the side of the buyer and on the side of the seller—in the sense that each has had available to him alternatives among which he could and did choose. As the Stoics said, freedom consists in the act of choice.

However, the champions of artistic freedom dwell on the freedom of the seller. That is consistent with rent-seeking. A sculptor who is offered a commission from the government will accept it only if it adds at least as much to his long-term income as a commission in the private sector would do, and the former may add more if the government is so extensively engaged in commissioning art as to raise its price. The amount by which the sculptor's income is increased, because the government buys art, from others as well as from him, is his rent but is not all of it. If he is permitted to make the sculpture in the way that best pleases him he has an additional rent in the form of the satisfaction the work gives him.

The freedom of the artist to create as he thinks best is not consistent with the freedom of the public to have its resources used as it thinks best. A representative government has the obligation (not always met) to do what the people it represents want done. They conceivably may want to support the art that expresses the artist who created it. The opposite is nearer to the truth according to such evidence as there is. An example is *Tilted Arc* by Richard Serra which was commissioned by the federal government and placed before a group of its buildings in New York City. Enough of the people who saw it disliked it enough to mount a campaign to have it removed. The art community rallied to its defense and to the sculptor's, partly on the ground that it was not ugly and partly on the ground of artistic freedom which means, if it means anything, that the sculptor had a right to make it ugly. The government heard both sides and wondered what could be done with it if it was moved since it is 120 feet long and 12 feet high. In France, there was a campaign to remove the columns which the sculptor Buren placed in the courtyard of the Palais Royal, and the French Ministry of Culture chose the course the General Services Administration chose in the United States. It promised to move the art but was hard pressed to know where to put it.

Among people who are quite on the side of the government assisting the arts, there are some who nevertheless believe it has a right to specify what the art shall be and indeed has an obligation to do so. In an article about the assistance given the arts in Britain, Nicholas Pearson argued that the British Arts Council was not fulfilling one of the two purposes for which it was meant, namely, to make art available to the wide public (the other being to assist in the creation and understanding of art). Making art available to the many requires subsidizing at least some art that pleases them. Mr. Pearson did not go so far as to say this. He did say the Arts Council should be subject to more Parliamentary supervision in order that it respect the will of the public or, in his words, conform to the "social democratic ideal"[10] (which however may not mean giving the people what they want but what their social-democratic betters know is good for them).

When the issue is spoken of by people in art, or by those outside of it who are solicitous of its freedom, what one hears, in addition to statements of high principle, is much about the badness of "official art," and one is given examples: the stadium Hitler commissioned Speer to do at Nuremberg, the monumental sculpture in Turin that was done under Mussolini, and the wedding-cake architecture favored by Stalin. One then is diverted with droll stories like that about Marc Chagall being asked by a commissar what those horses flying through the sky had to do with dialectical materialism. One does not hear what was thought of official art by the people who had to pay for it, the subjects of the dictators, except for an occasional whisper that comes through. In the early days of the Russian Revolution, the state commissioned avant-garde sculpture for public places where there also was work done in the traditional manner. The public preferred the latter and tried to pull down the former. That was wrong by the canons of artistic freedom and progress but not so by the canons of tax justice.

Rent-seeking is not a one-sided transaction. Those in government who dispense rent to people outside of it capture some of the rent themselves. The members of the Arts Caucus in the House of Representatives can at election time call on the arts organizations they support to support their supporters. The employees of the government agencies and offices that administer the arts and other cultural activity would, if that activity was abolished, very likely be doing something outside of government that paid less in money and in other forms of income. Consider the *Cultural Directory* and its 252 programs plus 47 advisory groups plus an uncounted number of others. These activities have been undertaken by the federal government because there are people outside of it who use it to acquire what the market will not provide them. But each of the activities provides employment within the government as well as outside of it. The amount of labor needed to do anything in the public sector usually is more than what is needed in the private sector, and the nonmonetary returns usually are higher in the public sector, though the total returns are higher only in those positions people are waiting to fill. Note should also be taken of the fact that the activities are administered by a large number of separate offices. Why is there not a single agency doing 252 different things instead of their being done separately? The answer, I suggest, is the 252 offices doing 252 different things use more labor and yield higher rents than would one office doing all of them.

RENT-SEEKING ABROAD

The "world" of art can be understood literally as well as metonymically, because art and artists move from country to country and make the market for art literally international. Not surprisingly, then, there is rent-seeking on an international scale. The countries that engage in it try through measures of government to have more and better art than they would have if they had to pay the market price to keep what they have or to acquire more. Not all countries engage in the practice or did they in the past. It is most noticeable today in countries that once were among the richest in the world and no longer are. In an absolute sense they are better off than they were but their wealth has not increased as much as that in other countries. Britain and France are the principal examples. When they were at their zenith they collected the art of Italy, of the Low Countries, and, to a lesser extent, of Spain, countries which themselves had been among the rich of the world at a still earlier time. The British seem to have collected more foreign art than the French did, certainly more foreign art than English art, and the reason must be that they valued their own art less than the French valued theirs. Both countries today have a great quantity of art, their own and foreign, and in each country there are people who want their government to do all in its power to keep as much as possible within the nation. Outside of Britain and France there are people who would like to buy some of it and are prepared to pay the market price. It can be very high, over $30 million for important Old Masters, over $50 million for Postimpressionism. That is not much as government spending goes but can be very much to a collector who would like to convert some of his assets to cash.

The government of each country has listened sympathetically to the importuning of those who do not want major works of art exported, but has not acceded completely to their demands. One reason is that to prohibit exports entirely would destroy the auction houses and dealers who themselves constitute a group that importunes government. In each country licensing is used to control the export of art of certain kinds. In England a license is required to export a work that is more than 100 years old, is valued at more than £8,000, was created in England, or has been there more than 50 years. In France, the restrictions are greater and have reduced the art market substantially. In neither country is there any restriction of the export of the work of living artists. In neither is as much attention given to the import of art as to the export. That is noteworthy because it is as consistent with reducing the price of older art as is the control of the export of such art. Also noteworthy is that the United States, which is the principal buyer of art of all kinds, has no restriction on imports of art of the past or the present (except some fussy customs regulations by which something might be taken to be an object of use and not of art, such as a vase). The American policy is consistent with reducing the price of art to Americans. It is noteworthy for another reason. It indicates that American artists, as distinct from dealers, collectors, and museums, do not engage in rent-seeking in the international market.

Within the policy of France, as restrictive as it is, there nevertheless is room for the price system to operate, in some instances obliquely. So one may infer from what is reported about the Wendy and Emery Reves Collection of French decorative arts and painting. In order to bring the collection from France to Dallas, where it was to be placed in the Museum of Art, the Reveses had to secure permission from the French government. The request was important enough to engage the attention of the head of state, at that time de Gaulle, and he granted it. Before the works were actually shipped, a new government came to power and rescinded the permission. Mrs. Reves then made a donation of $750,000 to the government for the purchase of a Bonnard for a French museum whereupon the new government permitted the export of the Reves collection, and it now is in Dallas. It is valued at $35 million, or something more than forty times the value of the Bonnard which can be thought of as an export tax of 2.1 percent paid in kind.[11]

In Britain when an important work is bought by a foreigner the export of it can be delayed while the British try to raise money to buy it for a public collection. If the effort is successful, the buyer is denied his purchase and is reimbursed. Another means of limiting exports is tax concessions to British collectors who might otherwise sell some of their holdings. They must agree "to care for them on behalf of the public and provide reasonable access to them." Another concession—this affecting estate and transfer taxes—is offered to people who own art of "heritage quality" that they are constrained to sell. Similar in purpose is the National Heritage Memorial Fund which receives money from the government and gives or lends it to nonprofit organizations so they may acquire "outstanding national heritage property." Among the acquisitions have been works of art, the papers of the Duke of Wellington, furniture, and vintage aircraft.

The British government, like the French and Italian, allows estate taxes to be paid in works of art and does so in the belief the works might otherwise be sold to foreigners. Some of the art itself is foreign, of course, and in Britain most of it is. In Italy, it must be valued for tax purposes, and if it is valued at its market price it will be undervalued because export control reduces the price. The control also reduces the foreign demand, and increases the transactions cost, a part of which comes from the risk of collectors not being able to retain the art once it is acquired.

People who own art are made worse off if they choose to pay taxes with it and they also are made worse off if they do not, except if they are indifferent to the market value of what they own. There are people who are indifferent because they are not permitted to sell what is in their charge or do not wish to sell it. They are museum people, and limiting the export of art is to the advantage of museums. It also works to the advantage of people who are more interested in adding to their holding of art than in reducing it. Among them would be young collectors. The principal beneficiaries seem to be museums, and they are so for two reasons. One is that the art they buy or are given is available at a lower price. The other is that they are the obvious repositories of art that is used to pay taxes. There must be a finance minister now and then, in England, France, or Italy, who sighs over the value of a work of art that comes into his treasury; he must wish he could convert it to money to meet the expenses of government. He could get the highest price for it only on the world market, and selling it there may be forbidden. Even selling to a collector in his own country would bring reproach if the artist is important except if there is so much of the artist's work in the museums that they do not want any more. The heirs of Dunoyer de Segonzac, the French engraver and naturalist painter, offered to pay the death duties with his paintings and were refused by the ministries of Finance and of Fine Arts. The artist during his lifetime had given so generously to museums that they had all of his work they cared to have. The matter was settled when his heirs offered a Courbet which he had owned and a museum wanted.

After Picasso died in 1973, the French Ministry of Finance took two years to agree to allow the estate taxes to be paid in his art and memorabilia. It did so only "in principle," only on the condition that it select the works before the heirs could divide them, and that their value constitute 25 percent of the estate instead of the statutory 20 percent if the tax is paid in money; that is, the tax was 25 instead of 20 percent of the estate. The heirs nevertheless agreed. Had they tried to sell the art in order to pay the tax in money, the value of Picassos might have fallen, including what the heirs retained.

One is not surprised to learn that officials of European museums are opposed to the export of art, of the older sort of course, because it is more valuable to them than the art of recent years. One would however be surprised to learn that museum officials of the United States also are opposed to the export of art from Europe. They do on occasion express sympathy with the position of their European colleagues but none, to my knowledge, endorsed the proposal, made in England, that Mrs. Thatcher and Mr. Reagan meet at the summit to limit the export of works from Britain to the United States, most of which at an earlier time were exported from the Continent to England. The proposal was made by Mr. Denys Sutton in 1983 when he was editor of *Apollo*.[12] An American museum had purchased at auction a drawing of Lord Grantham, which Mr. Sutton declared to be a part of the national heritage of Great Britain. The drawing was by Ingres, the celebrated Neo-Classicist—of France. The subject being British may have made it British. If so, Rembrandt's *Aristotle Contemplating a Bust of Homer*, now in the Metropolitan, would belong in both Greece and Turkey, spending a part of its time in each and rather more in Greece since Aristotle is more prominent in the painting than is Homer. The Greeks have not claimed it but have claimed the Elgin Marbles from the British who rather inconsistently have shown no inclination to give them up.

Mr. Sutton did not advocate limiting the export of art in order to keep its price down for museums or collectors in Britain, and he did not advocate prohibiting exports entirely but only those that are in the interest of Britain to keep. Nevertheless, what he proposed is beneficial to British buyers of art or others who want to keep it in Britain and is detrimental to the British who wish to sell their art and is detrimental to auction houses and British dealers. Of course, it is detrimental also to foreigners who would like to buy works from British collections. American museums probably would have more Italian art if the National Gallery of London had been permitted to sell to foreigners some of its vast holdings, said to be the largest in the world in any museum outside of Italy, and if it had been inclined to do so. The point restated is this: Limiting the export of art distributes it throughout the world in a way that reduces the benefit it can yield. If there was a free trade in works of art they would be distributed to the people who value them most highly and who express their valuation by the prices they are willing to pay.

That seems to mean art should be in the possession of people who will pay the most for it and indeed does mean just that. An economist of a neo-classical persuasion will agree if he believes art is purely a private good and is a poor vehicle for redistributing income. If he is not of this mind, however, he will not agree and if he is not inclined to neo-classicism he will find more reasons for disagreeing. They are examined in the next chapter. In the world of art, there probably is no one who would agree that art should belong to people who pay for it except collectors, painters, and dealers wanting to make a sale. The sale might repel even those who think the world of art makes too much of itself. One who does is J. V. Bowman, and he wrote, "What the Spiritual was to the nineteenth century, the 'artistic' or 'creative' is to the twentieth; an excuse for otherwise unfounded claims to a superior order of being; an easy and innocent humbug with which to distinguish oneself from the common run of humanity."[13]

The people of the museums of Britain and the Continent must think they are of a superior order if they believe what they write about the international market for art. Mr. Ian Finlay may be taken as representative of them, not unfairly I trust. He was associated with museums in Britain for forty years and was a principal figure among museologists when he retired. He asserts as a fact that while the purpose of a curator is to preserve the national heritage the purpose of art dealers and auction houses is antithetical to preservation. It is to make money, and in doing so they "in the last resort . . . are helping to destroy our real wealth." That is because the consequence of their activity is the export of art. He acknowledges it is paid for but dismisses the money as a "mess of pottage."[14] In another British commentary, Mr. Alistair Hicks proposed that the art which Britain exports be paid for in a way that is novel, at least to an economist. "No foreigner could buy a vital piece of our heritage without doing something for us in return," Mr. Hicks wrote, and he did not mean a return in money. He would require the buyers to keep a part of their purchase in Britain or return it from time to time for exhibition or to build a museum in Britain. "The Getty would be pleased to come to any arrangement with this country that would give it a free hand with its buying policy," he stated (on whose authority he did not disclose). He gave the xenophobia a final flick by recommending that admission to museums should be free to the British but not to foreigners.[15]

Mr. Thurston Shaw, an English writer on archeology (not art, to be sure, but a not-too-distant cousin) has carried the opinion of Messrs. Sutton, Finlay, and Hicks to its logical conclusion. He would have all art repatriated, including the Elgin Marbles. He deplores the acquisition of art from the Third World and asserts it is gotten "largely through stealing, smuggling, and illegal export. 'By right of wealth' has now superseded 'by right of conquest'; 'send a gunboat' has been superseded by 'send a cheque.' '"[16] His opinion is similar to that of Professor Trevor-Roper, noted in chapter four, who makes no distinction between voluntary and involuntary exchange, that is, buying and looting are one to him.

Neither Mr. Finlay nor Mr. Sutton would concur and neither favors prohibiting exports entirely. If they were, the magazine Mr. Sutton edited would lose the advertising that is placed by dealers and auction houses who address purchasers all over the world.

RESTRICTIONS IN THE ART MARKET

The proprietary manner of the British (and French and Italians) is not unusual. There are only a few countries today that permit the unlimited export of works of art. The United States does, along with Singapore, Denmark, and a few others. Elsewhere there is control in one form or another or (it would be more accurate to say) an attempt at control. In most of the countries where the attempt is made and there is little or no European art, the intent is different from that of the European countries. What the former want to do is to retain their own art and artifacts, like the pre-Columbian works in Mexico and the native sculpture in Africa (where Nigeria after becoming independent went onto the world market to buy Benin pieces that had been exported when Nigeria was a British possession). The moving forces in the effort to control exports are diverse. One is simply the people in government who administer the controls, who have obtained better-than-market employment by doing so, and who some of them add to their government salary the extralegal perquisites of office like bribes. In some countries the method of control is licensing, and in many parts of the Third World there is a market, illegal of course, in licenses. There is no reason to believe the licensing of art exports is any more effective than the licensing of other transactions in foreign trade. Another interested group is the people in financial organizations, including those of the government, who believe the art of a country will attract tourists and the currency they bring with them. There is also the tourist trade itself and, finally, there are the local museum people who must have an interest in making their collections larger than they would be if there was freedom of export.

Restricting it is said to have a benefit which is beyond that of keeping works of art and artifacts where they should be (their "native" or "natural" setting). The additional benefit is protecting them from damage or destruction by people in the art trade. There are graphic accounts of how looters rove the countryside, find stelae, and remove them with stone saws or heat them until they shatter, or of graves being plundered, of pottery being torn from archeological digs, and so on. In the outrage which the accounts are meant to provoke certain considerations are overlooked. One is that the protection of property is a problem in itself and is distinct from the control of exports. There are more direct and effective ways of protecting art than by preventing what is stolen from leaving the country. Some governments find keeping it in the country an impossible charge and so rely on other governments to return what has been illegally exported. This is not surprising in view of the insecurity of property of other kinds in the same countries and of the fact that art in all countries is insecure. The government of Italy, according to a report published in 1984, has estimated that about $50 million worth of art is stolen each year in that country.[17]

In conditions of uncertainty, works of art are more likely to be handled properly if the export of art is free. That is because people who trade in art have good reason to take care of it. The better is its condition, the higher is its price. One also may note that taking art from the country where it was created—from its native or natural setting—has been done for centuries and is a museum practice of long standing. If it did not have such a standing, the objects that the Myceneaens sold to the Etruscans that were a part of the burial ritual now would still be in Etruscan graves—or in Mycenae. Finally, one may note that dismantling a work of art and making separate pieces of it is also a practice of long standing. There are many diptychs, triptychs, and polyptychs that have been sundered and cast among as many collections as there are ptyxes. To be plain, they have been taken apart and distributed among museums. An example is Sassetta's altarpiece *Arte della Lana* done for the wool guild of Siena about 1426. In the passing of time, one of the seven panels was lost, two went into the Pinacoteca of Siena, and the other four were acquired by the Vatican, Durham, Budapest, and Melbourne, each of which now has one. In 1988 the panels were brought together and the altarpiece shown in almost its entirety (six-sevenths) at the "Painting in Renaissance Siena" exhibition at the Metropolitan. At the close of the exhibition, the panels were (one assumes) again parted and sent to their separate stations over the world, one of which, providentially, is a religious institution.

THE PROPRIETARY MANNER IN RETROSPECT

As the proprietary manner is not new, neither is it unusual. In the eighteenth century the authorities in Rome prohibited the export of statues in order to conserve "the profits flowing into the city by the concourse of strangers who travel to visit them." So wrote Horace Walpole.[18] He did not mean the authorities had no interest in conserving the statues for their own sake, and he expressed sympathy with the Italian collectors who in straitened circumstances had to sell their art. "How many valuable collections of pictures are there established in England on the frequent ruins and dispersions of the finest galleries in Rome and other cities!" He named several of the Italian collections that had been sold and he also named his father, Robert (the free-trade prime minister), as one of the British who were on the other, the buying, side of the transaction. He also remarked, no doubt accurately, that the Italian art in England was cared for better than the Italians had cared for it. The British, having less Italian art, could be expected to value it more than the Italians who, however, did not value it so little that they collected English art, something the English themselves were less inclined to do than to collect the art of other countries. The greater wealth of the English enabled them to buy more art, of all kinds, and to care for it better.

England bought still more when Italy was threatened by the

invasion of the armies of Napoleon. They were instructed to requisition art. The Italian owners expected less from the French and sold their collections to the English who early in the French Revolution had acquired works from the collections of Royalist emigrés and from the "curiosity shops" of Paris where art that had been pillaged found its way. If the laws of the present relating to stolen property in the United States had been in effect in England and France at that time, the British collectors would have had to return their bargains. In the annals of the proprietary manner, an instructive event is the restitution France had to make of the art it acquired during the wars of the Revolution and empire. In 1814 when Napoleon was first exiled and the monarchy restored, the victorious powers did not make France return the art so acquired and which had been placed in the Louvre. That which was in storage and had been gotten in the Low Countries and Prussia was returned to them. That which was on exhibit, the king said, belonged to France as testimony to the bravery of its military forces. Why the countries from which it came did not insist it be returned is a matter of conjecture. The Allied Powers may have thought the monarchy would be more secure if the art remained. So some historians say and in doing so suggest one of the more unusual arguments why a government should acquire art—to protect itself from being overthrown. Another conjecture is that the countries from which it was taken did not have a strong case for wanting it returned. France had acquired it by treaty as reparations and as the spoils of war. Some however must simply have been stolen. Usually it is all described as "plunder" or "loot" which certainly misses the important distinction between property gotten by means considered legitimate at the time and that not gotten legitimately. In France the art was cared for, much of it, better than it had been by the churches, monasteries, and the royal collectors from whom it came. That the French wanted to keep it is not surprising. What is surprising is that outside of France, there were voices raised on behalf of its remaining in France. One was that of the British painter Thomas Lawrence.

In the event, restitution was made of some 2,000 paintings, 130 or so pieces of sculpture, and a number of other objects. What the works returned represented as a proportion of all that were acquired is not stated by Edward Alexander from whose account this is taken.[19] He says the Allies demanded the art because they wanted to teach France "a lesson" for allowing Napoleon to return and for the considerable trouble he put them to at Waterloo. What an economist finds interesting is not reported by Mr. Alexander but is in the unsigned entry on museums in the *Encyclopedia of World Art.* Napoleon, as Mr. Alexander does report, established a number of museums outside of Paris—in Brussels, Geneva, Mainz, Milan, Turin, and Venice—where the art he acquired was placed and became a part of the public collections of those cities. After Waterloo and the restitution of the art, the encyclopedist writes, "the legitimate governments continued this activity." Why, one may ask, was the art not returned to the collections from which it was said to have been wrongly taken? What became of the rights of the churches, monasteries, the royal and other collectors who once owned the art? Had they been compensated by the governments that treated with Napoleon and transferred the art to him, and was the compensation satisfactory to the owners? It hardly could have been to the members of the religious orders that Napoleon abolished. It may have been to the people in the conquered countries whose share of the tribute paid to Napoleon was less because the share was more for the owners of art. What is evident in this transfer of art—from the defeated to the victors and back when the victors became the defeated—is rent-seeking on an international scale.

Later in the nineteenth century the proprietary manner took the form that is familiar today. It is the defense a country makes against countries that have surpassed it in wealth and can pay higher prices. Germany, after its unification in 1871, rapidly became a power, and its wealth enabled it to compete for art as well as for other things. The private collections increased, but more noticeable was the expansion of the museums, particularly those in Berlin, and the energy of Wilhelm Bode, the major figure in them. As Dickens said of Pancks, so it can be said of Bode, that what he did, he did indeed. The Germans bought European art, as was to be expected, and they also acquired the art of Asia, Oceania, Africa, and the Americas. The collectors, the museums, and the art historians in other European countries believed they were threatened, and they were right in the sense that if they wished to keep the art they had and to acquire more they would have to pay higher prices. However, the issue was not stated in this way but was described as an assault by Germany on the sensibility of Europe and as an attack on the national heritage of the countries where the Germans were buying art. What was said about them resembles what is said today about the acquisition of art by Americans. A century ago the prospect of an Italian painting finding its way to Berlin (from France or England as well as from Italy) was as disturbing as its finding its way to California or Texas today, and the name Bode was anathema as Getty now is.

In time it was Germany's turn to be threatened, and after the First World War it lost art to the United States. Bode could have been expected to speak of Americans as Roger Fry had spoken of Germans. He did not. "As European collections became poorer," he said, "so did Americans become richer in their collections. It is regretful for Europe, but when one sees what enthusiasm for art reigns in America . . . from East to 'Wild West' . . . then one cannot really regret this development from the European standpoint. . . . over there, this new enthusiasm for art may nourish a native art from this strong pulsating life, which may one day help improve European art."[20] His remarks were as prescient as they were generous.

THE MILLENARY MOVEMENT OF ART

The art of the world is moving west and has been for millennia. Works passed from the Middle and Near East to Greece, then to Rome, and with them came the influence they imparted to the artists of the places to which they went. When the movement was resumed toward the end of the Middle Ages it was most noticeable from Byzantium to Italy and from there to northern Europe and England. There was, to be sure, French gothic and Flemish painting that had an effect on Italy. But the greater movement was in a westerly direction. It crossed the Atlantic in the nineteenth century and in time moved from the east to the west where it now is flourishing in Texas and California, much to the dismay of the British and to the benefit of those states. There is no reason to believe it has come to rest. The Japanese have high and rising incomes and, like others in history who have been so favored, they are collecting art. The National Museum of Tokyo is building a collection of Oriental art and defines it extensively to include works from Greece to Oceania. The director has stated, "To get works from these countries will be no easy task . . . good works are not found easily on the market. But when something does show up we must be careful to grab [*sic*] it."[21] If, as the editor of *Apollo* proposed, the prime minister of the United Kingdom and the president of the United States are to meet at the summit to control the export of art they perhaps should invite the prime minister of Japan to join them. He in turn might note that real income per person is rising rapidly in South Korea, Taiwan, and Singapore, and that in Hong Kong it has been high for some time. No one of them is large enough to buy a substantial part of the stock of art in Japan but together, say in a buying cartel, they might be able.

The westerly movement of art, if it continues, will eventually reach Europe, and some of the art will return to where it was created. That will happen if Europe once again becomes the richest area of the world. It would be richer than it now is if it released the resources held in check by restraints on markets of all kinds. The power of the rent-seekers being what it is (in the Communist as well as non-Communist countries) that is unlikely. However, in other parts of the world also there is rent-seeking, and it conceivably could become so effective that the economy of Europe would find itself the strongest by reason of the greater weakness of others.

There is more—much more—that can be said about government and art. What seems to one person to be rent-seeking can to another seem to be no more than an act of simple justice while to a third it can be doing what is politically called for. Beyond these views are the ideas of the economists who believe art should not be left entirely to the market. They are the subject of the next chapter.

SUMMARY: THE RENT IN THE FABRIC

Rent-seeking is not among the arguments economists have made on behalf of government assistance to the arts and is not the only way to account for the assistance. But it is plausible and appears to be the most important. In the arts—among the people who create, perform, and enjoy them—the reason most often given for their being assisted is that the arts are of an order of things that is superior to the market. But that belief, although hallowed by time and use, cannot withstand analysis, as this and the other chapters of the book have been at pains to explain.

A person engaged in rent-seeking importunes the government to tax, spend, or regulate—or all three—in a way that makes his income and wealth larger than they would be if he had to earn them on a competitive market. His "rent" is the difference between what he actually receives and what he would receive on the market. The arts engage in rent-seeking by soliciting favorable tax laws, subsidies, and regulations of certain kinds. The visual and other arts have secured assistance for centuries, not as much as they would like, certainly not as much as they believe they merit, and they have not always received it in the form in which they prefer to have it. But they have been assisted. The consequence is that in all likelihood there has been more art than there would have been had the amount been determined only by what people who value it were willing to pay for it with their own money. That is the way of the market. This does not mean the market has been unimportant in the history of the visual arts or does it in any way qualify what has been said earlier about the importance of the market. All that is meant is that the market alone has not determined the course of the visual arts.

On the other hand, not all of the benefit they have received from government can be attributed to rent-seeking. There have been times when what government has done it has done for its own reasons, among them the glorification of the state. That, more than rent-seeking, seems to explain much of what was done by the government of Louis XIV, in particular what was done under the direct supervision of Colbert, and it also explains why the Communist governments direct resources to the arts (and the non-Communist governments, unhappily, choose to compete with them). Also to be noted is that the visual arts do not lend themselves to rent-seeking as well as the performing arts do (for reasons an economist does not have to be told). One notices that government is more inclined to subsidize orchestras, opera, and theater than to lend a hand to painters. Museums receive assistance, and commissions are awarded to painters and sculptors. But the principal beneficiaries on the supply side are probably architectural firms because government spends so much on construction of all kinds which increases the cost of private construction including the design cost. Whether architects are engaged in rent-seeking is arguable. There is no doubt that museums are.

In the United States, the arts are assisted in a multitude of ways. There are 300 or more programs and activities of the federal government that affect them. The state and local governments provide additional assistance. Government buys art for itself when it places sculpture and painting in public buildings; it buys art for other people when it gives cash subsidies to museums to acquire works for their collections; it gives subsidies in kind when it provides museums with the land and buildings in which they are located; it provides services to the visual arts in the form of information, insurance for traveling exhibitions, and specialized assistance of various kinds. The most noticeable program is the National Endowment for the Arts, and it has become more extensive and expensive since it was begun in 1966. But what it spends and the spending of the other programs is less than the cost of the assistance the arts received from the tax laws by which individuals could deduct from their taxable income the contributions they made to the arts. This indirect expenditure was about twice the direct (or money) spending of the government in 1973, and together they totaled about $700 million. (The indirect assistance was reduced by the Tax Reform Act of 1986.)

The total came to only twelve dollars per family, too little for any one of them to mount a campaign against rent-seeking. Whether the American people truly objected to subsidizing the arts can be discovered by asking, What would most taxpayers have done if they had been permitted to deduct twelve dollars from their taxes on the understanding that the arts subsidies would thereby be eliminated? Such a conjecture is as reliable, if not more reliable, than opinion polls. Yet even they, despite their upward bias, show that a majority of the population does not favor subsidizing the arts.

Rent-seeking in the arts differs from that in other areas in being more confident of its legitimacy. Farmers, while they must believe they are entitled to a higher income at the expense of consumers and taxpayers, do not come before them as public benefactors. Another difference is the belief of the arts that they must be free to use what they receive from the public in the way they themselves see fit. The freedom of art, as it usually is defined in the world of art, does not permit interference by government (even though a representative government should, by definition, attend to how its money is spent). Rent-seeking in the arts is similar to that in other areas because it is reinforced by government as well as being made possible by it. People in government who administer assistance to the arts have an interest in sustaining it because it can provide rents to them as well as to the people who receive the assistance.

With one exception, government in the United States has lent itself to the rent-seeking of the arts in every important way that governments in other countries have done. The exception is the control of the export of works of art. The governments of Western Europe impose such control. It is not complete, because to prohibit exports entirely would destroy the business of dealers and auction houses. But limiting exports to any extent means the price of painting, sculpture, and art objects is lower in the controlling countries than it would be if there were no limits. Lower prices are to the advantage of buyers in those countries, including the museums, and to the obvious disadvantage of collectors who have their art there. The control constitutes a partial embargo on the export of capital. As such it interferes with distributing capital over the world in a way that secures the greatest benefit from it. The control also happens to be inconsistent with the elementary principles on which countries have agreed to engage in trade, the General Agreement on Trade and Tariffs.

The control is defended as a means of preserving the national heritage of the countries imposing it, which is to say, it is meant to conserve their stock of art. In Britain, where the control is vigorously defended, the stock of art consists more of the art of other countries than of the art of Britain. The British and French acquired art when they were the richest people in the world. They no longer are and they are losing their art to those who can afford to pay more in order to acquire what they want and to keep what they have. The movement of art from the once-rich to the now-rich has taken place for thousands of years and has been mostly in a westward direction, from Asia Minor to Europe to America and now to Japan. The underlying cause of the movement, as well as the effort to arrest it, can be explained by economics, and the explanation is another example of its relevance to the history of art.

7

Should Government Assist the Arts?

They tell me we have no literature now
in France. I will speak to the Minister
of the Interior about it.
—Louis Napoleon

GOVERNMENT ASSISTANCE to the arts has its advocates among
economists. Indeed most who have thought about it have concluded
it is desirable in some form or other. They do not all of them make
the same argument but almost all say it will increase the welfare or
total satisfaction which the resources of the economy can produce.
They ground their argument on efficiency, which is the primary, actually the only, ethical premise in neo-classicism. They are not of
course prohibited from holding other values, and there are economists who advocate assistance to the arts on the ground of equity.

Altogether they have made eight, fairly distinct, arguments.
This chapter analyzes the arguments and explains why, in my view,
they are not convincing. The form of assistance most often recommended is a subsidy, and it can be made directly in money or indirectly by way of tax reductions to private donors; it can be in the
form of services, or a capital good like a building, land, or work of
art. Five of the arguments rest on an assumption about the demand
for art, that is, about the benefit it yields to people who experience

it. Three rest on one property or another of the supply of art, that is, about the way art comes into being and what it costs. Some of the arguments are not consistent with others. No economist who goes before his peers to argue for a subsidy would, if he wished to be heard, argue in all of the eight ways. Each of the arguments, so far as I know, has its origin in an analysis of the economics of the performing arts. But each is also relevant, though possibly not as plainly, to the visual arts; and the relation of each to the visual arts is what is examined here. My objections to the arguments have nothing to do with where they originated. I object to them when they are made on behalf of the performing arts as much as when they are made for the visual arts.

The purpose of this chapter is not to engage my colleagues in a debate over government assistance to the arts. It is to place before the general reader my belief that the case for government assistance has not been established and that until it is the arts should support themselves with whatever assistance they can secure from the private sector. If what I have to say invites debate, let the invitation extend to everyone: to people in the arts, in economics, and every other place where there is interest in the question.

Actually, what economists have said on behalf of government assistance is, when put in ordinary language, much like the arguments made for it by people outside of economics. The difference between them is that the economists have stated the case for assistance in greater detail, more carefully, and usually in a form in which it can be confronted with the facts. This seems to say the economists have argued more effectively for assisting the arts than have people in the arts, and that is what it does say.

EIGHT UNCONVINCING ARGUMENTS

The arguments will first be stated in summary form, then described in detail, and analyzed. The five that rest on a property of demand are:

1.   Art is a public good, which means its benefit is so extensive (like the benefit of maintaining public order) and at the same time is

so difficult to price (as again public order is) that it cannot be left to the market. If there is to be a sufficient amount and it is to be distributed properly, it must be subsidized.

2. Art yields positive externalities, which means that in addition to the people it benefits directly, it benefits others indirectly, hence to assure that the total benefit is as large as it should be art must be subsidized.

3. Art is a merit good, which, as explained earlier, is a good people believe they should have more of but do not demand more even though they can afford it. If they are to have what they believe they should have, it must be subsidized.

4. The demand for art depends on the supply, in the sense that without art being made available to people they never would know its value, and in order that it be available in the proper amount it must be subsidized.

5. Art should be available to everyone, for reasons of equity as well as efficiency, and not available only to those who can afford it. To make it so, it must be subsidized.

The arguments that rest on a property of supply are:

6. Art is made under conditions of decreasing average cost. Theaters and concert halls are large, so are museums. If they are to be utilized fully the price of admission must be low. But at a low price they cannot pay for themselves. A subsidy is called for to make up the loss.

7. Art is labor intensive, which means it requires a large amount of labor relative to that needed in many other activities. Labor becomes expensive over time, hence the cost and price of art rise correspondingly. Without a subsidy to keep the price down, the amount of art demanded and the amount available diminishes.

8. The stock of art must be maintained, and as maintaining it is not a profitable activity there must be a subsidy.

The arguments of the economists can be put alongside what others have said about the market for art and about the need for government assistance. Mr. Ian Finlay, whose strong views on several subjects have been reported in previous chapters, is of the opinion that a country which allows its art to be sold in unlimited amount to foreigners is a country that is permitting dealers to destroy its "real wealth."[1] What Mr. Finlay claims is claimed in the eighth argument, that without government assistance the stock of art cannot be properly conserved. The measures taken by Colbert as minister of economic affairs under Louis XIV were meant to make the art of France the greatest in the world. He enlarged the Gobelin factory and made it a public enterprise for the production of paintings and works of decorative art as well as of tapestries. Through the intermediation of Charles Le Brun he laid down the particulars in the manner of a manager laying down product specifications which in fact they were. Colbert, in using art for the purpose of placing the glory of France before the world, used art as a public good. His purpose was not altogether realized. French painting did not surpass Italian, did not, in the opinion of some, equal it, and in the opinion of others was distinctly inferior. That was 300 years ago.

Colbert's effort is still being made. The Communist countries do it on a grand scale. But the first argument, the public good claim, is to be noticed in other places also. An English television executive, Mr. Melvin Bragg, said in 1986, "Clearly we want orchestras, opera and dance and theater companies; we want art galleries and exhibitions, whether we see these undertakings as the essential ornaments and proper civilized features of our society or consider them chiefly as educational and social imperatives" (*Daily Telegraph,* November 15, 1986). Mr. Bragg said this is an indignant reply to a proposal by Mr. Martin J. Anderson, of the Institute of Economic Affairs, that the market should have greater authority over the arts and the British Council less. What Mr. Bragg said comes also within the third argument, that art is a merit good (if "essential ornament" is an oxymoron).

What governments today say in justification of assisting the arts comes, most of it, within the same argument, that the arts are something people should have more of even though they do not care to pay for more (or even for what they have). Professors Throsby and Withers have observed the policies of governments the world over and report the merit good argument is the most common.[2] One notices however that other arguments are also mustered. When the National Endowment for the Arts was established in the United States, one of its stated purposes was to inform the world that Americans valued the arts as well as the sciences and technology. That makes the arts a public good in America. They also have been made out to be a public "bad," as indicated in the preceding chapter which reported the ideas of Brian Wallis and others that American art is the opiate of the American people and a weapon in the Cold War. Whether the idea strengthens or weakens the argument that art has public qualities, the reader is authorized to decide.

The Presidential Task Force on the Arts and Humanities made its report of 1981 in a minor key. It began, "The strength of America's arts and humanities is essential to the well being of the nation."[3] That makes them a public good, of course, but suggests they have a prosaic quality, that they are a kind of necessity. Lionel Robbins in "Art and the State" said the fostering of the arts by the state was to the benefit of much wider sections of the community than the market can serve in much the same way as the benefits of "the apparatus of public hygiene or of a well-planned urban landscape."[4] Not everyone in art would be pleased to hear it compared with public hygiene but no doubt would rather hear that than to be told it is an instrument of war and imperialism. Lionel Robbins is the English economist who was noted above for the opinion that while some works of art never should leave the country where they were created (read: Italy) those which had gotten to England should remain there, the state should provide money to keep them there, and should provide more money to add to them.

The merit good argument is used outside of government as well as in it. The French dealer used the idea—he who, while acknowledging he was a merchant, wanted to make clear that he was not the kind who merchandized frozen peas.[5] So was de Stuer, the Dutch writer of the nineteenth century, who accused his countrymen of being small-minded when they "lumped together in our index of interests" their art and their colonies, Rembrandt and Java coffee.[6]

The merit good argument was used by William Morris, the socialist of the chair and archenemy of "competitive commerce" (which he held responsible for, *inter alia,* the misplacing of aitches). In "Art, Wealth, and Riches" (1884), he argued that to leave art to the market was to assure the triumph of the cheap and the nasty, a common notion in England for centuries and given new life at the beginning of the nineteenth century by William Cobbett.[7] Morris also argued that art brings benefits in addition to those of an aesthetic kind. It is life enhancing, it improves the taste of the common people, it cultivates pride of workmanship, and others[8]—all of which mean it yields positive externalities, a term Morris might have thought barbaric and if he had one would understand why. He also argued for making art available to the great mass of people, hence touching on the fifth argument, that subsidies are called for on grounds of equity.

Morris, disciple of Ruskin that he was, took a more realistic view of the great mass of people than do most advocates who want to bring art to it. He said, "People need some preliminary instruction before they can get all the good possible to be got."[9] He was not realistic enough however. "Preliminary instruction" in the arts had been offered for centuries before he wrote, without its having the desired effects, and it continues to be offered.

One who espoused it recently in Britain was Professor Richard Hoggart. In *Speaking to Each Other,* he stated, "The basis of the case for spending more public money on the arts" is that they make the imaginative life more diverse and open and that they can lessen the "damp, illiberal" quality of British society. This is so, he argued, because the arts, being acts of love, celebrate life, and because being about truth they are a force that liberates.[10] Most of this was said before Mr. Hoggart said it. Holman Hunt said the principle of the Pre-Raphaelite Brotherhood was "Art is Love." If no one before Mr. Hoggart had ever said art fosters the imaginative life the reason could be that it is like saying the creative life is creative. Any number of people have said art is liberating though few have explained what that means. What is unique in Mr. Hoggart's remarks is the thought that art can lessen the "dampness" of society. That seems to place them outside of anything economists have said about the case for spending more public money on the arts. He may have meant that if there was more art in Britain, there would be some sparkle and bubble in the British, or if not all that, then a little zip and zest. Having undergone this alteration the people of Britain might conceivably come together in a union of fellow feeling and thereby satisfy the human craving for solidarity.

By this free association, for which Professor Hoggart is *not* responsible, his ideas can be brought into correspondence with what was said by an economist and a very celebrated one. Keynes in 1936 opened a BBC series on the subject and came out strongly for subsidies.[11] He derided the idea that the arts should pay for themselves, calling it "the utilitarian and economic ideal," saying it had no place in history and claiming the sponsorship of art by government was more common than was the practice of art supporting itself on the market. He made particular mention of "public shows and ceremonies" and said they were the means by which people could come together and show their fellow feeling. He did not say they dispelled the dampness of society, but if one may glide to that from the craving for solidarity one then may place Mr. Hoggart beside him. Or perhaps beside Lord Robbins whose likening art to public hygiene conceivably could include its removing dampness.

Keynes was cavalier with the facts, a not unusual thing for him to be. There is no evidence the arts have gotten more support from the state than from the market. They have been assisted by government for ages but there is no information about what proportion that assistance has borne to the income received from the market and private donors. He said democracies had abolished public shows and ceremonies in the belief they were fit only for children or savages. Could he have been thinking of Roman spectacles? They were savage certainly but just as certainly gave people an opportunity to express their solidarity. The "utilitarian and economic ideal" that he scorned was his term for classical economics. One would have to look at it very closely to find it stating that things always must pay for themselves and, excepting in Ricardo, one in the end would not find anything. Ricardo was a *bête noire* of Keynes, and while he was the greatest member of the classical school (in the view of one professional) he was by no means all of it.

The BBC series continued with talks by people in the arts of the Soviet Union, France, Germany, Italy, and the United States.[12] The Russian said the function of art was to contribute to the building of socialism, and his talk included the obligatory praise of Stalin. The Frenchman was pleased to say the artists in his country had rallied around the Popular Front government of the day. The German praised the control of art by the National Socialist government and condemned "experimental art" in the way the Russian did. The Italian said nothing about the relation of art to the state and much about himself as a founder of the Futurist movement. The American representative was the cultural historian and critic Lewis Mumford, and he could only say the Works Projects Administration had given employment to artists and that the Depression of the time, which had brought the WPA into being, had made them class conscious. The series was concluded by Clive Bell, one of the Bloomsbury group and a friend of Keynes, who called the Italian a coxcomb bawling out praises of himself, called the art of the Soviet Union "penny dreadful," and said, "All that the state can do for art is to give the artist enough to eat and leave him alone." That is a principle which few artists who have been supported by the state, or the market, would find satisfactory. They have not objected to being left alone (and hoped they would be) but they wanted more than enough to eat.

The "public shows and ceremonies" which Keynes called for may be taken as public goods, hence what he said on behalf of subsidizing them places his remarks in the first argument. A detailed consideration of it and of the others is in order. It is best done by examining first what they have in common.

All of the arguments share an assumption about the benefit of subsidies and all but one of them share another about how the cost should be borne. The assumptions usually are not made explicit but they nevertheless are necessary to each argument.

A. All must assume that a subsidy or other form of government assistance to a specific art activity will yield as much benefit as would be gotten from subsidizing something else, another art or non-art activity, or from not subsidizing art at all but leaving it to the market. This is merely a condition that must be met if money—or, better, resources—are not to be wasted, whether they belong to the government, a business firm, or a household. In the language of economics, the condition is that the marginal rate of return to capital should be the same in all employments of a given risk.

B. The other assumption is that the subsidy should be financed in a way that makes the people who benefit from it the people who pay for it. If a subsidy benefits everyone, it should be paid for by taxing each person in proportion to his benefit; if it benefits only particular people, they and they alone should bear the cost of it. This is an application of the principle of just taxation that was stated by the Swedish economist Eric Lindahl. [It is that the marginal tax burden on each person should be proportional to that person's marginal benefit from the way taxes are spent. The two assumptions are identical if returns and costs are defined as realized and foregone utility respectively.] The principle stated in ordinary language is that things in a supermarket are best arranged if each person in the checkout line pays for his own groceries, not for someone else's, and the store's overhead is included in prices. The principle applies to all of the arguments except the fifth, which calls for the redistribution of art.

Economists and others who favor subsidies could say, and probably would, that these two conditions never can be met in the world of here-and-now but are meant for the never-never land of the seminar room. To insist on them, one is told (as if one didn't know), would rule out almost any conceivable policy. That may be so, but the argument for subsidizing the arts is not made stronger by showing the argument for other subsidies is just as weak. The advocates of subsidies of any kind, if they wished to be candid, could say the claims they make are conceivably true (which also means they are conceivably not), then invite the public to pay for them on the principle that if there is no way of knowing the outcome of an event one may as well suppose it is as likely to be favorable as to be unfavorable. Half of the subsidies then would be expected to justify themselves and the other half to be a mistake. A defense of this kind is not however in the rhetoric of advocates.

ART AS A PUBLIC GOOD

1. Art is a public good. In its pure form, a public good has three properties: one person can use more of it without there being less of it available to everyone else; no one can be denied access to it; and everyone must use it or be affected by it whether one wants to be or not. An example of a pure public good is a measure of foreign policy like a treaty that is meant to increase the security of a nation from foreign attack. If it makes everyone feel more secure, the additional security experienced by any one person is not acquired at the cost of making another person feel less secure. That corresponds to the first property. The second is indicated by the impossibility of denying the benefit of the treaty to any one person (except by making him leave the country). The third is indicated by the fact that the treaty affects everyone. If it doesn't make everyone feel more secure, but makes some people feel less while making others feel more secure, everyone is nevertheless affected by it, and it is a public "good" that is a "bad" to some people.

There are several ways, economists have said, in which art is a public good. Lionel Robbins made it a part of the cultural heritage of a country, hence a value that by definition should be preserved.[13] To ask each person to contribute voluntarily to preserving it would be impractical or impossible. Each person receives the benefit of its being preserved whether or not he contributes and each person knowing this will wait for others to contribute. So the "free rider" notion claims. The cultural heritage is in two parts. One is the art of the past that a nation possesses: the paintings in public and private collections, the sculpture, architecture, and decorative arts, the music that has been written, the drama, and the choreography that has been created. The other part is the tradition of doing such things: painting, constructing, composing, performing, dancing, writing, acting, and the like. The latter part is what properly belongs in the argument that art should be subsidized as a public good because only in that way will the activity be perpetuated. The former makes art a part of the store of valuable objects that a nation should preserve and properly belongs in the eighth argument, that only by subsidies will the store be maintained.

Another reason why art is a public good has been offered by Thomas G. Moore and William J. Baumol.[14] They claim art is an activity of which the people of a country are proud and want to see assisted. When government does assist it, people have (in Baumol's words) "the pleasure one feels when one's political system produces results which we consider virtuous." But people will not come forward and voluntarily contribute to the assistance, even though the gratification it yields is something they are willing to pay for. They will not because they will expect others to come forward and pay (that is, they will wait for a "free ride").

A third conception of art as a public good is that it is something people value not because they continuously experience it, as they do the cultural heritage, but because it is available as an option open to them, to have if they should want it. In this conception, the people of Australia (where opinion about art options has been polled[15]) think of the Sydney opera with pleasure, not because it is evidence of the nation's culture but because it is something that is there for them to attend should they wish (putting to one side the ticket price, the distance, and time). Here the definition of a public good turns entirely on its first property, that it is a good one person can use without reducing the amount available to others. Every Australian can take pleasure in the knowledge that should he want to go to the opera, Sydney is available to him. The other properties—that access to the good cannot be denied anyone and that everyone must use it—are not present. What the idea describes is, in the language of economics, an option demand.

A fourth conception of art as a public good makes it a source of national pride (which is enhanced by the admiration and the envy of people of other nations). In this view, the Australians value the Sydney opera not because they may want to attend some day, but because it is respected over the world. It is valued by people who have no interest whatever in opera, but are proud of their country. Paul said of Cilicia, "I am a resident of no mean city"; and (some of the) people of Chicago have said that about their city for its architecture, its football team, and its mayors. The Australians have carried the idea further and say art can give a nation an identity. They speak of the "Australia-ness" of their art. They did not originate the idea. It is quite old and has been expressed in one form or another in many places. Russia is associated with its distinctive music, Britain with its literature (and economics), Austria with the baroque, the Scandinavian countries with contemporary design, and Italy of course with its painting. This fourth conception comes near to that of Messrs. Baumol and Moore but is not in all respects the same. A man in Chicago might believe that a sense of respect—a form of virtue—calls for preserving the city's architectural heritage, hence take pride in its being preserved. He might also take pride in its football team or symphony but not because of their virtue.

There are still other ways in which art is said to have the properties of a public good. It is said to stimulate creative thinking; to encourage a critical attitude toward social institutions, thereby to make them better; to improve manners and morals; to refine taste; to be a public amenity; to engender fellow feeling; to take the dampness out of society.

In whatever way it is made a public good, that way entails a subsidy or some other form of government assistance. That is so, the argument says, because public goods by their nature cannot be supplied by the market in the proper quantities. The same is said about goods that yield positive externalities. To leave either kind to the market is to make the total output of the economy less than it could be, hence to allow waste. Why this must be is a fairly intricate question. The answer, put as simply as possible, is that to leave such goods to the market, which is to leave them to voluntary action, is either impractical or impossible. People will be uncertain about which goods of a public nature should be produced privately, will wait for each other to provide them, will not know how to price them when provided or be able to collect the price if they do know, will be unable to specify the rights attached to the goods, and will be unable to enforce contracts or protect the rights if they are known.

So the argument contends, and it claims that if goods of a public nature are to be had at all they must be supplied by government. To examine each of the contentions would take the chapter beyond its intended scope, and I shall only say that among economists they are *sub judice.*

What economists have said has mainly to do with the allocation of resources, that is, with how the labor and capital of the economy can be used to best advantage. The public, on the other hand, is likely to be more interested in another issue presented by public goods and by goods that yield externalities. It is how they affect the distribution of income. The two issues are actually one in pure economics where costs and returns are defined as foregone and realized utility respectively and are viewed with the Olympian detachment the theorist is expected to have. That is not the way other people view the matter. They are less interested in how allocation affects the total income of the population than in how it affects their own. So that when subsidizing the opera (or anything else) is proposed, people are less likely to think of how the measure will enhance national pride than in how much it will add to their taxes if they don't like opera or how much it will reduce the price of tickets if they do.

I am not convinced by the public good argument in any of its forms. To say that art benefits everyone is to say next to nothing, because the same statement can and has been made about many things—about American Science, Technology, Medicine, Higher Education, Religion, Morality, the Rocky Mountains, the Stars and Stripes, et al., each of them suitably capitalized. Just what is the benefit, how much of it should there be, and what will it cost? Or to restate the point, there is no evidence brought forward to show that subsidizing art because it is a public good (or for any other reason) would yield as much benefit as there would be in subsidizing something else or nothing at all. What is said is that the public at large believes it benefits from art and is willing to have some of its taxes used to subsidize it. Professor Baumol, for example, says a Harris Poll gives "strong evidence that a considerable portion of the public is prepared to lay out considerable amounts of money to support the arts" on the ground of their public benefits. The poll he cites may be interpreted differently. It showed that 38 percent of those asked said they favored cultural subsidies, 34 percent did not, 14 percent were not sure, and another 14 percent said "it depends." There was a little more support, 41 percent, for subsidies expressly to art museums.[16] But surely neither 38 nor 41 percent is "a considerable portion" if the words are meant to imply a majority. If they do not, what do they imply? Elections usually are decided by majorities, not by considerable portions. The portions could be increased by adding half of those in the groups that were not sure or said it depends, but the proportion would be only a little over half of the respondents.

Polls taken in other countries show that a higher percentage of the public than in America favors additional spending by the government on the arts: in Australia 72 percent, and of them four-fifths said it should be made by reducing the spending of government on other things. E. G. West reports this information along with the results of a poll conducted in Canada in which people were asked if they believed the arts yielded benefits in addition to the satisfaction of experiencing them directly. The respondents said they did believe there were such external benefits and cited the capacity of the arts to elicit national pride, to be of educational value, to help local business, etc.[17]

Even if this information is accurate, it is by no means enough to justify subsidizing the arts (and Professor West does not claim it is). One also has to know what people believe the external benefits are worth, and that is expressed by what they are willing to pay for them (just as the worth of a private good sold on the market is expressed by what they are willing to pay for it). The way people pay for the external benefits of subsidizing the arts or anything else is to pay higher taxes or to receive fewer government services of some other kind. Their willingness to pay—or WTP—for the *external* benefits of the arts is distinct from what they pay for the *private* benefit to themselves. If a person would pay $50 for a ticket to the opera, he expects the performance to be worth that much to him and to him alone. That is his private benefit. If in addition he is proud of his city's having an opera company, he would be willing to contribute something towards its support (assuming it could not support itself from ticket sales). The amount he would contribute is the value he places on the external benefit. He actually would pay that amount voluntarily and willingly if he knew that without his contribution the opera company could not exist. He would do this because by doing so he obtains something of value that is worth what it costs [and more if there is consumer surplus].

However he would not make a contribution if he believed there were other people who would contribute enough to keep the opera in existence. He might indeed not admit he was willing to pay anything at all—even though he certainly was—if he believed his admission would lead to his actually having to make a contribution. Therein is one of the difficulties in subsidizing the arts or anything else. The difficulty is to know just what the external benefits would be worth to the people who receive them, hence what all are willing to pay if each believes that without his contribution there will be no external benefits at all.

This difficulty has been the subject of economic research done in the past twenty years or so. Various ways have been devised for getting people to reveal just how much they are willing to pay if they believe that without paying they will not get what they want. The object of the research is to discover the "true WTP" of each person, hence the amount that all of them together are willing to pay. One way of discovering it has been devised by Peter Bohm of the University of Stockholm, and his method was used by the central government of Sweden to decide whether it should provide statistical information to local governments.[18] Once the true WTP of the external benefits is discovered, or the range within which it falls, it is compared with the amount the government must spend in order to bring them about. For example, the money value that people, all of them taken together, place on the external benefits of an opera company is compared to the amount the government must spend to keep the company in existence. If the cost is less than the aggregate WTP, the subsidy then is deemed to be justified; if the cost is more, the subsidy is not justified.

One may question each of the three steps of this procedure. The first and most obvious is whether the willingness to pay has in fact been discovered. If it has, then one wants to ask why a subsidy is justified simply because the amount of it is less than the WTP. May there not be other activities for which the excess of willingness to pay over cost is even greater? Surely the government should try to get as much as it can from the money it spends. A family that decides to spend X dollars a month for a five-room apartment does not move into the first five-room apartment it sees that rents for X dollars. People may very well believe the external benefits of an opera company are greater than the Z dollars needed to subsidize it by an amount equal to A. The same people should also be asked if the net external benefits of spending Z dollars on medical research are greater than A. And whether spending that much on a third, fourth, or *n*th object is still greater. The third question is how the financing of the government's spending is to be arranged so that the financing satisfies the condition (which it must satisfy in order to be fair and efficient) that each person shall pay for the external benefits an amount that is proportional to the value he places on them. Neither the second nor the third question is addressed by Professor Bohm.

THE PUTATIVE POSITIVE EXTERNALITIES

2. Art yields positive externalities. This is logically related to the preceding argument, that art should be subsidized because it is a public good, but the arguments are not identical. The benefits of a pure public good cannot be separated from its private benefits because they are the same, for example, the light cast by a street lamp on everyone who passes under it. The benefits of the kind of good considered in this, the second, argument can be divided between those received by the person owning it and those received by the public at large, for example, the placing of a house on a site in such a way that it does not obstruct the view other houses have although it may not itself have a view, the private benefit being whatever amenity it provides the owner and the external benefit being its not obstructing the view of the neighbors. An opera company is this kind of a good, since its benefits are separable. It was also used as an example in the examination of the public goods argument; but there the issue was that of estimating its public good value only.

Some of the externalities that have been attributed to art are "real" in the economist's sense of the word. They are said to increase the total quantity of goods and services which the economy is capable of obtaining from the resources it has. A "real" positive externality, properly managed, increases efficiency. Other externalities which have been attributed to art are "pecuniary" in the sense that they are said to increase the money income of people who are affected indirectly as well as directly by the payment of subsidies (all of which will be explained in a moment). The distinction between pecuniary and real is not made by all of the economists who employ the argument. It is made here because it should be.

The pecuniary externality most often credited to the arts is that they attract people to a city or country. More spending ensues, and the income of the community increases. An example is a study of the effect on New Orleans of the exhibit of the Treasures of Tutankhamen (a blockbuster among blockbusters). The study was made by the director of the New Orleans Museum of Art in collaboration with the director of the University of New Orleans School of Hotel, Restaurant, and Tourism Administration and was reported by the director of the Urban Arts program of the U.S. Conference of Mayors Institute for the Development of Urban Arts and Sciences (which as an acronym would be UAPUSCMIDUAS, a jawbreaker). Visitors from outside of the city spent $89,028,262. There were 540,445 of them who did not come in groups (came "singly"), and each spent $150.50; there were 72,724 who came in groups, and each spent $105.76. That may mean those who came in groups spent less time in the queue, and the inference is supported by the fact that the singles stayed 2.42 days in New Orleans, while the others ("groupies"?) spent 1.42 days or 24 hours less. The total spending generated by the visitors was not the $89 million noted above but (the study claimed) was $267 million, a figure reached by "using the accepted multiplier effect, which has shown that for every dollar spent for the arts, approximately three dollars are directly or indirectly generated for the city." And, the study did not report, three dollars less for every visitor who comes from every other city. [One notes there is an arts multiplier to take its place besides the investment multiplier, the foreign trade multiplier, and the balanced budget multiplier in the kitchen midden of Keynesianism.]

Arguments of this kind, even if they are carefully made (and this one is not), are weak at several points. What one community gains from a subsidy another loses by having fewer visitors and by possibly having to pay higher taxes to finance the subsidy. The losses are most evident, although not necessarily greater, within a country where (*a*) the arts are subsidized in some cities and not in others and (*b*) the subsidies are provided by the national government. One would not expect a national government, if it acted on economic grounds, to subsidize only some communities for the purpose of increasing their income. One would expect local and state governments to compete with each other in offering subsidies to the arts as they do in offering subsidies to business firms, to professional sports, and the like. The effect of the competition is to reduce the external benefits of the arts and to render even less what is at best a money illusion. The effect is also to hold each government hostage to all of the others. What may be said of the competition between cities or states may also be said of that between countries, except that while the unsubsidized city loses both visitors and tax money the unsubsidized country loses only visitors. A country that wanted the arts to pay their own way might for this reason be deterred from making them do so even though it would lose only a pecuniary externality. If the British wanted to make Covent Garden support itself they no doubt would wonder how many visitors, along with singers and conductors, they would lose to Vienna. Vienna, on its part, would welcome the removal of subsidies in Britain and could then reduce its own. Or could if it was able to overcome the opposition of the Austrians who are employed in the Stadtoper and others. The problem is analogous to that of disarmament; the consequences are less grave fortunately.

The externality argument usually includes the claim that the increase in the number of visitors to a community will not only increase total spending and employment but also will increase real wages or purchasing power of each worker and the profitability of the firms that sell to the visitors—the hotels, restaurants, and the like. Actually there can be no increase in the profitability of capital if new restaurants and hotels can be opened and the subsidy is anticipated. If the subsidy is not anticipated, there will be an increase for a time but it will disappear as new establishments are opened and compete with the old in selling to visitors. Any significant increase in real wages will draw labor to the subsidized community until wages are no more attractive there than elsewhere. Moreover, whatever gains accrue, and most will be temporary, will accrue at the expense of communities elsewhere and also of the residents of the subsidized community who do not sell to visitors and do not themselves care for art but must help pay for it.

There is however one group in the subsidized community that will gain permanently, and it consists of people who own something of which the supply cannot be increased or cannot be increased without raising its cost. A subsidy can increase the demand for land of certain kinds, like that in the vicinity of an arts center and of course the land on which a center is located. One is not surprised then that the owners of such property are in favor of subsidizing the arts or anything else that will increase the value of their capital. Or is one surprised to be told the subsidizing of art has a place in urban renewal.

There is another group of people who gain permanently from art subsidies, but they are not alluded to in the externality argument and mentioning them would not strengthen it. Some of them gain quite directly, not in any external way at all. They are the people in the arts whose talent or ability is scarce and is much in demand and would be even if the arts were not subsidized but is in greater demand because they are. The leading conductors of the world would have high incomes if each orchestra had to pay its own way but not as high as they now have as a result of orchestras being subsidized. There also are people in the museum world, as mentioned earlier, whose abilities are exceptional, and they too benefit from subsidies but apparently not as much as conductors or tenors. Museum subsidies, as explained, raise the price of art everywhere, whether it is on the market or not, so long as there is any substitutability among the works [i.e., any cross elasticity]. That redounds to the benefit of private collectors and dealers with a significant inventory and to the embarrassment of museums that are asked about the value of their collections.

Another claim within the externality argument is that the arts of a community make it attractive to new firms. If that is so, the community is subsidizing the firms and should ask itself if subsidizing other attractions would be more effective, like putting fish in the lake, or creating a lake to put fish in, or providing a theme park, or racquetball courts, or just giving money to the new firms to pay their workers or stockholders. A European firm is reported to have refused to establish a branch in a Florida city because it had no symphony orchestra. The fact was used to argue for subsidizing orchestras. It could also be used to argue that a firm which needs a symphony to attract employees should bring one with it. Such are the pecuniary externalities attributed to art.

The other class, those which economists call real externalities, are considerably different. Three are described by Dick Netzer in *The Subsidized Muse:* (1) each art form is better, the greater is the amount of art in other forms; (2) each will itself be better in the future, the more there is of it in the present; and (3) the greater is the amount of art in any form at any time, the more likely is some of it to be experimental.[19] Each of these claims is plausible and may be factu-

ally correct. But cannot the same statements be made about unsubsidized goods and services? The more automobiles there are, the
greater will be the demand and output of tires and the greater will be
their durability. If there are many computers today, there probably
will be many tomorrow, and they may be better because of efforts to
improve them.

The same question may be asked about the novel argument of
Hans Abbing of Holland. Mr. Abbing, who is both a sculptor and an
economist, contends the benefit of a work of art extends beyond its
buyer and reaches out to the world at large. He claims it does so in
numerous ways, for example, by influencing taste (he cites shower
curtains that look like op art), by the work of art having a user other
than the buyer (a library book), by its being reproduced without the
artist being compensated (the tape of a concert) and, beyond these
ways, by affecting culture in its entirety, viz., "Giotto and Rousseau,
. . . changed the face of the world."[20] For these additional benefits,
which are positive externalities, he believes the artist should be
compensated by public subsidies or private payments. What he
dwells on is the distributional effect of externalities, and he implies
that artists are treated unjustly if they are not paid for all of the
benefits their work yields to those who are touched by them. (If
justice was symmetrical, the artist would have to pay those on whom
his work had a negative effect.) There is another issue, however, as
explained a few pages back. It is the allocational effect of externalities. Goods that yield a positive externality are not produced in
sufficient quantity if their output is determined solely by the market.
Economists who argue for subsidizing such goods stress that the
result is to increase output.

The ideas Mr. Abbing proposes are acknowledged in a curious
practice of the British. Their law requires, in effect, that authors
receive higher royalties for the copies of their books that are sold to
libraries. The royalties, moreover, vary directly with the number of
readers of each library copy. In the visual arts, the analogue would
be for museums to pay a painter or his heirs a sum that would be
determined by the interest the public shows in his painting. The
technology for measuring the sum has been available for some time
in the churches of Italy where important pictures cannot be seen
without artificial light. It is provided by the visitor putting a coin in
a box whereupon a light goes on for a few minutes. There is a free
rider problem of course. When the light goes on, other visitors flock

around (sheepishly) to gaze on what someone else has illuminated. The problem might be lessened, though not eliminated, by making the painting invisible, even when lighted, except through stroboscopic spectacles which the visitor would rent at a fee and on deposit of an amount greater than their cost (to discourage his making off with them to use in other churches). The net proceeds of this pricing system (which would be the total revenue less the amortization of the coin boxes, the spectacles, the cost of the electricity, and administrative overhead) would go to the painter or his assigns. (There would be no need for this folderol if a museum was operated for a profit. It would buy or rent paintings and pay for them what they were expected to add to admission receipts, the highest payment being made for those that would add most, and if any was the work of a living artist he would receive in one grand sum an amount that represented the public's interest in it. The electric company would get nothing or would the makers of meter boxes. What would become of the important art that is not popular? Are the recordings of Beethoven's late quartets subsidized? Possibly—by the record company with the profits from the Fifth Symphony.)

There is another and older practice in Britain and elsewhere. It is for people who want to get the greatest benefit from art to pay the artist to supply it to them. An interesting example from the visual arts is related by Louise Irvine in a study of the connection between the potteries of England and the sculptors of the nineteenth century.[21] The firm that became Royal Doulton engaged sculptors; their designs improved the quality of pottery and raised the income of the sculptors who were paid out of the receipts from the sale of what they designed. Another example is George Stubbs who for a time was associated with Josiah Wedgwood (horses enamelled on earthenware). Just as interesting is what is implied by an observation John Walker made about Vermeer, that the vitreous surface of his painting could have been suggested by the high glaze of Delftware. Would Mr. Abbing say Vermeer should have compensated the pottery workers?

A different sort of externality has been cited by economists in Australia. It is that people who appreciate art are more law-abiding, hence art reduces the cost of maintaining order. The effect was remarked on by Plato, and Congreve said music could soothe the savage breast. Where the evidence for the claim is to be found has not been disclosed. If it exists, it would have to show that a given expenditure on the arts reduces crime more than the same amount spent on enlarging prisons or adding to the police force. A clue might be gotten by asking companies that issue theft insurance which is more likely to reduce the premium: X dollars spent on (a) enlarging the city jail, (b) hiring more policemen, or (c) establishing a symphony orchestra.

A real externality has been made of the observation of A. C. Pigou, also cited earlier, that while most people add to the welfare of others by producing something for them there are people who by being just what they are add to the welfare of others. The idea may have been suggested by what Mill said about nobility of character in *Utilitarianism:* "If it may possibly be doubted whether a noble character is always happier for its nobleness, there can be no doubt that it makes other people happier, and that the world in general is immensely a gainer by it." Pigou went beyond Mill and said that certain kinds of consumption, like the enjoyment of art, raise people from the class of those who produce welfare to the class of those who radiate it. Other kinds of consumption (the use of demerit goods presumably) degrade people. This argument is of the group which makes art a public good as well as that which attributes externalities to it, hence what may be objected to in the public good argument may be objected to in this also, namely, that it offers no evidence about costs and benefits. To say that art diminishes the coarse fibres of human nature may be true, or may not, but is no guide to how to spend the public's money. A lesser but not a trivial objection is the difficulty of deciding which people are in which class or who produces welfare and who emanates it. By the terms of the argument, the lesser, not the nobler, should receive the subsidy because those who provide welfare simply by being what they are do not need improvement (or as much of it). This could lead to rivalry over who was most in need of it, hence most entitled to assistance. In India after it became independent, communities were subsidized in proportion to their backwardness, and they vied with each other in claiming to be backward.

They did, however, mean to use the money to bring themselves into the present. The U.S. government in the 1970s offered a number of subsidies that were an inducement to cities to return to the past. The city of Eureka Springs, Arkansas, asked for three-quarters of a million dollars in order "to make itself look older," which it proposed to do by bringing back streetcars and constructing buildings in the style of the 1890s.[22] The report comes from G. Ellis Burcaw (to whom I am also indebted for information reported in chapter three). He relates that the education director of the Smithsonian Institution, when explaining why it proposed to recreate a slum apartment as an exhibit of American life, said, "It's the nasty side of life that we're in danger of losing today."[23] The exhibit was to be fetid, warm, and touched off with a few live rats. In the Department of the Interior, the National Trust for Historic Preservation proposed to restore the abandoned cotton mills of Lowell, Massachusetts, and make them "living museums" which showed the conditions of work in the past. The Lowell and Eureka projects, it was claimed, would have beneficial external effects, the former by attracting 750,000 visitors each year and the latter by renewing the (*fin-de-siècle*) quality of Eureka. Neither come within the scope of the National Endowment for the Arts, but both indicate that history competes with art in the production of externalities.

The NEA itself has subsidized some unusual undertakings. The Alvarado program in forty San Francisco schools engaged pupils and their parents in "art activities." One was "educational beautification." On vacant lots near the schools it instructed the children and their parents in farming and animal husbandry, the twofold purpose being "to train people to address the critical problem of food shortages and, in fact, future survival" and to demonstrate "the social value of creative work."[24] Another branch of the federal government, the Department of Agriculture which is considerably larger and more expensive than the NEA, spent $25 billion in 1986 to address what it called the critical problem of food surpluses.

ART AS A MERIT GOOD

3. Art is a merit good. The argument has a forthright and ingenuous quality that makes it attractive. It declares that art is a good thing, that people do not want enough of it even though they can afford it, and that the state should see that they get more. This seems to take things out of economics and to relieve one of having to follow the ambages of the arguments that employ it. Tibor Scitovsky has said as much, and he is an economist. "None of the standard arguments in favor of financing is really applicable to the arts. The only valid argument for government aid to the arts is that it is a means of

educating the public's taste and that the public would benefit from a more educated taste," he said.[25] One is not permitted to object that if art is actually to the benefit of people they will themselves acquire a taste for it. The merit good argument is that they will not do what is to their benefit either because they do not know what it is (the reason implied by Professor Scitovsky) or because they simply will not while nevertheless acknowledging that they should (which is the reason more often given).

The argument comes near to being an Irish bull and would be if it was said to have a justification in economic theory. It then would imply that although each person knows best what is good for himself he is better off if someone else tells him what it is. This may be why Professor Scitovsky says the argument cannot be justified by economic reasoning. Other economists have not been as prudent. Professor Netzer makes it the principle argument for subsidies. Roger J. Vaughan advances it.[26] It was made a century earlier by Stanley Jevons who said museums of all kinds have a "civilizing effect."[27] That merges the idea of art as a merit good with the idea of its being a public good. In either form, the argument invites the question: If art is truly meritorious or truly beneficial to everyone, should not the subsidy do more than make it available to the people to use or not as they wish? Should not the subsidy be large enough to pay them to use it? In some countries people are paid to submit to medical treatment. In the United States, some people are paid to attend school. The stated justification is that health and education are public goods or have positive external benefits. But if a person can be paid to benefit someone else, surely he can be paid to benefit himself. If a subsidy that reduces price to zero is permissible, then a subsidy to reduce it below zero must be also.

That is not all. If there is reason to pay people to benefit others or themselves, as the three arguments imply there is, can a reason be found to compel them to do so? Compulsory vaccination against contagious diseases is justified on the ground that health and sickness have external effects. To compel people to obey the law is defended because law is a public good. Is there a reason to compel a person—not merely pay or make it easy for him—to do that which is good for him and for him alone, as the merit good argument says the appreciation of art is? The answer could take us into the deeper waters of normative economics but need not. It is, No, if we believe that whatever has an effect on the individual must have his consent and if it affects him alone then only he has the right to decide if it shall be done. That is the premise of rights theory. By the premise of utilitarianism, or what it implies about an act that affects only one person, compulsion is permissible if the consequence is to make the person happier. The utilitarians, and Mill especially, probably would object to the word compulsion, nevertheless what they advocate entails it.

SUPPLY AS THE CREATOR OF DEMAND

4. The demand for art depends on the supply. The argument here is not that art should be subsidized permanently in order that it can be given away or offered below cost. That, of course, is one way to induce people to notice it but is not the way of this argument or does this say the supply of art creates a demand for it. To be sure, that is suggested by the form in which it has been stated [as if it were Say's law applied to art]. What is claimed, by Karen King and Mark Blaug, is that "Tastes, and hence, demand, tend to be stimulated by the mere provision of artistic facilities."[28] This implies the purpose of the subsidy is to inform people that there is an object of value available to them.

But in this respect, art is no different from anything which is unfamiliar (which in fact art is not). When a new product is offered for sale by a private enterprise, information is offered with it and comes in the form of advertising and other marketing devices. Unfamiliarity is no more reason to subsidize art than to subsidize anything else, except if art is more than a private good which, however, the argument does not claim. It does say the arts cannot afford to advertise and, moreover, may find it ineffective. Actually they do advertise, as a glance at the arts section of the Sunday *New York Times* shows. If the advertising is ineffective, it is evidence of a stunning waste of money and suggests that there are better ways to invite the attention of the public.

The argument comes near to being another Irish bull. It says that subsidies to art increase the amount available to the mass of people who in turn acquire a taste for it. If the amount was not increased they never would come to know art and not knowing it never would want it. Not wanting it they would be worse off than if they did want it but would not know they were.

Enclosed in the fourth argument is the idea that art is a merit good without the idea being made explicit. It is implied by the assumption that ignorance and ignorance alone keeps the masses from art. We are to believe the museums of Italy must be subsidized because (among other reasons) the Italian people have not had sufficient time to become familiar with their Renaissance in the 700 years that have passed since it began. The government of Greece subsidizes the theater today even though the Greeks have had some 2,500 years to take notice of Sophocles. Is not indifference or uninterest rather than ignorance the correct description of the attitude of the Italians, the Greeks, the Americans, the Australians, and of people everywhere?

Another feature of this and also of the merit good argument is a curious notion of how the human mind works. It never initiates or anticipates. It only responds. We never would know what hunger is until food was made available (by subsidized farmers presumably) and we would not know the difference between being wet and dry until we opened an umbrella. Moreover, we need ever so long a time to grasp this information.

ART FOR MORE PEOPLE AND PLACES

5. Art should be made available to everyone, or at least to many more people than now have it. The argument makes two factual assumptions. One is that there now are only a few people who have an interest in art, and the other is that there would be more if its price was reduced (lower ticket prices, smaller museum admission charges, etc.). About these assumptions so much has already been said that here it need only be summarized in the briefest way. By the evidence of opinion polls and, even more, the evidence of attendance figures, the interest in art is indeed limited. The first assumption then is entirely warranted. The other is not, and it is the more important of the two. There is no evidence that by making art less expensive the interest in it would be increased substantially. The evidence indicates that in the United States a reduction in price of, say, 10

percent would increase attendance by less than 10 percent. There is no evidence that lower prices would transform the arts into a mass phenomenon (leaving aside negative prices).

Prices are not low in Europe, even though the arts there are heavily subsidized and have been for a long while. There are, to be sure, negative prices on occasion. On certain days when there is no admission charge, the Kunsthistorisches Museum of Vienna gives away postcards and small reproductions to visitors. The gifts would not be expensive to buy but they do have a value and at other times are sold at the museum store. Giving them away makes the effective admission price less than zero. Yet there is no crowding, as there probably would be if the museum cafe offered free coffee and strudel.

There is a stronger indication that admission prices do not limit the audience or interest in the arts. It is the high prices and large audiences of popular entertainments like rock concerts. They can fill the 100,000 seats in Soldiers Field in Chicago, something not even Pavarotti could do several times a year. Of course this does not prove the poor can afford to go to the opera and would go if they cared for it. But the fact is suggestive. Moreover, one would be surprised to learn that the median income of the opera audience is no higher than that of a rock audience and still more surprised to learn that the average education of the two was the same. Actually, the point could be made stronger by setting popular music against something other than opera because, by the findings of one poll, opera is the least unpopular of the performing arts among the working class.

In any event, the size of the audience has another bearing on the argument for redistributing art via subsidies. The purpose of such redistribution, one would suppose, is to provide for the poor, that is, to give them something that adds to their welfare as they themselves think of it. The purpose of redistribution cannot, by this argument, be to improve their taste. That is the merit good argument. Moreover, if art is meritorious it should be used by everyone, rich as well as poor. To single out the Philistines among only the poor would be extraordinarily insensitive. By the redistribution argument, the poor are singled out not because they have no taste but because they have no money. Would not the most effective remedy be to give them money? That is not the way of governments or reformers, of course. Why not then give the poor something they would buy if they had more money, like tickets to a rock concert or Disneyland, not tickets to the Philharmonic or the Cloisters? Admittedly, this would not help the arts. But helping them is not the purpose of redistribution. Helping the poor is.

About subsidies and prices and the poor there is more to be reported. It is that large subsidies do not always result in low ticket prices. In Vienna, Paris, London, and Munich, where opera is heavily subsidized, the price of tickets is about the same as in New York, San Francisco, and Chicago where it is not. Moreover, in the European cities there is, despite the high prices, queueing, so that the subsidies manage to bring about the worst of worlds: expensive tickets that are unobtainable. There is queueing in the United States also but not as much. That there is any at all indicates prices could be raised and the opera subsidies, though small, could be still smaller.

A queue signifies excess demand, but that should not be taken to mean the population would swarm into opera houses if there were more of them. The excess, while it means there should be more opera, does not mean there should be a quantum increase even if that were possible. It probably is not because there are not enough performers of the first rank; there are others who can sing but they might not be willing to do so at the price the public would pay to listen. That public is, by all accounts, a relatively small number of people. An indication of how large it is relative to the public that is not interested in high art is offered by information about television audiences. Need it be said that more people watched "Dallas" than "The Ring"? The prices were equal.

The argument for redistribution not only proposes to make art available to more people but also to make it available in more places. What may be said about redistributing art for reasons of equity seems to be equally apposite to redistributing it for reasons of geography. Yet the objection may appear to have less weight when made about geographic redistribution. In the receiving communities it would be welcomed by local interests that benefit, however briefly, by a theater, museum, concert hall, or, grandly, by an "arts complex." Subsidies for construction are said to be helpful in renewing the inner cities. But to justify them for this reason is to move the argument from equity and geography to externalities, and their claim has already been examined. There is, however, another objection that applies to this externality alone. The problem the subsidies are meant to alleviate—the concentration of art in a few cities—seems actually to have been made worse in countries where art subsidies are substantial. The performing arts and museums of London, Paris, Vienna, and several other major cities (excepting Rome and Berlin for reasons having nothing to do with the point) are not only more extensive in an absolute sense because they are subsidized but are also more important relative to the arts of other cities in the same countries. The others continually complain that the capitals take the giant's share of the subsidies.

A novel solution to the problem has been offered by the British economist Alan T. Peacock.[29] It is to take the audiences to the arts instead of the other way around. People in the provinces would be given round-trip railway tickets to London as well as being provided with theater and concert tickets (the museums were free when the proposal was made). There is an additional cost of enjoying the arts, and the policy seems to overlook it. It is the time needed for enjoyment which includes the time spent on the train and getting to and from the stations. The travelers would have to be compensated for that as well, or at least for the difference between the time they spend getting to the theater and that spent by people living in London. Care would also have to be taken to assure that the people who got the travel vouchers used them for the arts and not for shopping in London; perhaps they should be required to give evidence of having been in an arts audience before being reimbursed for the expense.

Yet how the problem of the concentration of the arts is to be solved has nothing to do with whether it should be, no more than the method of redistributing it in favor of the poor has anything to do with whether there should be redistribution. About that question—the question of whether or not, rather than how—I expressed my opinion a few pages back.

The arguments that so far have been described and commented on are arguments that attribute a property of some kind to the demand for art and to the utility or benefit it yields. My principal but not only objection to them is that they do not provide information that would substantiate the benefits that are claimed. The three other arguments that have been made for subsidies, while they touch on demand, dwell in the main on some property of the supply of art.

ART AND SCALE ECONOMIES

6. Art is made under conditions of decreasing average cost. The argument can be illustrated by the seats in a theater although it applies also to the number of visitors a museum can accommodate. If a theater has 100 seats and each performance has a total cost of $100, the price of a ticket must be at least $1 in order that the theater support itself. But if in order to fill all of the seats the theater must price the tickets at 75 cents, the total cost will not be covered. If at a $2 price, 50 tickets would be sold, the total cost would be covered but there would be 50 empty seats that could be occupied to the benefit of 50 people without adding anything to the cost of the performance. There appears, then, to be a flaw in the market. If the theater is to support itself, which is the way of the market, there will be waste in the form of empty seats. If there is to be no waste, which is also the way of the market, the theater cannot support itself. Avoiding waste, that is, maximizing satisfaction, is the more important consideration (the argument continues), hence the theater should play to a full house. It can do so by pricing the tickets at 75 cents, and there should be a subsidy of $25 to cover the loss.

But soft, Gentles, as was said in the theater of Elizabeth. If each person in the audience paid as much as his seat was worth to him—more than 75 cents to some and less than that to others—would the total amount they would be willing to pay come to as much as $100? If not, the performance is not worth its cost; it is using resources that would be worth more elsewhere; and it certainly should not be subsidized. That is not all. There would be a loss even if the subsidized performance was worth $100 in the aggregate but a service or good of some other kind, in or out of the theater, would be worth that much and could be produced for less than $100.

The weakness of the declining average cost argument, stated simply, is that it does not include information of this kind, that is, information about what the subsidized art is worth to those who receive it and about the cost of an alternative that would be worth as much.

The argument is still weaker when it is taken from the realm of theory, where it conceivably could be valid, and is examined for the use that could and probably would be made of it. A subsidy granted because average cost decreases should be used only to reduce the price of admission to a museum or arts performance. It should not be used to increase spending on what is shown or performed and certainly should not be used to increase the size of the arts organization. Yet those are the uses to which subsidies almost always are put, irrespective of why they have been granted. Museums grow ever larger, adding to their collections, their buildings, and their staff. Theaters produce more expensively and venturesomely as do opera companies. The size of symphony orchestras is limited but the number of them is not; and all of the performing arts spend more on performers. That makes the decreasing cost problem greater, because it raises costs and increases the seats and space to be filled. Yet it is the predictable outcome of subsidies that are sought for the purpose of securing rents in the economic sense explained in the preceding chapter.

ART AS LABOR INTENSIVE

7. Art is labor intensive. The argument is that art can be made only by people and they cannot be assisted by machines, as people making other things can be. As a country becomes richer, the income from an hour's work increases in all occupations including art, and if people are to engage in the creation and performance of art they must be paid as much as they can earn elsewhere. In many employments there are substitutes for labor, and their cost does not rise as much as the cost of labor rises. So that if hourly wages rise 50 percent in manufacturing, the cost and price of a manufactured product will rise less than 50 percent. Relative to the income of people who work, the product will become cheaper. In art, however, the cost will rise in the proportion that labor becomes more expensive. A string quartet always requires four string players, and if they must be paid 50 percent more the cost of performing the quartet and the price of hearing it will rise 50 percent. As the price of art increases the amount demanded decreases until, at the limit, the price is higher than anyone will pay. If art is not to pass out of existence, it must be subsidized. So the argument goes.

It usually has been applied to the performing arts. Although it also applies to painting, sculpture, drawing, and design, it rarely has been mentioned in connection with them, and the reason may be that painters, sculptors, and designers usually have not been subsidized. The exhibition of their work has been subsidized of course for the reason explained in the preceding chapter. (The fewer are the rent-seekers relative to the number of rent-payers, the more likely is rent to be sought and obtained.) The argument is not strictly applicable to museums because they use much more capital than labor. But the accounting procedure of museums does not correspond to economic logic and makes labor cost seem more important than it is. Hence they too can plead for a subsidy on the ground that what they produce is labor intensive.

Irrespective of what it is applied to, the argument is objectionable on two grounds. The more common is that in the performing arts there are substitutes for labor, not for all labor of course, but for enough to prevent total cost from rising as much as the price of labor rises. For example, the cost of a single orchestral performance can be reduced by the program's being performed more than once. In the visual arts there have been many ways by which the cost of painting a picture has been reduced, as explained in chapter three. There also are ways in which museums can reduce costs (and increase their earned income) as explained in chapter five.

A more important objection is that the argument encloses (or conceals) an unwarranted assumption about demand. It is that the value of the arts is greater than that which the market places on them. There is nothing in economics that says an increase in relative cost and price is itself a condition that calls for a subsidy. The increase could indicate that production should be reduced rather than maintained or enlarged. Handmade shoes become relatively expensive as time goes on, but that is no reason to subsidize them. Closer to the nerve again is popular music. The cost of rock concerts increases over time relative to the cost of things that can be made with capital that is a substitute for labor, yet subsidizing rock concerts has not been proposed.

Most of what has been said about the labor intensity argument has been about whether labor cost in the arts does, in fact, rise relative to the labor cost of other things and whether the arts can do anything to mitigate the increase. But this has nothing to do, really, with whether art should be subsidized. That depends on its benefit or utility in relation to its cost and on its benefit–cost ratio relative to that of other things. If there is proof that the return to art is higher than to other things and that the return cannot be realized on the market, then there is a good reason to subsidize art and the reason is valid whether the labor cost of art is rising, falling, or constant.

ART AS ENDANGERED CAPITAL

8. The stock of art must be maintained. This, again, is an argument which was first used on behalf of subsidizing the performing arts. It claimed that if the theater was left to the market the drama of the past would be forgotten and even the ability to perform it would vanish. Applied to the visual arts the argument is that there must be museum subsidies in order that the stock of painting, sculpture, and the like be properly preserved. It has been extended to include architecture in order to preserve landmarks, and in many countries there are laws that limit the changes that may be made in such buildings. Had the papacy been subject to such a law, the basilica of St. Peter never would have been built because in order to make place for it a church on the site had to be demolished. It was cherished by the Christians of Rome, and they protested its being taken down.

The argument as applied to either the performing or the visual arts does not claim they are public goods or provide external benefits or are merit goods or should be supplied in order to create interest in them or should be made available to everyone everywhere (the first five arguments). The argument can be joined to some of them, but it can also be made independently. When it is, it is of the class that asserts the market is shortsighted about the capital stock, hence undervalues it, the consequence being that too little is invested and too little care is taken to maintain what has been invested. The argument is parallel to the argument made by conservationists, viz., that the market undervalues natural resources as evidenced by their being depleted and substitutes not being found for them.

The principal objection to this argument is the same as that to the others that proceed from a characteristic of the supply of art but contain the assumption that the utility or the benefit art yields is not fully expressed by the demand for it. The same can be said of the other five. All assume art is worth more than people are willing to pay for it. I am in no way convinced but cannot deny the possibility.

Anything is conceivable. But to say it does not prove it is. One would not care to live under a legal system where no distinction was made between what could be true and what is.

Another objection is that the argument would have one believe art held by the state or by a nonprofit organization will be better taken care of than art held by an individual or by a profit-seeking firm. If this were so, paintings held by dealers and collectors would be in a condition inferior to those in museums. Just how well museums take care of their collection, or neglect to do so, is described in chapter five. We are told less about how well dealers do that, possibly because like other people they can be expected to take care of what they have had to pay for. A dealer who did not take proper care of his stock would have to sell it for less than he paid and would not be a dealer for long. When one does hear from the private sector, the report is often about the lady from the provinces who appears at Sotheby's with something she found in the attic and would like to know if it is important, whereupon Sotheby's examines it, declares it to be a Gellée, and sells it for several hundred thousand pounds. The story is a parable and would be quite misunderstood if it is taken to mean paintings in private hands are neglected. The Gellée did, after all, get to the auction house and did so because the owner stood to gain by taking it there, the auction house by selling it, and the buyer by exchanging his money for what was more valuable to him.

The owner of a painting or of anything else will take better care of it if it belongs to him than to someone else. So economic theory predicts. It would be a poor subject if it did not and departed so far from common sense as to predict people will take better care of what does not belong to them. Yet that is what is implied by the argument that the conservation of art cannot be left to private collectors. There is a comment on the point that is noteworthy in an article by Walter A. Liedtke in *Apollo* (January 1983) about a painting by Michiel Sweerts, the Flemish artist of the seventeenth century: "Seclusion in one family collection for more than 250 years accounts in good part for the painting's excellent state of preservation." Another comment that is noteworthy was made about the London dealer Partridge, by Jo Durden-Smith and Diane deSimone in *Connoisseur* (January 1983). It touches on more than the preservation practice of museums and merits quoting at length: " 'William Hunt furniture should be kept very bright. And we should do what we can to return it to its original brilliance. Museums can't do this—these pieces need to be gilded every twenty years, and museums don't take care of their furniture. But we can do it,' he (Partridge) says with conviction. 'If a piece is important enough, then I've no feeling about it going to a museum—even though its never handled and even though the museum may take rather poor care of it, . . . museums say they have no money and they can't compete. But they have hoards of things downstairs, out of the public eye, things that are never seen. And there's no chance of getting them out.' " (When Mr. Partridge said he had "no feeling" about a piece going to a museum, he must have meant no feeling in favor of its going there.)

Where in fact the important art of the world is—in private hands or elsewhere—is a question for which there is not much information. A clue is in *Fine Art Reproductions of Old and Modern Masters,* a catalog of the New York Graphic Society published in 1976. It represents itself as "a comprehensive catalog of art through the ages," and along with information about the size and price of each reproduction it also gives the location of the original. About half of them appear (from a swift count) to be in private collections, and some of the others in museums that are not subsidized by government. If the eighth argument is correct, the cultural heritage is in peril. Advocates of the argument may however take comfort in the fact that my count may have been wrong. Comfort can also be gotten from the information in *Les Pientres Célèbres* (1953–54), a compilation made by Bernard Dorival of the great artists from the Master of Daphne in the twelfth century to El Greco in the seventeenth. It indicates that most of the works are in museums (but again my count was swift).

The location of art, although it has a bearing on the argument, is not particularly important. More important is whether the stock of art is better cared for if it is privately owned and exhibited or if it is in public collections that are supported by the state. Still more important is what form of ownership, care, and exhibition will allow art to confer its greatest good on the greatest number. In my opinion, private ownership is the better arrangement.

CODA: SHOULD ART SUPPORT ITSELF?

The arguments for government assistance—made by economists, by people in art, and by their advocates who are not economists—have one idea in common. It is that art costs more and is worth more than the public at large is willing to pay for it. Because of its cost, it is unable to support itself, and because of what it is worth it should not be asked to support itself. If art is left to the market, there will be less of it than there should be, of some kinds possibly none at all. So the arguments claim.

Those that have been made by economists try to explain the nature of the costs of art, its benefits, and why if it is left to the market it will not be what it should be—not for the people who create, perform, and exhibit art, not for the people who value and want it, and not for the many others who benefit from it whether or not they are aware of the fact.

The arguments that have been made outside of economics and that are to be taken seriously, while they may seem to have nothing to do with it, are nevertheless similar and are quite the same on the critical point that art is worth its cost and worth more than its market price.

There are, admittedly, arguments that cannot be harmonized with economics but I do not take them seriously, however distinguished are the people who make them. The reason is not that a statement, if it is to be taken seriously, must be in harmony with economics but that the premises of economics are most of them self-evident and widely acted upon, whether knowingly or not. To say, "Art is not just a good thing among other good things," as Jacques Barzun said, is meaningless if it is a demand for art at any cost whatever. Science also is a good thing; so is health, so are the Scriptures.

Another statement that is meaningless, and for the same reason, is the common assertion that the arts are an essential part of every civilized society, always have been, and must continue to be. The claim could be made for a dozen other activities and has been. No such claims can be taken seriously until they offer a standard for choosing among them. Our interest is not engaged by being told the arts should be subsidized because they take the dampness out of social relations. Or is it to hear "Art is Love," which Holman Hunt said was the principle aspired to by the Pre-Raphaelite Brotherhood of which he was a member.[30] In fairness to the Brotherhood, one must report it did not confine itself to the principle; readers with a long memory will recall the complaint of Burne-Jones (reported in chapter three) that the Brotherhood was getting none of the money spent on Victoria's Jubilee.

Governments, when they have undertaken to foster art, have not rested their case on its intrinsic value. They have been guided by considerations of state although they have not always expressly acknowledged them. Colbert wanted to use art to make France glorious in the eyes of the world. Three hundred years later, the National Endowment for the Arts was begun in the United States and stated it meant to inform the world that America had more than its science and technology to be proud of. The governments of both countries claimed that art is a public good. It has been said to be that by economists and for that reason to call for a subsidy. Their reason is that a public good is worth its cost and worth more than people will voluntarily pay for it.

There are seven other arguments economists have made for subsidizing art. They claim it yields positive exernalities, that is, it benefits people who do not use it directly as well as those who do; that it is a merit good, which is a good people believe there should be more of than the market provides; that the demand for art depends on its first being supplied by a subsidy; that art should be available to more people in more places; that it is made under cost conditions such that if it is to be made efficiently it cannot pay for itself and if it is to pay for itself it cannot be made efficiently; that it is made with more labor than many other things, hence becomes relatively expensive over time; and that the stock of art must be conserved and can be only if it is subsidized.

In order to justify the subsidizing of art, or of any form of assistance to it, or to anything else, the assistance and the way it is financed must be shown to satisfy two conditions, each of which is necessary and which taken together are sufficient. One is that the assistance directs capital to a use in which its return is as high as it would be in any other use to which it can be put by government, or private enterprise, or by households. More must be shown than that a subsidy to a museum or orchestra yields a return that is positive, for example, say, 4 percent. What also must be shown is that an equal expenditure elsewhere that is subject to the same risk does not yield more than 4 percent. The other condition is that the money which pays the subsidy is obtained by taxing the people who benefit from it in the proportion to which they benefit. This condition does not apply, however, to a subsidy for the purpose of redistributing art for reasons of equity. Applied to other subsidies the condition means no more than that people should pay for what they receive from government just as they should pay for what they obtain in the private sector, except if they are too poor to do so, if they want what the government provides, and if they are entitled to it.

None of the eight arguments made by economists presents evidence that it meets either condition. The most that is claimed for any of them is that the public is in favor of subsidizing art. In fact, it is not in the United States, and the poll that is cited to support the claim shows that only 38 percent favor subsidies. Even if 100 percent did, that would not be evidence the public would favor subsidizing art if the return from doing so was less than the return from subsidizing something else or nothing at all. The public was not polled about its opinion of the best use of capital in all possible employments, and if it had been it could not have answered since it does not know, any more than do the advocates of subsidies know.

The arguments made outside of economics offer even less evidence. Numbers are cited but they are pointless or inconsequent. In the first fifteen years of the NEA "the arts have begun to flourish all across the country. . . . In all of this the National Endowment serves as a vital catalyst," its chairman reported in 1980, by which he meant there was more then than in 1965.[31] One would like to know how much the additional art was worth—surely more is not better simply because it is more—and how much it cost. The question (if it occurred to the NEA) was not thought important enough to answer or perhaps was thought not prudent to consider. It is not to be dismissed on the ground that the value of art cannot be measured as economics measures value, even if the ground were valid, because the question is entailed by the benefits attributed to the subsidy, namely, that it brought about an increase in the production and consumption of art. If economics is to be excluded from the arts, it should be excluded completely, and if it is to be admitted it should be admitted altogether. As was said of a great religious order, you must take it as it is or not at all.

If you do not take it, you must believe that what is given up in order to support the arts is of no consequence and believing that about the arts you must allow other people to believe the same about things they want, then among yourselves try to decide who gets how much of what. You also must believe it is of no consequence that the people who bear most of the cost of supporting the arts are not the people who have the greatest interest in them. Finally, you must believe there is nothing amiss about taxing people to pay for what most of them do not want.

On the other hand, if you do take economics as it is, you then must make the arts one of the many things that people want and are entitled to have in whatever amount and quality they are willing to pay for with their own money. You then may be assured that what they have is worth what is given up in order to get it, because no one pays more for anything than it is worth to him. That, in brief, is why one economist believes art should support itself.

NOTES

Chapter 1: Art and Economics Reconciled

1. Quoted by François Duret-Robert, "The Verdict of the Sale-Room," in *Phaidon Encyclopedia of Impressionism,* ed. Maurice Serullaz (New York, 1977), p. 249.

2. Barbara Scott, "Letter from Paris: The Triumph of Degas," *Apollo* (April 1988): 283.

3. John Ruskin, *Modern Painters,* Illustrated Cabinet Edition (Boston, n. d.), vol. 5, pt. 9, ch. 12; vol. 5, p. 350.

4. Jacques Maritain, *Art et Scholastique* (Paris, 1927), ch. 8.

5. Clovis Whitfield and Jane Martineau, *Painting in Naples 1605–1705* (London, 1982).

6. Eloise Spaeth, *American Art Museums, An Introduction to Looking,* 3rd ed. (New York, 1975), p. 348.

Ambroise Vollard, *Recollections of a Picture Dealer,* trans. Violet M. MacDonald (Boston, 1936), pp. 62, 71, 24.

7. T. R. Adam, *The Civic Value of Museums* (New York, 1937), p. 2.

8. Robert Hughes, "Art and Money," *New Art Examiner* (October 1984): 23–27; (November 1984): 33–38.

9. John Walker, *Self Portrait With Donors* (New York, 1974), pp. 49–50.

10. L. J. Olivier, Letter to the editor, *Times* (London), October 22, 1968.

11. J. Bruyn, B. Haak, et al., *A Corpus of Rembrandt Paintings* (London, 1982). See also *The Burlington Magazine* (November 1983): 661–63.

12. Fritz Neugass, "The Art Market," *Arts Magazine* (June 1966): 19.

13. Jacqueline Damien, "19th and Early 20th Century American Art, the Boom Continues," *ARTnews* (December 1986): 66.

14. Lee Rosenbaum, "Can the Art World Live with the Tax Reform Act?" *ARTnews* (January 1986): 96.

15. "Kunstkompass 1976, Il listino valori dei cento artisti pui famosi degli anni '60 e '70," *Domus* (November 1976): 21–24.

16. Louise Lippincott, *Selling Art in Georgian London: The Rise of Arthur Pond* (New Haven, 1983), pp. 98–99.

Chapter 2: The Acquisition of Art

1. Ambroise Vollard, *Renoir An Intimate Record,* trans. H. L. van Doren and R. T. Weaver (New York, 1925), p. 62.

2. M. L. d'Otrange Mastai, "The Sale of the Century, Indeed," *Apollo* (December 1961): 220.

3. G. Ellis Burcaw, *Introduction to Museum Work* (Nashville, 1975), p. 76.

4. Alan L. Feld, Michael O'Hare, and J. Mark Davidson Schuster, *Patrons Despite Themselves: Taxpayers and Arts Policy,* A Twentieth Century Fund Report (New York, 1983).

5. Francis Haskell, *Patrons and Painters, A Study in the Relations Between Italian Art and Society in the Age of the Baroque* (New York, 1963).

6. John Michael Montias, *Artists and Artisans in 17th Century Delft* (Princeton, 1982), p. 190.

7. Graham Reynolds, "The Elegance of George Stubbs," *Apollo* (January 1985): 22–23.

8. John Walker, *National Gallery of Art,* rev. ed. (New York, 1984), pp. 440, 544.

9. Frederick Antal, *Florentine Painting and Its Social Background* (London, 1947), p. 378.

10. Giorgio Vasari, *The Lives of the Painters, Sculptors, and Architects* (London, 1827), pt. 2.

11. Haskell, *Patrons and Painters,* ch. 1.

12. Robert Goldwater and Marco Treves, eds., *Artists on Art* (New York, 1945), pp. 145–46.

13. Walker, *National Gallery of Art,* p. 369.

Rene Gimpel, *Diary of an Art Dealer,* trans. John Rosenberg (New York, 1966), p. 243.

Walker, *National Gallery of Art,* pp. 380, 383.

14. Ambroise Vollard, *Renoir,* pp. 50, 56.

15. Daniel Grant, "Is There Recognition after Death?" *American Artist* (July 1987): 72.

16. Justus Dahinden, *New Trends in Church Architecture* (New York, 1967), p. 78.

17. C. D. Throsby and G. A. Withers, *The Economics of the Performing Arts* (New York, 1979), pp. 183, 174.

18. *Americans and the Arts. A Survey of Public Opinion* (New York, 1975), p. 59.

19. Paul DiMaggio, Michael Useem, and Paula Brown, *Audience Studies of the Performing Arts and Museums,* NEA, Research Division Report No. 9 (Washington, 1978), p. 20. See also Marilyn G. Hood, "Staying Away. Why People Choose Not to Visit Museums," *Museum News* (April 1983): 50.

20. DiMaggio, Useem, and Brown, *Audience Studies,* p. 31.

21. Thomas G. Moore, *Economics of the American Theater* (Durham, 1968), p. 90.

Dick Netzer, *The Subsidized Muse, Public Support for the Arts in the U.S.,* A Twentieth Century Fund Study (Cambridge, 1978), p. 29.

22. Harrison C. White and Cynthia A. White, *Canvases and Careers, Institutional Change in the French Painting World* (London, 1965), p. 83.

23. Kenneth M. Clark, "The Value of Art in an Expanding World," *The Hudson Review* (Spring 1966): 12.

24. Burcaw, *Introduction to Museum Work,* p. 76.

25. Bryan Robertson, "The Museum and the Democratic Fallacy," in *Museums in Crisis,* ed. Brian O'Doherty (New York, 1972), p. 87.

26. Edward B. Henning, "Patronage and Style in the Arts: A Suggestion Concerning Their Relations," *Journal of Aesthetics and Art Criticism* (June 1960): 467.

27. Antal, *Florentine Painting,* pp. 274–77.

28. Fairfield Porter, "The Prendergast Anomaly," *ARTnews* (November 1966): 36–39, 78–79.

29. Horst C. Gerson, "The Age of the Lowland Giants," ibid., p. 78.

30. Gerald Reitlinger, *The Economics of Taste* (London, 1961), vol. 1, pp. 43, 111.

31. Denys Sutton, *Christie's Since the War 1945–58, An Essay on Taste, Patronage and Collecting* (London, 1959), p. 65.

32. Don Hawthorne, "Saatchi and Saatchi Go Public," *ARTnews* (May 1985): 95–100.

33. Anthony Storr, "The Psychology of Collecting," *Connoisseur* (June 1983): 35–36.

34. Maurice Rheims, *Art on the Market,* trans. David Pryce-Jones (London, 1959), p. 610.

Chapter 3: The Art of Painters and the Craft

1. Ambroise Vollard, *Recollections of a Picture Dealer,* trans. Violet M. MacDonald (Boston, 1936), pp. 191, 193.

2. Maurice Rheims, *Art on the Market,* trans. David Pryce-Jones (London, 1959), p. 79.

3. "Peter Paul Rubens to W. Trumbull," January 16/26, 1620–21, in *Original Unpublished Papers . . . of Sir Peter Paul Rubens, etc.,* ed. W. Noel Sainsbury (London, 1859), p. 56.

4. Mary Lago, ed., *Burne-Jones Talking. His Conversations 1895–98 Preserved by His Studio Assistant Thomas Rooke* (London, 1982), p. 146.

5. *Times Literary Supplement,* July 10, 1987.

6. Bernard S. Myers, *Problems of the Younger American Artist* (New York, 1957), pp. 10–13, 59.

7. John Michael Montias, *Artists and Artisans in 17th Century Delft* (Princeton, 1982), pp. 205–6.

8. Ivan Gaskell, "Gerrit Dou, His Patrons and the Art of Painting," *Oxford Art Journal* 5 (1982): 15.

9. Montias, *Artists and Artisans in 17th Century Delft,* ch. 3.

10. Gerald Reitlinger, *The Economics of Taste. The Rise and Fall of the Picture Market 1760–1960* (New York, 1961), p. 484.

11. Francis Henry Taylor, *The Taste of Angels, A History of Art Collecting from Rameses to Napoleon* (Boston, 1948), p. 322.

12. Ambroise Vollard, *Renoir An Intimate Record,* trans. H. L. van Doren and R. T. Weaver (New York, 1925), p. 56.

13. Harrison C. White and Cynthia A. White, *Canvases and Careers, Institutional Change in the French Painting World* (London, 1965), pp. 30–31.

14. Ibid., p. 13n6.

15. Bernardo de Dominici, *Vite de pittori, scultore ed architetti napoletani, etc.* (Napoli, 1742), vol. 3, ch. 1.

William Feaver, "Atrocity Pictures," *ARTnews* (February 1983): 134.

Harold Acton, Preface, in *Painting in Naples 1605–1705,* ed. Clovis Whitfield and Jane Martineau (London, 1982).

16. Bernardo de Dominici, *Vite de pittori, scultore ed architetti napoletani, etc., pagine scelte ed annotate da Felice de Filippis* (Napoli, 1970).

17. Francis Haskell, "The Patronage of Painting in Seicento Naples," in *Painting in Naples,* ed. Whitfield and Martineau, p. 61.

18. Ibid., p. 61.

19. Montias, *Artists and Artisans in 17th Century Delft,* p. 164.

20. William Feaver, "Clashing Furniture and Whatnot," *ARTnews* (February 1987): 38.

21. Carlo Ridolfi, *The Life of Tintoretto, etc.,* trans. Catherine Enggass and Robert Enggass (University Park, 1984), p. 48.

22. David Rosand, *Painting in Cinquecento Venice: Titian, Veronese, Tintoretto* (New Haven, 1982), p. 207.

23. Anne Rorimer, "Up, Down, In and Out, Step by Step, A Sculpture, A Work by Daniel Buren," in Art Institute of Chicago, *Museum Studies,* pp. 140–41.

24. Stephen H. Goddard, "Brocade Patterns in the Shops of the Master of Frankfurt: An Accessory to Stylistic Analysis," *Art Bulletin* (September 1985): 401–17.

25. Ellis Waterhouse, *Reynolds* (London, 1973), pp. 39–41 passim.

26. Tancred Borenius, "A Venetian Apotheosis of William III," *The Burlington Magazine* (December 1936): 245–46.

F. J. B. Watson, "An Allegorical Painting by Canaletto, Piazzetta, and Cimaroli," ibid. (November 1953): 326–65.

27. J. G. Links, *Canaletto and His Patrons* (New York, 1977), pp. 12 et passim.

28. Neville Wallis, ed., *A Victorian Canvas: The Memoirs of W. P. Frith, R. A.* (London, 1957), pp. 101, 107.

29. Thomas G. Moore, *Economics of the American Theater* (Durham, 1968), p. 13.

30. Wallis, *A Victorian Canvas,* p. 16.

31. Martin Bressler, "Counsel on the Arts," *American Artist* (June 1983): 89.

32. Montias, *Artists and Artisans in 17th Century Delft,* pp. 306, 70.

33. Quoted by John E. Bowlt, "The Failed Utopia: Russian Art 1917–32," in *Museums in Crisis,* ed. Brian O'Doherty (New York, 1972), p. 50.

34. Nick Pearson, "More on the Economic Situation of the Visual Arts," *Art Monthly* (April 1986): 5.

35. Duncan Kinkhead, "Juan de Luzon and the Sevillian Period of Francesco Zurbarán," *Art Bulletin* (June 1983): 305–11.

Chapter 4: The Art Market

1. Ernest Samuels, *Bernard Berenson* (Cambridge, 1987), vol. 2, pp. 314–18.

2. Frank Arnau, *The Art of the Faker* (Boston, n. d.), p. v.

3. Hope B. Werness, "Han van Meegeren *fecit,*" in *The Forger's Art,* ed. Denis Dutton (Berkeley, 1983), pp. 1–57.

4. Alvar Gonzalez-Palacios, "The Flight from Boredom. Italian Writing on Art Since the War," *Apollo* (May 1988): 345.

5. Colin Simpson, *The Partnership: The Secret Association of Bernard Berenson and Joseph Duveen* (Oxford, 1987).

6. John Walker, *Self Portrait With Donors* (New York, 1974), p. 149.

7. Richard Hislop, *1970–1980 Auction Prices of Old Masters* (Weybridge, 1982), pp. 431–32.

8. Walker, *Self Portrait With Donors,* p. 147.

9. Gonzalez, "The Flight from Boredom," p. 344.

10. Alfred Lessing, "What Is Wrong with a Forgery," in *The Forger's Art,* ed. Dutton, p. 62.

11. Quoted by Denis Dutton, "Artistic Crimes," in ibid., pp. 173–74.

12. Gonzalez, "The Flight from Boredom," p. 346.

13. J. Paul Getty, *The Joys of Collecting* (New York, 1965), p. 27.

14. Ben W. Bolch, "There Is No 'Just Price' for Art," *New York Times,* October 28, 1987.

15. Richard L. Feigen, Letter to the editor, ibid., January 2, 1988.

16. Daniel Grant, "Is There Recognition after Death?" *American Artist* (July 1987): 70–73.

17. Jean Renoir, *Renoir My Father* (Boston, 1958), pp. 177–78.

18. A summary of the dissertation is in John Picard Stein, "The Monetary Appreciation of Paintings," *Journal of Political Economy* (October 1977): 1021–35.

William J. Baumol, "Unnatural Value: or Art Investment as a Floating Crap Game," *American Economic Review* (May 1986): 10–14.

Robert C. Anderson, "Paintings as an Investment," *Economic Inquiry* (March 1974): 13–26.

Geraldine Keen, *The Sale of Works of Art: A Study Based on the Times–Sotheby Index* (London, 1971).

Bruno S. Frey and Werner W. Pommerehne, "Is Art Such a Good Investment?" *The Public Interest* (Spring 1988): 79–86.

19. Maurice Rheims, *Art on the Market,* trans. David Pryce-Jones (London, 1959), p. 151.

Chapter 5: Art Museums

1. C. D. Throsby and G. A. Withers, *The Economics of the Performing Arts* (New York, 1979), p. 53.

2. W. E. Williams, Secretary General, British Council, quoted by Hugh Jenkins, *The Culture Gap, An Experience of Government and the Arts* (London, 1979), p. 44.

3. Benjamin Ives Gilman, *Museum Ideals of Purpose and Method* (Cambridge, 1918), p. 373.

4. Ian Finlay, *Priceless Heritage. The Future of Museums* (London, 1977), p. 11.

5. Kenneth Clark, *Another Part of the Wood. A Self Portrait* (New York, 1974), p. 225.

6. E. S. Robinson, *Behavior of Museum Visitors* (New York, 1928).

7. E. S. Robinson, "Exit the Typical Visitor," *Journal of Adult Education* (October 1931): 422.

8. Peter Andrews, "A View of Toledo," *Connoisseur* (November 1982): 110–11.

9. National Endowment for the Arts, *Museums USA: Art, History, Science, and Others* (Washington, 1974), p. 577.

10. Germain Bazin, *The Museum Age,* trans. Jane van Nuis Cahill (New York, 1967), p. 274.

11. Detlef Heikamp, "Florence, the Future of the Uffizi Gallery and the Florentine Museums," *The Burlington Magazine* (January 1983): 50–51.

12. National Bureau of Economic Research, *Measuring the Nation's Wealth, Studies in Income and Wealth* (Washington, 1964), vol. 29, app. 2, annex A, pp. 788–90.

13. Robert Tillotson, *Museum Security* (Paris, 1977), p. 184.

14. Penelope Hunter-Stiebel, "The Great Art Inventory," *Connoisseur* (July 1984): 16, 18.

15. Tillotson, *Museum Security,* p. 118.

16. Thomas Hoving, "How Many Sublime Works of Art Are There in American Public Collections? 30," *Connoisseur* (July 1984): 44–49.

17. W. H. Daugherty, Jr., and M. J. Gross, Jr., *Museum Accounting Handbook* (Washington, 1978), p. 125.

18. Throsby and Withers, *The Economics of the Performing Arts,* pp. 54–55.

19. Ford Foundation, *The Finances of the Performing Arts* (New York, 1974), vol. 1, p. 5.

20. Ibid., p. 5.

National Endowment for the Arts, *Museums USA*, p. 139.

21. *Financial Times*, May 21, 1988.

22. *Daily Telegraph* (London), May 11, 1988.

23. Art Institute of Chicago, *Annual Report, 1978–79*, p. 7.

24. *The Museum: Its First Half-Century* (Baltimore, 1966), p. 77.

25. Burton B. Fredericksen and Federico Zeri, *Census of Pre-19th Century Italian Paintings in North American Collections* (Cambridge, 1972), p. 555.

26. *Americans and the Arts. A Survey of Public Opinion* (New York, 1975), p. 36.

27. Heikamp, "Florence," pp. 48, 51.

28. John Walker, *Self Portrait With Donors* (New York, 1974), p. 305.

29. Sherman E. Lee, "The Idea of an Art Museum," *Harper's Magazine* (September 1968): 78–79.

Quoted by Daniel Catton Rich, "Museums at the Crossroads," *Museum News* (March 1961): 37.

30. Quoted by Theodore L. Low, *The Museum as a Social Instrument* (New York, 1942), p. 8.

31. Quoted by Dillon Ripley, *The Sacred Grove: Essays on Museums* (New York, 1969), p. 61.

32. Eva Cockcroft, "Abstract Expressionism, Weapon of the Cold War," in *Pollock and After,* ed. F. Franscini (New York, 1985), ch. 7.

33. Rich, "Museums at the Crossroads," p. 38.

34. Alan Shestack, "The Director: Scholar and Businessman, Educator and Lobbyist," *Museum News* (November/December 1978): 89.

35. Jean Chatelain, "Dedication from the Louvre," in *Louvre Paris, Great Museums of the World* (Milan, 1968), p. 9.

36. Hiroshi Daifuku et al., *The Organization of Museums: Practical Advice* (Paris, 1960), p. 77.

37. D. R. Prince, "Museum Visiting and Unemployment," *Museums Journal* (September 1985): 85–90.

38. D. R. Prince and R. T. Schadla-Hall, "The Image of the Museum: A Case Study of Kingston-upon-Hull," ibid. (June 1985): 42.

39. Linda Nochlin, "Museums and Radicals: A History of Emergencies," in *Museums in Crisis,* ed. Brian O'Doherty (New York, 1972), p. 35.

40. Pierre Bourdieu and Alain Darbel, *L'Amour de l'Art: Les Musées d'Art Européens et Leur Publique* (Paris, 1969), app. 2.

41. Ayela Zachs et al., "Public Attitudes Toward Modern Art," *Museum* 3/4 (1969): 141, 144.

42. M. Blaug, "Rationalizing Social Expenditure—The Arts," in *The Economics of the Arts,* ed. M. Blaug (Boulder, 1976), pp. 141–42.

43. Anthony Hilton, "The Economics of the Theater," *Lloyd's Bank Review* (July 1971): 30.

44. W. J. Baumol and W. G. Bowen, "Arguments for Public Support of the Performing Arts," in *The Economics of the Arts,* ed. Blaug, p. 84.

45. Bazin, *The Museum Age,* p. 276.

Edward F. Fry, "The Dilemmas of the Curator," in *Museums in Crisis,* ed. O'Doherty, p. 113.

Franco Russoli et al., *Brera Milan* (Milan, 1970), p. 9.

Chapter 6: Why Does Government Assist the Arts?

1. William D. Grampp, "Rent-seeking in Arts Policy," *Public Choice,* no. 60 (1989): 113–21.

2. Fraser Baron, "A Mission Renewed: The Survival of the National Endowment for the Arts, 1981–83," *Journal of Cultural Economics* (June 1987): 22–75.

3. National Endowment for the Arts, *1986 Annual Report* (Washington, 1987), pp. 240–43. *Statistical Abstract of the United States: 1987* (Washington, D.C., 1986), pp. 222, 463. *New York Times*, March 26, 1989. (The adjustment for changes in the value of money was made with the Consumer Price Index.)

4. Alan L. Feld, Michael O'Hare, and J. Mark Davidson Schuster, *Patrons Despite Themselves: Taxpayers and Arts Policy,* A Twentieth Century Fund Report (New York, 1983), pp. 2, 24.

5. Jean Rudd, "A Banker's Novel Views on Nonprofit Money Management," *Museum News* (July/August 1979): 9.

6. *Americans and the Arts. A Survey of Public Opinion* (New York, 1975), pp. 105–6.

7. Denis Lees and John Coyne, "Can We Afford Our National Heritage?" *Lloyd's Bank Review* (January 1979): 131–32.

8. Thomas W. Leavitt, "From the President," *Museum News* (February 1983): 69.

9. Fred Mannering and Clifford Winston, "Economic Effects of Voluntary Export Restrictions," in *Blind Intersection*, ed. Clifford Winston and Associates (Washington, 1987), p. 65.

10. Nicholas Pearson, "The Quango and the Gentlemanly Tradition: British State Intervention in the Visual Arts," *Oxford Art Journal,* no. 1 (1982): 56–60.

11. Paul Gardner, "At Home in the Dallas Museum of Art," *ARTnews* (January 1986): 12–14, 156.

12. Denys Sutton, "The Getty Museum and the British Heritage," *Apollo* (June 1983): 497.

13. J. V. Bowman, "Supporting Culture," *The Cambridge Review,* May 25, 1979, p. 136.

14. Ian Finlay, *Priceless Heritage. The Future of Museums* (London, 1977), pp. 32, 37.

15. Alistair Hicks, "A Collector's Haven," *Spectator,* June 1, 1985, pp. 27–28.

16. Thurston Shaw, *Encounter* (March 1985).

17. *ARTnews* (April 1986).

18. Frank Hermann, *The English as Collectors: A Documentary Chrestomathy* (New York, 1972), pp. 83–84.

19. Edward P. Alexander, *Museum Masters, Their Museums and Their Influence* (Nashville, 1983), pp. 88–102.

20. Ibid., p. 226.

21. Nagatake Asano, "The Tokyo National Museum: Foreword," in *National Museum Tokyo, Great Museums of the World* (Milan, 1968), p. 10.

Chapter 7: Should Government Assist the Arts?

1. Ian Finlay, *Priceless Heritage, The Future of Museums* (London, 1977), pp. 36–37.

2. C. D. Throsby and G. A. Withers, *The Economics of the Performing Arts* (New York, 1979), p. 192.

3. Presidential Task Force on the Arts and Humanities, *Report* (Washington, 1981).

4. Lionel Robbins, "Art and the State," in *Politics and Economics: Papers in Political Economy* (London, 1963), p. 58.

5. François Duret-Robert, "Être Marchand à Paris," *Connaissance des Arts* (January 1985): 60.

6. Department of Paintings, Rijksmuseum. *All the Paintings of the Rijksmuseum of Amsterdam* (Amsterdam, 1976), p. 19.

7. William Morris, "Lectures on Socialism: Art, Wealth, and Riches," in *The Collected Works of William Morris* (1877), ed. May Morris (New York, 1966), vol. 22, pp. 143–63.

8. Ibid., pp. 143–63.

9. William Morris, "The Lesser Arts," in ibid., vol. 23, pp. 16–17.

10. Richard Hoggart, *Speaking to Each Other* (London, 1970), vol. 1, pp. 242–45.

11. J. M. Keynes, "Art and the State," *Listener,* August 26, 1936, pp. 371–74.

12. All of the talks were published in the *Listener,* 1986: N. Milyutin (Russia), September 2, pp. 423–26; Georges Duthuit (France), September 9, pp. 474–76; Hans Hinkel (Germany), September 16, pp. 514–17; Lewis Mumford (U.S.), October 7, pp. 649–52; F. T. Marinetti (Italy), October 14, pp. 730–32; Clive Bell (England), October 21, pp. 745–47.

13. Robbins, "Art and the State," p. 55.

14. Thomas G. Moore, *Economics of the American Theater* (Durham, 1968), p. 118. William J. Baumol, "On the Social Benefits of the Arts and Humanities," *Columbia/VLA Journal of Art and Law.*

15. Throsby and Withers, *The Economics of the Performing Arts,* p. 183.

16. *Americans and the Arts. A Survey of Public Opinion* (New York, 1975), p. 106.

17. E. G. West, "Rejoinder," *Economic Affairs* (December/January 1987): 44.

18. Peter Bohm, "Revealing Demand for an Actual Public Good," *Journal of Public Economics* (July 1984): 135–51.

19. Dick Netzer, *The Subsidized Muse. Public Support for the Arts in the U.S.,* A Twentieth Century Fund Study (Cambridge, 1978), pp. 22–25.

20. Hans Abbing, in *Economic Policy for the Arts,* ed. William S. Hendon et al. (Cambridge, 1980), p. 38.

21. Louise Irvine, "A Century of Cooperation between Sculptors and the Doulton Potteries," *Connoisseur* (August 1979): 252–55.

22. G. Ellis Burcaw, *Introduction to Museum Work* (Nashville, 1975), p. 156.

23. Ibid., p. 163.

24. National Endowment for the Arts, *Profile: The Alvarado School Art Workshop* (Washington, 1975), pp. 9, 8.

25. Tibor Scitovsky, "What's Wrong with the Arts Is What's Wrong with Society," *American Economic Review* (May 1972): 68.

26. Roger J. Vaughan, "The Use of Subsidies in the Production of Cultural Services," paper prepared for the 1976 meeting of the Southwest Social Science Association.

27. W. S. Jevons, "The Use and Abuse of Museums," *Methods of Social Reform* (London, 1883), p. 64.

28. K. King and M. Blaug, "Does the Arts Council Know What It Is Doing?" in *The Economics of the Arts,* ed. M. Blaug (Boulder, 1976), pp. 107–8.

29. Alan T. Peacock, "Welfare Economics and Subsidies to the Arts," in ibid., p. 80.

30. Holman Hunt, "Pre-Raphaelitism and the Pre-Raphaelite Brotherhood," in *Artists on Art,* ed. Robert Goldwater and Marco Treves (New York, 1945), p. 339.

31. Livingston Biddle, "Chairman's Statement," in *NEA Annual Report 1980* (Washington, 1981), p. 2.

INDEX